THE ROMANTIC AGE

THE ROMANTIC AGE

EUROPE IN THE EARLY NINETEENTH CENTURY

BY

R. B. MOWAT

PROFESSOR OF HISTORY IN THE UNIVERSITY OF
BRISTOL
FORMERLY FELLOW AND TUTOR OF CORPUS
CHRISTI COLLEGE OXFORD

THE FOLCROFT PRESS, INC.
FOLCROFT, PA.

First Published 1937

Reprinted 1969

THE ROMANTIC AGE

EUROPE IN THE EARLY NINETEENTH CENTURY

BY

R. B. MOWAT

PROFESSOR OF HISTORY IN THE UNIVERSITY OF
BRISTOL
FORMERLY FELLOW AND TUTOR OF CORPUS
CHRISTI COLLEGE OXFORD

GEORGE G. HARRAP & CO. LTD.
LONDON   BOMBAY   SYDNEY

First published 1937
by GEORGE G. HARRAP & CO. LTD.
182 *High Holborn, London, W.C.*1

Made in Great Britain.   Printed by Butler and Tanner, Ltd.,
Frome and London

TO

MAJOR-GENERAL SIR REGINALD HOSKINS
OF ASHRIDGE

PREFACE

THE charm of the fascinating study of history is largely in the opportunities it gives for transcending time and living the life of past ages.

The eighteenth century in Western Europe was a ' classical ' 1 age, an age of form and style and lucent reason. It had a quiet but pervasive and potent influence on the following century, particularly on that great achievement of the nineteenth century —universal tolerance.

Without, however, the Romantic Age—that strange, disturbing, brilliant era from the French Revolution to the revolutions of 1848—the work of the eighteenth century would not have been complete, and the many-sided splendour of the whole nineteenth century would not have been attained.

In the present book Germany and the Germans bulk largely. It is impossible, on any comprehensive view, to present the period otherwise. The Germans were—perhaps are—the most romantic of the Continental peoples, though, curiously, it required a French-speaking Swiss, a Génévoise, Madame de Staël, to interpret them at that time to Europe.

R. B. M.

CLIFTON
1937

CONTENTS

THE ROMANTIC AGE

CHAPTER I

"DE L'ALLEMAGNE" ("ON GERMANY")

THE celebrated remark of Albert Sorel in *L'Europe et la Révolution Française*—" There is a European atmosphere; the same ideas are spread everywhere; they are all French "—may be applied almost completely to the eighteenth century, and also, though less completely, to the nineteenth. For English ideas have, since the time of Hobbes and Locke, always had a certain vogue on the Continent. And there have been times when German ideas had something like an ascendancy in the intellectual world. Madame de Staël was the first person to discover Germany for the rest of Europe; and the effect of her work *De l'Allemagne* has never been wholly effaced. After the restoration of peace in 1815 there were no keener visitors to Germany than the active, intellectual Frenchmen of the Romantic period. Cousin, Hugo, Sainte-Beuve, and others found stimulus, interest, food for thought, in their German journeys. Sainte-Beuve wrote to A. F. Villemain, author of *Le Tableau de la littérature au XVIIIme siècle*, that he would like to obtain a professorship at Berlin, or at Munich *chez ce bon roi de Bavière*.[1]

Madame de Staël, *née* Anne-Louise-Germaine Necker, was forty-two when she began making studies for *De l'Allemagne*, and forty-four when she completed it. It is the work by which she lives. Others of her books are read occasionally, but people would scarcely think of reading them were she not remembered on account of *De l'Allemagne*. For it was she who first made people think of Germany as a whole, as a land of definite

---

[1] Sainte-Beuve, *Correspondance* (1935), i, 174 (January 31, 1830).

physical features, and of the Germans as a people of numerous and soaring, if not definite, ideas. It was not the loose collection of states called the Holy Roman Empire (*das heil'ge röm'sche Reich*), which, according to the Cellar Song in Goethe's *Faust*, held together so unstably. The Holy Roman Empire did not survive the victories of Napoleon over Austria and the distributions which he made of constituent states. It was dissolved in 1806. When Madame de Staël published her book in 1810 there was no longer a political Germany; but she saw deeply into things, and discerned a German land and a German soul. Napoleon's police seized the whole of the first edition and the book was not reprinted and safely launched until 1813, when it came out in London, in its original French tongue, from the publishing house of John Murray. It was naturally already a famous book, owing to Napoleon's seizure and barbarous destruction of the first edition. And when definitely published in 1813 it went the round of Europe, except at first in France, where Napoleon was still reigning; but he fell from power in 1814, and *De l'Allemagne* began its sway in France. Only in the last thirty or forty years, after the advent of Bismarck, did people begin to doubt whether Madame de Staël had truly discerned Germany, for her interpretation of it conveyed anything but an impression of " blood and iron."

De l'Allemagne is a work of sensibility, of Romanticism, and it depicts a Romantic Germany, a people of thought rather than action, loyal, gentle, introspective, industrious. The country " between the Alps and the sea, between the Rhine and the Danube," is covered with oaks and firs, traversed by rivers of imposing beauty, divided by mountains of picturesque aspect. In many places, however, heaths and sandy wastes, neglected roads and a severe climate, create an impression of sadness; but gradually the traveller begins to feel an attraction.

The south of Germany is very well cultivated; nevertheless, even here there is something serious, which makes one think of work rather than of pleasure, and of the virtues of the inhabitants rather than of the charms of nature. The land

and the people seem alike silent. The vegetation grows slowly, as do also ideas in the minds of the men. In time, however, observation convinces one that here is something interesting and poetic; one feels that gentle spirits and imagination have embellished these landscapes. The high roads are planted with fruit trees; the views on the Rhine are superb. One might call this river the tutelary deity of Germany: its waters are pure, swift, majestic, like the life of an ancient hero. Serious, varied, fertile, and solitary are the territories through which it passes; man seems to count for nothing; it is as if the river had cultivated the land itself. The Rhine tells, as it passes, the high deeds of former times; and the shadow of Arminius seems still to wander along these cliff-like banks.

Gothic is the characteristic architecture of Germany. All the museums recall the age of chivalry. Every town, every arsenal, possesses painted wooden monuments of knights, clothed in armour—helmet, shield, thigh-pieces, and spurs all complete. The traveller walks among these standing dead, their arms raised, ready to strike their adversary, who on his side has his lance levelled. These immobile images of actions once so lively make a painful impression.

The modern architecture in Germany is only mediocre; nevertheless, in general the towns are well built. The houses are well cared for, painted outside with diverse colours, ornamented with the figures of saints and other ornaments, not, indeed, highly artistic, but generally pleasing and cheerful. The little houses of the towns have a hospitable appearance. The gardens of Germany are almost as beautiful as English gardens: with scented flowers and Æolian harps and grottoes these inhabitants of the North endeavour to compose an Italian scene, and sometimes they nearly succeed. All this, however, is chiefly in the south.

The north of Germany is somewhat grim. The deserted countryside, the houses blackened by smoke, the Gothic churches, seem made for the stories of witches and ghosts. The commercial towns are big and well built, but they convey no idea of the real glory of the Germans, their literary and

philosophic spirit. And the little towns of North Germany
offer no amusement at all—nothing to see, no society. Little
English towns send representatives to Parliament; French
provincial towns have relations with Paris; but the citizens
of the little North German towns, with no great public affairs,
work in obscurity like miners, and exploit in silence the intellectual riches of the human race.

In spite of the differences of north and south and of the
various states of Germany, the Germans have some character-
istics in common. The defunct Empire had no capital; there
was no common centre of light and of the public spirit. The
Germans are not a compact nation. Their divisions, fatal to
Germany's political force, are nevertheless very favourable to
all sorts of undertakings which attract genius and imagination.
There is a sort of gentle and peaceful anarchy with regard to
literary opinions and metaphysics which allows every man
complete development of his individual point of view.

As there is no capital in Germany where the best company
assembles Society has little power: " the empire of taste and
the arm of ridicule are without influence." Herein Germany
of the late eighteenth or early nineteenth centuries greatly
differed from France, where the *salon* had an undisputed
empire and where ridicule killed. In Germany, continues
Madame de Staël, most writers and thinkers work in solitude
or surrounded only by a little circle which they dominate.
Each lets himself go, according to his unconstrained imagination. If there is any trace of the ascendancy of *vogue* in Germany it is only because everybody wants to be different from
everybody else. In France, on the other hand, everybody
aspires to deserve the praise which Montesquieu gave to Voltaire: " He has more than anyone else the spirit which is
common to the whole world." [*Il a plus que personne l'esprit
que tout le monde a.*]

In literature, as in politics, the Germans have too much
consideration for foreigners and too few national prejudices.
It is a characteristic of Germans individually to sacrifice their
own personality and to esteem that of other people; but, adds

the cosmopolitan Madame de Staël rather unexpectedly, the patriotism of nations should be egoist. Whether this can be accepted as a universal axiom or not, Madame de Staël thought that the Germans as a whole could do with a little more *sacro egoismo*. Perhaps they have made up for the defect since her time. The English pride, she pointed out, powerfully helped their political existence. The good opinion which the French have of themselves has always greatly contributed to their ascendancy in Europe. But the Germans are Saxons, Prussians, Bavarians, and the rest; the Germanic character is *morcellated*, split in fragments, like the land which has so many different masters.

Yet, despite all differences of states, and particularly despite differences of north and south, the Germans have certain characteristics in common. These are fidelity and sincerity. Deceit is foreign to them; breaches of faith scarcely ever occur. The Latin nations have often shown themselves singularly adroit in the art of freeing themselves from their duties. But, to the glory of the German nation, one can affirm that it is almost incapable of that bold suppleness which makes all truths give way to interests, and sacrifices engagements for calculations. The defects of the German nation, like its virtues, subject it to the honourable necessity of justice.

Capacity for labour and ability for reflection are distinctive traits of the German nation. It is also naturally literary and philosophic; on the other hand, the separation of classes, which is more pronounced in Germany than anywhere else, militates against what is properly called *esprit*. The nobles have too few ideas; the man of letters has too little experience of affairs. *Esprit* is a combination of knowledge of things and of men. Imagination, rather than *esprit*, is characteristic of the Germans. Jean Paul Richter has said that the English have the empire of the sea, the French of the land, and the Germans of the air. They have an eminent faculty of thought, but it tends to soar and to lose itself in the void.

Above the lowest class one easily discerns that inner life, that poesy of soul, which characterizes the Germans. The inhabitants of town and countryside, the soldiers and the labourers, practically all know music. " It has often happened to me to enter into poor houses, blackened by tobacco smoke, and suddenly to hear not only the mistress but the master of the house improvise on the *clavecin*, as the Italians improvise in verse." Once in winter at Eisenach, when the streets were blocked with snow, Madame de Staël saw a long procession of young people, in black mantles, passing along and singing the praises of God. No other people were in the streets, on account of the hard frost. They did not even dare open the windows; but behind the glass you could see faces, sad and serene, young and old, of people who were receiving with joy the religious consolations of that melodious sweetness.

Among such a tranquil people nothing can be more bizarre than the warlike aspect of entire Germany, the soldiers met at every step, in contrast with the domesticated lives that people lead. People shun the fatigues and asperities of the open air, as if the nation was composed of merchants and men of letters, and yet all their institutions tend to give the people military habits. But stoves, beer, and tobacco smoke form around the common people in Germany a thick and warm atmosphere which they do not like to leave. Their peaceable and regular habits are a bad preparation for danger, and they more willingly submit themselves to a methodical death than to an adventurous life. In the century after Madame de Staël wrote this a German statesman, Vice-Chancellor Von Papen, declared that pacifist opinion " could not understand the ancient German aversion to death on a mattress." [1] The facts of history, however, are on the side of Madame de Staël. Throughout the whole Napoleonic period the Germans (no more than any other people at that time) showed no preference for a violent death on the field of battle. The demarcation of classes, which is more positive in Germany than in France, tends to extinguish the military spirit among the *bourgeoisie*. But there is nothing offensive about this division of classes, for there is good-nature

[1] May 13, 1933; see the *Bulletin of International News* for May 25, 1933, p. 20.

mingled with everything, even with the pride of the aristocracy. The differences of rank amount in effect just to Court privileges; and there is no bitterness where there is little sense of the ridiculous. A serious and truthful people, they have always justice and happiness. The love of liberty, however, is little developed among them; they have never learned, either by enjoying it or by being deprived of it, to know what a prize it is. This carelessness of the Germans about their liberty, Madame de Staël thinks, was due to the independence of the states and the justice of the Imperial courts. As no power down to the time of Napoleon threatened the independence of the three hundred and fifty odd states the citizens were content with their existing institutions. But these antiquated feudal institutions are in striking contrast with the philosophical enlightenment of the Germans, who thus combine the utmost audacity of thought with the most obedient of characters. Their obedience is not servility; it is the spirit of regularity. Besides, old charters, city privileges, family history, all things that make the charm and the glory of small states, are singularly dear to the Germans. But to know all and to understand all is a great cause of uncertainty. Energy of action is developed, concludes Madame de Staël (with her eye upon England), only in a free and powerful country where patriotic sentiments are in the soul like blood in the veins, and only grow cold with death.

B

Chapter II

PHILOSOPHERS

PHILOSOPHY, the love of wisdom, is the noblest pursuit of mankind. Few persons, however, are really inspired by this love, and few have the intellectual capacity and firmness of purpose to maintain unflinchingly the search for truth all their lives. Besides, if the thinker starts with a system of given truths which he does not question he obviously has not freedom of search. Though some of the great philosophers have been religious men, only a very few have had a dogmatic theology—since the Middle Ages very few indeed. The great German philosophers of the Romantic Age—Kant, Fichte, Schelling, and Hegel—were members of the Reformed communion.

At all times the philosopher has been rare. Only in the Romantic Age can the species be called numerous, and then it was mainly German—Kant, Fichte, Schelling, Hegel; it was a kind of German dynasty. The French had lost the pre-eminence which Descartes had won for them in the seventeenth century; the brilliant and tirelessly industrious Victor Cousin could not restore it in the Romantic Age. The English had no great philosopher since John Locke; the Scots, on the other hand, had a very notable number in the eighteenth and early nineteenth centuries—Reid, Hume, Adam Smith, Dugald Stewart, Hamilton. Even Kant could not do without a Scottish ancestor, who came from the neighbourhood of Aberdeen. But the Germans in the Romantic Age held the palm.

German philosophic pre-eminence was entirely due to Kant, the greatest name in the intellectual history of the age; for though Kant, after he became a professor at Königsberg, never left the little Baltic city, his fame and influence were European. His *Critique of Pure Reason* (*Kritik der reinen Vernunft*), published in 1781, though not much noticed at first, within a few years won over all academic circles. It strengthened their love of truth, fortified their power of criticism, and deepened their views upon reality. Criticism, the exercise of reason, the unflinching facing of the truth, is the force which keeps mankind sane and wholesome. Kant's greatness was not in his conclusions, never very numerous nor definite, but in the method, the reasoning, which he employed.

Heine regarded Kant as something strange and terrible, a little *bourgeois* of dull, routine life whose thoughts, expressed in clumsy, involved, and, indeed, little-read writings, shook and shattered the foundations of belief.

The history of the life of Immanuel Kant is hard to write, inasmuch as he had neither life nor history, for he lived a mechanically ordered, an abstract, old bachelor life in a quiet, retired street in Königsberg, an old town on the north-east border of Germany. I do not believe that the great clock of the cathedral there did its daily work more impassionately and regularly than its compatriot Immanuel Kant. Rising, coffee-drinking, writing, reading college lectures, eating, walking, had all their fixed time, and the neighbours knew that it was exactly half-past three when Immanuel Kant, in his grey coat, with his Manila cane in his hand, left his house door and went to the lime-tree avenue, which is still called in memory of him the Philosopher's Walk. There he walked its length eight times up and down in every season; and when the weather was threatening or the grey clouds announced rain his servant, old Lampe, in anxious care walked behind him with a long umbrella under his arm, like an image of Providence.

Strange contrast between the external life of the man and his destroying, world-crushing thoughts! In very truth, if the citizens of Königsberg had dreamed of the real meaning of his thought, they would have experienced at his sight a greater horror than they would on beholding an executioner, who only kills men. But the good people saw nothing in him but a professor of philosophy, and when he at his regular hour passed by they greeted him as a friend, and regulated their watches by him.[1]

[1] Heine, *Germany* (*Works*, trans. Leland, v, 137).

This philosopher, who in Heine's eyes was so terrible, was certainly bold, even in that tolerant age, in proclaiming his views. In the Preface to the *Critique of Pure Reason* Kant writes :

> This may well be called the Age of Criticism, a criticism from which nothing need hope to escape. When religion seeks to shelter itself behind its sanctity, and law behind its majesty, they justly awaken suspicion against themselves, and lose all claim to the sincere respect which reason yields only to that which has been able to bear the test of its free and open scrutiny. . . .
>
> Morality requires us only to think freedom without self-contra-diction, not to understand it ; it is enough that our conception of the act as free puts no obstacle in the way of the conception of it as mechanically necessary, for the act stands in quite a different relation to freedom from that in which it stands to the mechanism of nature. From the critical point of view, therefore, the doctrine of morality and the doctrine of nature may each be true in its own sphere ; which could never have been shown had not criticism previously established our unavoidable ignorance of things in themselves, and limited all that we can *know* to mere phenomena. I have, therefore, found it necessary to deny *knowledge* of God, freedom, and immortality, in order to find a place for *faith*.[1]

Robespierre, wrote Heine, was the great destroyer in politics, and Kant in religion, though Kant " went far beyond Maximilien Robespierre in terrorism." In both there was the same cold, inexorable integrity. In both there was the same inveterate mistrust—in the one case mistrust of men, called by Robespierre republicanism, in the other of thoughts, called by Kant criticism. They were both really, says Heine, typical *bourgeois*. " Nature meant them to weigh out coffee and sugar, but destiny determined that they should weigh other things ; so one placed a king and the other a God in the scales. . . .

" And they both gave exact weight ! "[2]

Though Kant's thoughts were great, his literary expression was deplorable. He is responsible for the almost universal

---

[1] Kant, *Critique of Pure Reason*, Preface, in John Watson, *Selections from Kant* (1901), i, 6.

[2] Heine, *op. cit.*, v, 137–138.

belief that philosophers, when they put pen to paper, become unintelligible; and that no man who writes well is a really deep thinker. His early writings, however, were brief and stylish. " While Kant had his great work in his head he hummed these essays like little airs. He seems to smile like a soldier arming himself for a conflict in which he is sure to conquer." But when the great work appeared he conquered indeed, but at what a cost: He gave the *Critique of Pure Reason* " a grey, dry, wrapping-paper style." He seemed to fear that learning would lose its dignity if expressed in a light, attractive, and cheerful tone. " Therefore he gave his style a stiff, abstract form which coldly repulsed all familiarity from the lower classes of intellect." His unwieldy style, tolerable in a great thinker, is unbearable in the heap of dull mediocrities who have followed him, and who wrap up their intellectual common-places and nonsense in a devastating mass of verbiage. Kant's deplorable manner of writing affected even the poets and essay-ists; his philosophy " was very injurious to *belles-lettres*, on account of its dryness. Fortunately it did not get into cookery."[1]

Yet, when all is said and done, he is the Copernicus of meta-physics; he investigated the thing in itself. " He led back investigation into the human soul itself, and examined what was in it."

Fichte was Kant's immediate, though not most eminent, successor, less cosmopolitan than Königsberg's citizen of the world, more of a prophet, almost a politician, and therefore less of a philosopher. His teaching had a remarkable effect upon the Germans, particularly the Prussians, for whom he had a tremendous attraction; his piety, devotion to duty, and national patriotism struck sympathetic chords in them in the time of national regeneration between the battle of Jena and the battle of Leipsig. Fichte may almost be said to have met a soldier's death: he was infected by the fever of a military hospital in Berlin, and died (January 27, 1814) at the same moment as the French armies of occupation were cleared out of Germany.

[1] Heine, *op. cit.*, v, 154.

Kant was an East Prussian with a dash of Scottish blood. Fichte belonged to the Saxons, that good-natured, honest middle German people who respond, though never quite convinced, to the impulsion of the impetuous Prussians. Besides his Saxon ancestors, however, there was, according to tradition, a Swede in his genealogy, a soldier of the army of Gustavus Adolphus, who had settled in Rammenau. Perhaps it was from the Swede that Fichte's fervour and impetuosity came; these qualities are not characteristic of the Saxons, though not infrequently found among the Swedes.

Johann Gottlieb Fichte was born on May 19, 1762, at Rammenau, in Saxon Lusatia. His father was a small landholder and linen-spinner. The young Fichte was educated first at the village school. Later, chiefly at the charges of a friendly noble, Freiherr von Miltitz, he was sent to the celebrated and ancient foundation Schulpforta near Naumburg. Fichte was not very happy there, and once ran away, but returned, and ultimately rose to be one of the top boys when he found life more enjoyable. In 1780 he left Schulpforta and entered the University of Jena. After a year he transferred himself to Leipsig, where in three years he completed his studies, mainly theological. Fichte originally meant to be a Lutheran pastor, but he found difficulty in satisfying the Saxon consistory of his orthodoxy. He frequently preached in village churches, and though he was never ordained a minister, he remained essentially a preacher all his life.

The aristocratic patron, Freiherr von Miltitz, died before Fichte went to the university. His student years were years of poverty. On leaving the university he adopted the usual resource of the poor scholar of the period—a private tutorship. This sort of post was easy to obtain, was meagrely paid, and seldom lasted long. Fichte ultimately found his way in 1788 to the pleasant city of Zürich, to take up the post of tutor in the family of a hotel-keeper called Ott. He travelled from Leipsig to Zürich on foot.

Zürich was an intellectual centre at this time, Lavater, the famous preacher and phrenologist, being at the height of his fame. Lavater introduced Fichte to a cultured family called Rahn. Hartmann Rahn was brother-in-law to Klopstock, the author of the *Messiah*. Fichte fell in love with Rahn's daughter, and was betrothed to her in 1790, though the marriage could not take place until 1793.

In 1790 Fichte returned to Leipsig and engaged in private teaching there. One of his pupils asked for help in reading Kant's *Critique of Pure Reason*. Fichte took up this study thoroughly, and soon felt that something new had come into his life. " I have gained a nobler morality," he wrote to his betrothed. " It has given me a peace which I have not known before." In spite of this enthusiasm for the *Critique*, he adds, " It is difficult beyond all conception." He resolved to set himself to putting the principles of the *Critique* in a clear light before the public. Never, however, simply the pure philosopher, but also always the preacher-politician, he explains that his exposition of Kant is to be for the good of an age which has a morality corrupted at the fountain-head.

After a year's teaching at Leipsig Fichte went off in 1791 to a private tutorship in the house of Count Platen at Warsaw. This experience was brief and stormy. Fichte was dismissed summarily, but with enough salary in lieu of notice to keep him for some months. So, though he was now thirty years of age, he went back to the university as a student, this time to Königsberg, where the master whom he had never seen was lecturing. Fichte, when introduced to Kant, was received rather coolly. He attended the master's lectures, and did not think much of them: he considered Kant's delivery to be dull and drowsy. Nevertheless, he did not despair of the master. He shut himself up in his inn for five weeks, writing a long essay on Kant's critical philosophy. When it was finished and all his money spent he showed the essay to Kant, and asked for a small loan of money. Kant approved of the essay, refused to give the loan, but procured a post as private tutor for him in the family of Count von Krockow near Danzig. Although he had sworn never to be a private tutor again, he found the Krockow household thoroughly congenial, and this proved to be one of the happiest periods of his life. Kant also recommended Fichte's Kantian essay, which was called *A Critique of All Revelation* (*Eine Kritik aller Offenbarung*), to his publisher, Hartung, who accepted it and published it in 1792. This essay demonstrated at any rate the probability of revelation, and went through the eye of the needle of the theological censor of Halle, where it was printed. It appeared anonymously, and all the learned public took it for a work of Kant himself. It had such a success that it enabled Fichte to marry Johanna Rahn in 1793. He spent the winter of 1793–94 with his wife at Zürich, where the established political order, the tranquil valley, lovely lake, and majestic mountains, were congenial to thought. Besides carrying on his speculations on the Kantian system of philosophy, Fichte wrote a couple of political pamphlets defending the principles of individual and constitutional freedom expressed in the French Revolution. At Zürich also he began a lifelong friendship with Pestalozzi, who, having seen his school at Neuhof, near Zürich, fail, was living on there as a market-gardener and thinking out his schemes of education. In 1793 Fichte accepted an invitation to a chair of philosophy at the University of Jena, to succeed Reinhold, transferred to the University of Kiel.

It would be impossible to imagine a more intellectually stimulating place than Jena in the last ten years of the eighteenth century, or, indeed, for the next twenty or thirty years. Although Weimar, twelve miles distant, was, according to the rate of travel in those days, as far from Jena as Oxford is to-day from London or Cambridge from Oxford, the two places were practically one intellectual and social unit. Goethe, Herder, and Wieland at Weimar were in regular association with Schiller and other eminent scholars at Jena. Weimar was the unique capital of the republic of letters. Jena had almost unchallenged supremacy in the academic world. Schiller, professor of history and after Goethe Germany's greatest man of letters, was the bond of union between Weimar letters and Jena scholarship. August Wilhelm von Schlegel (famous still as the translator of Shakespeare) was at this time living at Jena.

Fichte, professional teacher and philosopher, but fundamentally romantic, poetic, and oratorical, was congenial to the men of letters and scholars, and equally congenial to the enthusiastic, eager students.

The philosophical works of Fichte in his Jena period (mainly editions of lectures) were numerous and imposing—*Foundations of the Whole Theory of Knowledge* (*Grundlage der gesamten Wissenschaftslehre*), 1794; *Foundations of Natural Law* (*Grundlage des Naturrechts*), 1796; *System of Morals* (*System der Sittenlehre*), 1798. Although Fichte set out to complete Kant's critical philosophy, the older philosopher (who apparently did not read his young follower's books) became alarmed at the reputation of Fichte's works for atheism, and in the *Allgemeine Literaturzeitung* in 1799 repudiated any connexion with him. In this year Fichte's Jena period came disastrously to an end. He was a public-spirited but undeniably somewhat rash professor. He got into trouble with the religious authorities by making 10 A.M. on Sunday one of his regular hours of public lecture. He conducted a vigorous and justified but maladroit campaign to dissolve the students' orders—clubs which seemed to have a corrupting and deadening influence upon their members. Finally a contribution of his own to the *Philosophisches Journal*, which he edited—nearly every energetic professor in Germany had his own journal—brought upon him the censure of the Upper Consistory Court of Saxony. Fichte answered this with an impetuous letter to a Privy Councillor of Saxe-Weimar, which the ducal Government accepted as a letter of resignation (March 1799). Thus losing his Jena chair, he left Saxe-Weimar and went to Berlin, where the Prussian Government upheld the principle of freedom of thought and expression.

Berlin had no university at that time, but it had a brilliant, if eccentric, galaxy of men of letters and scholars and a vivid, cultural social life in the drawing-rooms of clever and romantic ladies not unworthy of comparison with the *salons* of Paris. Fichte, matchless for his combination of learning and oratory, soon had his vigorous public lecture course in operation by which he made sufficient income for the modest needs of himself and his family. His high philosophical studies produced *The Vocation of Man* (*Die Bestimmung des Menschen*) in 1800, and in the same year his studies in politics produced *The Closed Commercial State* (*Der geschlossene Handelsstaat*), the counterblast to Adam Smith's *Wealth of Nations*, the philosopher's plan for a self-sufficing state, with a planned economy and no foreign trade.[1] In 1805 Fichte accepted a call to the University of Erlangen, in the territory of Bayreuth, which belonged to Prussia.[2] It was only a part-time professorship, and required residence of half the year at Erlangen. Fichte was able to reside for the winter at Berlin and to continue his public lectures there. His Erlangen course of lectures was published under the title of *On the Nature of the Scholar* (*Über das Wesen des Gelehrten*). Fate, however, did not for long allow him to enjoy this professorial leisured Elysium, for in 1806 the Prussian Government threw off its neutrality and entered on war with Napoleon. Fichte, who had offered his oratorical services as a lay preacher to the military authorities unsuccessfully, was at Berlin when the terrible news of the battle of Jena (October 14, 1806) came, of the defeat of the Prussian army and the march of the French upon the capital. Leaving his wife and family to look after the house in Berlin, he fled with the Court and officials to East Prussia—to Stargard, to Königsberg (where the university remained open and he gave courses of lectures), to Tilsit, finally to Copenhagen. In August 1807, peace with Napoleon having been secured by the Treaty of Tilsit, Fichte returned to Berlin.

By the Treaty of Tilsit Napoleon placed a French garrison in Berlin, took a war indemnity, payable by instalments, and limited the Prussian army to 40,000 men. This was the time of " Germany's deep humiliation," as described in the previous year (1806) in a pamphlet, *Deutschland in seiner tiefen Erniedrigung*, for selling which a harmless Nuremberg bookseller had been shot at Napoleon's orders. Fichte had even before Jena

---

[1] See below, pp. 33 and 42–43.

[2] Bayreuth territory was annexed to Bavaria in 1810, and is still part of the Bavarian state.

analysed and bewailed the corruption of the times in *Character-istics of the Present Age* (*Grundzüge des gegenwärtigen Zeitalters*). Now he was more alive than ever to the demoralization of society, increased by the moral shock of the defeat of Jena and the occupation of the country by foreign troops. Feasting, gambling, dancing, all the horrible cabaret life of reckless, disillusioned, pessimist people, was painfully obvious to him. His patriotic soul revolted against all this, and, as usual in trouble and difficulty, he turned his philosophy to the service of society and politics. Disunion, lack of purpose, lack of national consciousness, had, in Fichte's view, ruined Prussia and ruined Germany. As the statesman Stein was combating this degeneracy by legal reforms, the school-teacher Jahn by gymnastics, and the soldier Scharnhorst by military organiza-tion, so the philosopher Fichte set out to rouse the public and national spirit by idealistic addresses. The addresses to the German nation (*Reden an die deutsche Nation*) were delivered to crowded audiences in the hall of the Berlin Academy on Sunday evenings throughout the winter of the year 1807–8. The addresses, which were perfectly well known to the French military authorities, were not considered to be politically im-portant; nor did the audiences which listened to the impas-sioned orator appreciate their political significance. Yet, along with Stein's, Jahn's, and Scharnhorst's reforms, and along with the general vague yearning for ' regeneration ' which animated many public men, Fichte's addresses must be given their place in the national revival of the next five years. The public men and scholars at Berlin (increased by those who came from Halle when Napoleon closed that university after the battle of Jena) pressed the royal Government to establish a university in the capital. Planned and organized in 1809, the University of Berlin was opened in the autumn of 1810, Schmalz, late of Halle, being the first rector, and Fichte, Schleiermacher, Savigny, and other eminent men professors. Thus anchored once more in an established university, Fichte continued his philosophical discourses, steadily expanding and developing his great system of *Wissenschaftslehre* until the greatest moment of his life came, the opening of the War of Liberation upon the ruin of the Moscow expedition. Fichte ended the winter's course of lectures (February 19, 1813) with a fervent address to his students on the great national effort, on the nobility of the cause to which they were now going to devote themselves.[1] The young men went off to the war, and Fichte would fain have gone with them as lay preacher, but again his services were declined by the Army authorities. Soon the wagons began to bring back trains of sick and wounded to the capital. Fichte's wife became a nurse in hospital, caught the soldiers' fever but after a terrible illness recovered; Fichte, however, had caught the fever from his wife, and died on January 27, 1814.

Heine said that Fichte in philosophy merely carried on the Kantian reign of terror, demolishing the past with a *Critique of Pure Reason*. It was an orderly demolition, like Napoleon's after the rule of the Convention in the French Revolution. Fichte too, says Heine, was like Napoleon in so far as he made the ego, self-consciousness, the measure of all things: " Napoleon and Fichte represented the great inexorable I." He adds, with more generosity than perhaps Fichte deserved:

> If the whole transcendental philosophy was an error there still lived in Fichte's works a proud independence, a love of freedom, a manly dignity, which exerted, especially on youth, a wholesome influence. Fichte's ' I ' was perfectly in accordance with his un- bending, stiff-necked, iron character. The doctrine of such an almighty ' I ' could perhaps only spring from such a character, and that character must, rooting itself more deeply in such a doctrine, become more inflexible, more unyielding, more iron-like.[2]

Madame de Staël was of a similar opinion. When she was in Germany in 1807, collecting material for *De l'Allemagne*, she met Fichte, and asked him if he would give her a sum- mary, or *aperçu*, of his system in fifteen minutes. Although a little taken aback by this request to explain his life-work of metaphysics in *un petit quart d'heure*, he began in rather bad French to do the best he could. But he had not proceeded

[1] *Werke* (1845), iv, 603–610.
[2] Heine, *Germany* (*Works*, v, 182).

for more than ten minutes when Madame de Staël, who followed him with the greatest attention, broke in with, " *Ah! c'est
assez ; je comprends, je vous comprends parfaitement, M. Fichte.*"
She then told the discomfited professor that his philosophy
reminded her of the way in which Baron Munchausen had
jumped over a river by holding on to his sleeve. " Now, M.
Fichte, this is just what you have done with your *ich*."

Friedrich Wilhelm Joseph Schelling, a Württemberger, was
Fichte's successor at Jena. He was only twenty-three when he
became professor at Jena in 1798. Crabb Robinson went to
his lectures at Jena in 1802, and found in the lecture-room
one hundred and thirty students listening to the exposition of
a system " which not one in twenty comprehends." [1] Afterwards he received many calls, and held chairs at Würzburg,
Erlangen, Munich, and, finally—this one came in 1841—at
Berlin. He died in 1854, having profoundly influenced the
speculative thought of his time, though now he is little read.
His system developed the philosophy of Fichte, basing it, like
Fichte, on the ego, but aiming at more positive results. He
believed that over and above the knowledge which comes from
experience, from phenomena, there is a mysterious power of
apprehension in men—intellectual intuition. His great work,
Transcendental Idealism, set forth a " philosophy of identity "
which is believed to have contributed to Hegel's system of
logic. Fichte, though a friend of the young philosopher, came
ultimately to despise Schelling's work: " one of the most
muddled heads that the general muddle of the age has produced," Fichte called him.

Schelling appears always to have been prosperous. Fichte's
life was a long struggle. " The history of his youth," Heine
wrote, " is a series of sorrows and anxieties, as it is with that
of all our great men. Poverty sits by their cradles and rocks
them till they are grown up, and this squalid nurse remains
their true companion through life." At any rate, poverty seems
never to have restricted their intellectual output, in the case

---

[1] *The Diary of Henry Crabb Robinson* (1869), i, 69. The Madame de Staël
story which precedes is from *The Life of George Ticknor* (1876), i, 498.

of a philosopher like Fichte or a novelist like Balzac. But Schelling, though in easy circumstances, was as prolific of books as all the philosophers of that age.

George Ticknor, writing from Göttingen in 1816, said that since 1809 there had been no single philosophic ascendancy.

> From 1790 to 1800 Kant ruled unquestioned through all Germany. For three or four years succeeding Fichte was lord of the ascendant, till Schelling pushed him from his stool, and kept it a few years. But before 1809 had closed a rebellion of common sense through the land has dispossessed them all, and since that no one has succeeded to their influence.[1]

But, in fact, if unnoticed, a new dictator of philosophy was arising.

Georg Wilhelm Hegel was born at Stuttgart in 1770 of a family of small *bourgeoisie* which had been employed for generations in the lower branches of the Württemberg Civil Service. He grew up with the tidy and methodical habits of the clerkly bureaucracy, read widely while still a boy, and made copious extracts in notebooks. After some years in the *Gymnasium*, or high school, at Stuttgart Hegel went, at the age of eighteen, to the University of Tübingen, intending to be ordained as a clergyman of the Reformed Church. He made friends with the brilliant Schelling, five years his junior, attended lectures regularly, went on reading and thinking, obtained his diploma, and left the university in 1793 without having made any particular mark. Being not yet ready to enter the ministry, he too followed the line of other poor graduates: he became a tutor in a series of well-to-do families in Switzerland and South Germany, until 1799, when his father died and left him a sum equal to £300. This modest competence appears to have sufficed for Hegel's wants and studies until January 1801, when, with the help of his friend Schelling, he obtained lecturing work at the University of Jena.

Hegel had from his schooldays been an ardent scholar of Greek literature. Regarding the problem of reality as one of seeing the universal in the particular and unity in difference,

[1] *The Life of George Ticknor*, i, 96.

he thought that the solution was to be found in the Greek outlook. " Greek life presented itself to Hegel as a solution of a problem which to Kant had been only approximately soluble—the problem of combining the universal with the particular, the reason with the feelings." [1] His Jena lectures on the " philosophy of identity " were largely a criticism of Fichte and a defence and exposition of Schelling, with whom he entered into partnership, editing with him the *Critical Journal* until Schelling left Jena in 1803.

After lecturing at Jena for four years as a *Privat Dozent* Hegel became extraordinary professor in 1805. Next year he was working quietly in his lodgings on *Phenomenology* when French soldiers broke into the house and drove him into the street. This was a prelude to the battle of Jena, which not merely caused the fall of Prussia, but, involving a French occupation of the duchy of Saxe-Weimar, for the time being broke up the University of Jena. Hegel was glad to obtain a livelihood as head (rector) of a *Gymnasium* at Nuremberg, once a free Imperial city and recently annexed by Napoleon to the friendly state of Bavaria. Hegel, though he owed the loss of his professorship to Napoleon, regarded the Emperor as an artificer of fate who was remoulding the world: " All now wish good fortune to the French army," he wrote to a friend a few days before the battle of Jena.

As a schoolmaster Hegel was conscientious and successful. Although living on the heights of philosophy, he was practical and businesslike. He was a strict disciplinarian, and had no sympathy with the *laissez-faire* system of education which Pestalozzi to some extent advocated. In the middle of his period as schoolmaster Hegel married a lady of a noble Nuremberg family, Marie von Tucher, artistic, a friend of Jean Paul Richter. The Nuremberg period was happy. He had two sons; he found time to write his *Logik*; he enjoyed the quiet, cultured *bourgeois* life of Nuremberg and the opportunity of making little expeditions into the country with his family. He was glad, however, when in 1816, just before the last volume

[1] Edward Caird, *Hegel* (1883), p. 24.

of the *Logik* was to be published, he received a call back to university work—three calls, in fact, to chairs at Erlangen, Heidelberg, and Berlin. He chose Heidelberg, and held a chair of philosophy there from 1816 to 1818, when he passed on to Berlin, to the chair which Fichte had held.

Hegel was forty-eight when he went to Berlin. For the rest of his life, until carried off by the cholera of 1831, he was the great educator of Germany, or at any rate of Prussia, the schoolmaster-philosopher, careful, punctual, orderly, systematic. He was by no means the unworldly scholar, remote from common things, although he is said once to have left his shoe in the mud as he walked, deep in thought, from his home to his classroom. He was profoundly interested in politics, and in his Heidelberg period wrote an excellent pamphlet on the Württemberg Estates question, advocating hereditary constitutional monarchy and Parliamentary government. One of his last works was an article on the English Reform Bill of 1831. He was, in fact, a good liberal, as nearly all the academic and professional people of Germany were in those years. He believed in orderly freedom and in self-disciplined free will. His influence, during his lifetime and for forty years afterwards, was all on the side of liberalism. His lectures contain occasional references to current politics, the last being to the July Revolution of 1830 in Paris, which he criticized as disturbing the established peace. The truth is that Hegel, after the end of the War of Liberation and with the restoration of the orderly Prussian state, thought that there was nothing more in politics for Germans to do. They should return to their inner life, to philosophizing, which was free. Content with this freedom of the inner life, he and his like seemed to be unconscious of, or at any rate to accept a little obsequiously, the external political limitations on the citizens' freedom.[1] After 1870, in the Bismarckian period, his philosophy came to be regarded as idealizing the State, as supporting the Prussian Junker theory that the State was a supreme personality against which no

[1] B. Croce, *History of Europe in the Nineteenth Century* (trans. H. Furst, 1934), p. 77.

individual personality had any claims. Actually it was Fichte, in his work *Der geschlossene Handelsstaat*, who was the philosophical father of this theory.

As is common in the academic profession, Hegel drew no hard-and-fast distinction between his teaching life and his private life. He was interested in people and everyday things. He was a good business-man, and, though never affluent, he made a comfortable living. He liked his students, and if he met one on the way to the university they would go the rest of the way together. He enjoyed student parties, and went to theatres and concerts, and discoursed on the merits of his favourite actors and singers in his broad Suabian accent. He gossiped on the small things of Berlin life, always followed politics closely, and was fond of the company of ladies. He had a gift of pithy, picturesque and often poetic phrase-making which comes out in his philosophical works. He had robust common sense, and disliked sentimentalism and ' Wertherism,' though his name was commonly coupled with his great contemporary Goethe, who, as a matter of fact, did not really like Wertherism himself. Hegel was a teacher to the end. In the last week of his life he lectured as usual on Thursday and Friday, attended to some affairs at the university on Saturday, and died on Monday.

Heine wrote that every philosopher of the age complained that he was misunderstood by his contemporaries. Fichte did, indeed, declare that Reinhold (his predecessor at Jena) understood him best; but when the elder man turned away from the Fichtean philosophy Fichte declared that Reinhold had never understood him. Where Kant's writing seemed to contradict Fichte's Fichte declared that Kant had never understood himself. When Hegel lay on his deathbed he said, " Only *one* man ever understood me "; but he added immediately afterwards, " and he did not understand me either." [1]

Philosophers in Germany have either been unpolitical or else, like Fichte and Hegel, they have, either directly or indirectly, supported official policies. The philosophers have

[1] Heine, *Germany* (*Works*, v, 157).

cultivated the inner life, and have been satisfied with the limitless freedom of thought. Lack of individual political freedom apparently irked them not at all; " German philosophy had no martyrs." [1] Out of touch with external conditions, concerned only with abstractions, German philosophy deserved its reputation for pedantry and heaviness. When due consideration is given to the mental power of its professors and the industry with which they laboured it will probably be concluded that German philosophy has contributed nothing to the political life of the people, or has contributed only an element of weakness.

[1] Croce, *op. cit.*, p. 77.

CHAPTER III

FICHTE AND THE ORIGIN OF
NATIONAL SOCIALISM

IT is generally recognized that National Socialism, the 'Nazi' movement, is the child of humiliation. The proudest military people in the world, who relied upon might, trusted the State without reserve, and openly gloried in all this, were struck down in 1918 amid circumstances of unutterable bewilderment. Everything had gone wrong. *Machtfreudigkeit*, the joy of power, had proved a snare. The State seemed to have betrayed them. Their army was broken up; a contemptuous, dictated peace treaty was thrown at them; their country was occupied by foreign troops; they were forced to pay a vast indemnity of annual tribute. The German people, having thus lost their philosophy of life (for belief in might and reliance upon the State were nothing less than this), were like a ship without helm or moorings. They lost all steadiness. Party strife, faction, civil war, political murders, suicides, pessimism, all denoted simply the absence of co-ordination in society after the War. From this pessimism and disillusionment, from this mental, moral, and political anarchy, the German people have found escape in the ideal of nationalism, which merges differences in unity and absorbs individuals' freedom in the freedom of the State. As the New Monarchy in France and England towered up in lonely grandeur on the ruins of the Middle Ages, so the Totalitarian State has arisen on the ruin of Bismarckian Germany and of the Weimar Republic—supreme, sovereign, all-absorbing, terrible, the embodiment of power and the centre of *Machtfreudigkeit*.

It is not commonly realized that the Germans, or at any rate the Prussians, passed through just such another experience between 1806 and 1813 as between 1919 and 1932. Napoleon had broken whatever pride there was in the German nation. He had laid the Austrian armies low at Marengo in 1800 and at Austerlitz in 1805. He had destroyed the Holy Roman Empire, extinguished whole states, cut and carved up and consolidated others, and had erected a Frenchified *Rheinbund* (' Confederation of the Rhine ') to do his bidding. At last the Prussians, who seemed to have waxed mightier than ever during the neutrality, drew the sword to meet the foreign conqueror. " There are several generals in your Majesty's army," said a councillor to Frederick William III, " each one of whom is the superior of Bonaparte." It was a magnificent army which was mobilized and marched off to Jena and Auerstädt. The shade of Frederick the Great hovered over it ; the matchless discipline of the panoplied host was the admiration of all Germany. A few hours' fight sufficed for the total rout of the whole army. A single hammer-blow of Napoleon smashed the complete military machine of the great Frederick. A few weeks saw the surrender of all the Prussian fortresses. Then came the occupation of Berlin, the pursuit of the fleeing Prussian Court into East Prussia, the Treaty of Tilsit, and the dismemberment of the kingdom.

When Fichte, who had fled from Berlin before the French soldiery, returned in 1807 to the capital he found all the signs of demoralization after a great defeat and a great disillusionment. People had no longer faith in the State. Its might had failed them. The army on which they rested had broken. Their land was in foreign occupation. Their illusions were shattered ; their mind was in chaos. Thus robbed of their philosophy of life, thrown back upon themselves, they adopted the only resource of the children of this world, and said, " Let us eat, drink, and be merry." Berlin intensified its night life. Prussia was on the verge of moral and political disintegration.

It was in these circumstances that Fichte took up his lecturing again, on Sunday evenings in the auditorium of the Berlin Academy. But he was no longer lecturing on philosophy, at any rate not directly. He had a political purpose—the revival of Germany, not only of Prussia. He was giving addresses to the German nation—*Reden an die deutsche Nation*.

Fichte had already, in previous lectures delivered in 1804–6, and therefore well before the battle of Jena, declared his political views about Germany. In these lectures, called *The Character-istics of the Present Age* (*Grundzüge des gegenwärtigen Zeitalters*), he explained the aims which condition the existence of states, the place of honour and heroism in their lives, the absolute power of the State and its command of all the individuals' energies. " The absolute State in its form is an artificial organization to direct all individual powers for the life of the species and to merge them in it." And as the individuals " have indeed no desire, but rather great unwillingness, to sacrifice their indi-vidual life for the species, this organization [the State] has to be a *compulsion*-organization [*so versteht es sich, dass diese Anstalt eine Zwangs-Anstalt seyn werde*]." [1]

Having demonstrated the Absolute Compulsion-State, Fichte says, quite sensibly, that it must have an object—not, however, a rather vague object, to keep order or to make possible the better life. The aim of the State should be precisely conceived, and then all society will be co-ordinated and directed to that end.

If only the aim of the State is envisaged as clearly as it is possible to be in its particular age, and if all available powers are directed to the realization of this best object, then the system of government is right and good, whether it is in the hands of all, or of the many, or only of one. [2]

Here already in the lectures delivered while Prussia was still neutral and strong there appears in Fichte's teaching the idea of the Totalitarian State, absolute, compulsory, aiming at definite results, claiming to direct the total activities of the citizens to this end, and demanding, against their particular desires, the sacrifice of their lives for this purpose. Then, after all this explanation, comes the frightful collapse at the battle of Jena and all the bewilderment and mental, moral, and political chaos following on that great catastrophe. Fichte takes up the thread

[1] Fichte, *Werke*, vii, 144.   [2] *Grundzüge* (*Werke*, v, 155).

of his discourse, and before the vast concourse in the Academy auditorium patiently and in moving words re-explains his thesis.

The French Revolution and Napoleon had shattered the Europe of the eighteenth century, an age, in Fichte's view, of individualism and the concomitant evils of individualism—that is, selfish morality and selfish statecraft. In the ruin of this individualist system Germany now had the opportunity of entering upon her noble inheritance. " No God and no man and no opportunity within the domain of possibility can help us, but we must help ourselves." [1]

Moral regeneration will come through the education of the individuals, so that they shall serve the general interest. This integration (to use a modern word) of the individual with the community is possible only where there is a free and living national spirit. *Nationalism* is the binding driving-force, as, for instance, among the French of the Revolutionary period, when their ideas, as explained by Joseph de Maistre, were " all national and all passionate."

The *laissez-faire* State has no answer to the pressing problems of to-day. " The State's gentle grip of the bridle, called in foreign words *humanity, liberalism, popular government [Popularität]*, are in German speech to be called laxity and a worthless contribution " (*Schlaffheit und ein Beitragen ohne Würde*). If a nation so sunken is yet to save itself it must be through a quite new, a hitherto unused, means, through the creation of a quite new order of things. The discovery and exposition of this are the object of the *Addresses*, " in order that the sunken nation may raise itself to a new life [*damit die gesunkene Nation sich aufrichte zu einem neuen Leben*]."

The German nation has remained in its original home, preserved its original language, and, although intermingled to a considerable extent with other races, has remained distinctly German; and this has happened, too, wherever the Germans have gone as conquerors; " for the victors, masters, and creators of the new people made through this mingling were all German [*denn Sieger, Herrscher, und Bildner des aus der Vermischung*

---

[1] *Reden an die deutsche Nation,* " Erste Rede " (*Werke,* vii, 268).

entstehenden neuen Volkes waren doch nur die Germanen]."
Language is the great spiritual force of nationality. The German tongue distinguishes the nation clearly from all other races.
The German nation will never find itself unless it decides to be
German. " So long as we are German we show ourselves as
men, as others do also. Yet when we talk half or more than half
un-German, and put on imported manners and clothes . . . then
we think ourselves very distinguished." This is an error.
" Foreign countries are the earth from which fruitful vapours
separate themselves and rise to the clouds. . . . The Motherland is the surrounding, everlasting heaven on which light
vapours thicken into clouds which . . . falling as fructifying
rain, join heaven and earth together."

The Germans, then, are an original people (*Urvolk*), and one
which has had to fight. Generations of Germans have given
their lives in order that their sons may be free. " It was heaven
and eternal blessedness for which they poured out their blood.
. . . The freedom for which they fought was to continue to be
Germans [*Freiheit war ihnen, dass sie eben Deutsche bleiben*]."
And on the existence of Germany depends the existence of the
whole modern civilized world. There is no barbaric nation coming forward, as in the time of the late Roman Empire, to renew
declining Europe. " There is no way out. If you sink all mankind sinks with you, without hope of restoration." [*Es ist daher
kein Ausweg : wenn ihr versinkt, so versinkt die ganze Menschheit
mit, ohne Hoffnung einer einstigen Wiederherstellung.*] So ends
Fichte's *Reden an die deutsche Nation.*

It seems fair to consider that Fichte is the philosopher of
National Socialism. His philosophy established nearly all the
dogmas of the ' Nazis.' His thought is not to be confused with
' Hallerism.' He did not glorify the Middle Ages like Haller,
who " opened the door and gate wide for a cult of power [*öffnete
er nun freilich Tür und Tor für einen Kultus der Macht*]." [1]

Karl Ludwig von Haller (1768–1854), author of *Die Restauration der Staatswissenschaft,*[2] was born of a Protestant family in

[1] F. Meinecke, *Weltbürgertum und Nationalstaat* (1928), p. 225.
[2] Published at Winterthur, 6 vols., 1816–34.

Bern. Becoming first an official of the state of Bern, he subsequently undertook important diplomatic missions for the
whole Confederation of Switzerland. In 1806 he accepted the
chair of jurisprudence (*Rechtswissenschaft*) in the Academy of
Bern, a position which he held until 1817. He was a member of
the Great Council of the city of Bern. His aristocratic and
feudalist outlook was in conflict with the rising liberalism of the
age. In 1820 he lost his official position in Bern through his
conversion to Catholicism, which was regarded almost as a
' European event.' His *Restauration der Staatswissenschaft*,
which was read at any rate in its first volume of 1816, became
for a time a kind of gospel for the Holy Alliance and for all who
sighed, in politics as in religion, for authority and medievalism.
He stood for monarchy, aristocracy, the priesthood; it was, so
to speak, the *anti-Rousseau*, an elaborate attempt to undo the
work of the *Contrat Social*. But the day of the patriarchal monarchy was over, and Haller's *Restauration* lies in the dust of un-
touched bookshelves, while the limpid sentences of the *Contrat
Social* still charm and convince succeeding generations.

Neither Haller nor Rousseau, however, had much effect upon
Fichte. For Fichte was nationalist and ' racist ' in politics, and
nothing else; Haller hated nationalism, and Rousseau ignored
it. Fichte argued, with intellectual power, with impressive
historical instances, and in moving language, that the revival
or resurgence of a people will come through an elevation, in-
tensification, and concentration of the national spirit. He exalted
the ego of the German people, in order to cure the humiliated
and inferior consciousness which afflicted them after the defeats
of the war of 1806–7. He distinguished the Germans from other
nations, pointed out their originality and racial purity, and
exalted their language to a mystical attribute which made any
use of foreign words or phrases contemptible. He made the
State the supreme, all-powerful means of leading the citizen to
the highest life, endowed the State with absolute, compulsive
powers, and asserted the categorical duty of every citizen to
sacrifice himself for the future generations. He raised unity to
the position of an article of religious faith, and consecrated

nationalism with religious fervour. He made patriotism the
mainspring of action. He gave the State the claim to the complete activities of the citizens, and demanded that education
should be national, co-ordinated, and directed towards the end
and aim of the State. He denied, indeed ignored, the value of
the classical and cosmopolitan culture of the Germany of his
age, and made *Deutschtum* or *Deutschheit* and national egoism
the all-in-all of civic consciousness. And, having proved that a
nation is the thing of supreme value in the sight of itself, he left
the German nation, thus deified, with a ' mission ' by means
of national self-assertion and survival, to save the world. A
humane man, a thinker and scholar, he nevertheless idealized
war as the unique opportunity offered to the citizen for sacrifice
and unity. To the young men departing for the campaign of
Jena he declared, in one of his finest orations, " You have and
will now hold fast *the opportunity* to make yourselves certain of
this your worth. . . . In the battle, in the tumult, to keep firm
thought in your breast; even in death to think only victory,
fatherland, eternity. This opportunity no others have like
you." [1] Also " through war and through the common effort of
a campaign a nation becomes a nation. He who will not go
through with the present war will not be able by any decree to
be incorporated in the German nation." [*Auch im Kriege und
durch gemeinschaftliches Durchkämpfen wird ein Volk zum Volke.
Wer den gegenwärtigen Krieg nicht mitführen wird, wird durch
kein Decret dem deutschen Volk einverleibt werden können.*]

In his system of politics and of education Fichte was National
Socialist. Equally striking is his anticipation, or rather his
foundation, of the economic theory of National Socialism, which
is ' autarchic.' His work *The Closed Commercial State (Der
geschlossene Handelsstaat)* has fortified a tendency to which un-
informed people are always too prone, to think that all imports
are loss (instead of being, in fact, gain), and that to exclude
foreign trade is the way to the wealth of nations. " By an
exclusive commercial state Fichte understands a union of
citizens under common laws, in which no international trade

[1] *Werke*, vii, 512.

is permitted."[1] The metaphysical and economic argument contained in the long and closely reasoned parts (or books) of *Der geschlossene Handelsstaat* has been summarized by Professor Adamson as follows:

> The right of property does not extend over things, but only over modes of action. The State, therefore, has to assign to each of its members the sphere within which his free activity may be manifested. Hence it is requisite that the State should determine the distribution of the citizens into the three grand classes of producers of raw materials, manufacturers, and merchants; should regulate the scale of production and consumption; should fix the natural ratios of value in accordance with the principles that the intrinsic worth of a thing is the amount of its life-supporting property; and should issue a money of its own which could be contracted and expended in amount so as to cause no detriment by fluctuations of prices.
>
> In the second book, where the actual economic conditions of communities are considered, the ruling ideas are those so commonly met with in Socialist writings: that in trade left to its natural course one party benefits at the expense of another; that the use of money confers a new and beneficial power on some classes of society; and that among interchanging countries the poorer, to its certain loss and harm, will gradually be drained of its metallic wealth.
>
> In the third book the way towards the exclusive State is shown to be the rejection of the use of metallic currency and the adoption of a circulating medium which shall be valid only within the community itself. From this would naturally follow the restriction of the State to its own resources and the fostering of its own industries.[2]

Fichte was a man of the study, with no experience of commercial affairs, no training in economics. His *Closed Commercial State* is the worst type of elementary economics, appealing with elaborate philosophical equipment to the passions of national greed and xenophobia. It is as if Adam Smith (to whom Fichte made no reference) had never written. Taken up again by Friedrich List (1841), the miserable doctrine has gone on in

[1] R. Adamson, *Fichte* (1881), p. 79.   [2] *Ibid.*, pp. 77–78.

Germany until it has met National Socialist sentiment and the modern movement for ' autarchy.'

Fichte cannot escape the charge of being a militarist and extreme nationalist. He and Carlyle, who drew much of his inspiration from Fichte, helped to produce bitter fruit, though it did not mature until after their time. The Romantic Age was free from militarism, but the seed had been sown. Renan, whose youth was passed in the Romantic Age, and who later observed the rise of militarism, has a remarkable passage upon it in his *Souvenirs d'enfance*:

> To force everybody to obedience is to kill genius and talent. Whoever has passed years shouldering arms after the German manner is dead so far as fine work is concerned. Thus, Germany, since she has given herself entirely to the military life, would no longer have talent if she had not the Jews, towards whom she is so ungrateful.[1]

It is a remarkable fact that the Romantic movement took two opposite directions. In its earlier manifestations it was, on the whole, cosmopolitan. The Schlegels, Novalis and Tieck, and all their school or kind were *weltbürgerlich*: they believed in the existence of the republic of letters, in world literature, in the common aims, the common views, of civilized mankind. The later Romantics, however, the Brentanos and their like, were highly national, and apt to insist on the genius of race. Fichte, though contemporary with the earlier Romantics, was an ardent nationalist, ' étatiste,' and ' racist,' and had nothing fundamentally in common with these cosmopolitans. Fichte and the later Romantics seem to anticipate the post-War, twentieth-century nationalism. Herr Hitler's *Mein Kampf* is Neo-Romantic; National Socialism is a kind of Neo-Romanticism, without, however, as yet the Romantic distinction in literary form and expression.

[1] E. Renan, *Souvenirs d'enfance* (*Œuvres complètes*), p. 190.

CHAPTER IV

THE ROMANTIC MOVEMENT

HEGEL, tracing the development of civilized mankind in his *Lectures on the Philosophy of History*, came to the conclusion that the outstanding fact was the development of self-consciousness and will. From these two things, self-consciousness and will, comes freedom; and from freedom proceeds the idea of rights and duties. This development reached a high stage in the period of *Aufklärung*, or *éclaircissement*, before the French Revolution. In France the *éclaircissement* took a practical form—the Declaration of the Rights of Man (1791). In Germany, on the other hand, there were almost no domestic politics; the *éclaircissement* remained in the domain of abstract thought.

Hegel asks the question why the French, who had been so eminent in metaphysics in the time of Descartes, passed over from the theoretical to the practical. The common answer—because the French are hot-headed (*ont la tête près du bonnet*)—is, he says, not satisfactory. The real reason is that in the circumstances of the time the French thinkers were in opposition to the Church, and so turned away from theology and speculation to practical matters. The Germans, on the other hand, having adopted the Reformation, had no quarrel with their Church, and therefore continued naturally to associate their intellectual freedom with abstract thought and theology.

> The principle of thought, therefore, had been so far conciliated already; moreover, the Protestant world had a conviction that in the harmonization which had already been evolved the principle which would result in a further development of equity in the political sphere was already present.[1]

[1] Hegel, *Lectures on the Philosophy of History* (1892), Part IV, Chapter III.

44

While German and French thought proceeded in different directions towards the end of the period of *Aufklärung*, England too followed a way of her own, although " in no country has the question of liberty been more frequently a subject of reflection and public discussion." In England, according to Hegel, the Constitution was just a collection of particular rights:

> Each particular Church, parochial district, county, society, takes care of itself, so that the Government, strictly speaking, has nowhere less to do than in England. . . . Arrangements, based on particular interests, render a general system impossible. Consequently abstract and general principles have no attraction for Englishmen.[1]

Accordingly, the influence of Germany upon the Romantic Age was less obvious than that of France or England. The Germans did not, like the French, make and unmake states, wipe away feudalism, establish legal codes. Nor did they, like the English, provide a pattern of Parliamentary government and introduce constitutions in place of the old despotisms. The Germans had no political or social influence at all outside their own country; only their thought was pervasive, leapt over frontiers, entered into Europe's being. Since the Reformation Germany had lived through rather a barren time. But in the Romantic Age the influence of German literature was remarkable, because the literature was universal in character. There being no one capital city of all Germany, literature was followed as a calling in dozens of little princely, ducal, or free cities and university towns. But patronage was not common, " for the people are too poor and the Governments too inconsiderable." Thus, a real literary democracy established itself, independent of Governments and untrammelled in thought and form. It spread over all Germany, irrespective of state frontiers; and outside historic Germany German literature was practised in Denmark, Poland, Russia, and Switzerland.

In this way, without noise and almost without notice, from Bern to St Petersburg and from Munich to Copenhagen, a

[1] Hegel, *op. cit.*, Part IV, Chapter III.

republic has been formed, extending through all the great and small Governments, and independent of the influence of them all, which by its activity unites all the interests of learning, while by its extent it prevents low prejudice from oppressing individual merit; and, finally, by its aggregate power, resting as it must on general opinion, it is able to exert a force which nothing that naturally comes under its influence can resist.[1]

It was the publication of *Werther* in 1774 that made German literature European. Goethe, surprised and not a little annoyed at the ' sentimentalizing ' result of his book, had found a sympathetic audience in Europe whose natural sensibility was evoked and developed by the tale of Werther's heart-sickness and suffering. Although Goethe himself was classical, not Romantic, *Werther*, with its appeal to common sentiment and its attention to everyday things, struck a blow at the classical system in literature. And he had one characteristic in common with the Romantics: he was universal. Literature for him, though expressed in national tongues, was universal; its universal qualities made it great. He believed in, aimed at, world literature (*Weltliteratur*).

" If I were to say," said Goethe towards the end of his life, " what I had really been to the Germans in general, and to the young German poets in particular . . . I should say I had been their liberator." The republic of letters was free and cosmopolitan. Pursuing this interest of universal culture, Goethe along with Schiller, founded and edited *Die Horen* (not a great success) in 1794, and himself founded (or refounded) *The Universal Literary Journal* (*Allgemeine Literaturzeitung*) of Jena in 1804, and edited it for three years. He welcomed translations as bringing the intellectual riches of various peoples into the common treasury. He himself translated the *Autobiography of Benvenuto Cellini* and *Le Neveu de Rameau* of Diderot for *Die Horen*. He greatly appreciated A. W. Schlegel's translation of Shakespeare and Tieck's *Don Quixote*. Interest in translations was, however, almost his only link with the Romantics, to whom

[1] *The Life of George Ticknor*, i, 100–101.

in general he was inflexibly opposed. They were altogether, in mind and conduct, too ill-regulated for him.

Another noble champion of universal literature, who exercised great influence upon Goethe, was Johann Gottfried Herder, an East Prussian. Herder was born in 1744, studied in the University of Königsberg under Kant, became a teacher in the Protestant cathedral school at Riga (under the Russian Empress Catherine II), was Court preacher (Lutheran) at Bückeburg, and later Court preacher at Weimar. There he associated closely with Goethe, though they sometimes jarred on each other; he died at Weimar in 1803. In Herder's mind all literature was one. " His was the innate faculty, fostered in a great measure by the study of Shakespeare and Homer, of throwing himself into the noblest parts of the inner life of all nations; of bringing these foreign elements home to the hearts of all others. He was a universalist in the highest sense." [1] His universalism did not make him despise ' popular ' or ' natural ' poetry; quite the contrary. He held that the truest poetry was the poetry of the people. His finest work is his critical interpretation of the Psalms—*Vom Geiste der hebräischen Poesie* (1783). His *Ideen zur Philosophie der Geschichte der Menschheit* is part history, part philosophy of history, and has germs of the evolutionary theory of Darwin in it. He preached that man's essential quality was his *humanity*, the quality which man had in common with the spiritual powers and higher existences. Herder was the German Emerson; like the great New Englander, Herder was noble, eloquent, rational, poetic, *humane*. The young Englishmen and Frenchmen (or Frenchwomen), like Henry Crabb Robinson or Madame de Staël, who conceived it their duty to visit Weimar in this age felt that here indeed was the capital of the republic of letters, and that Germany, in Herder and Goethe, possessed in utmost purity the universal spirit of the Renaissance. " It is pleasant," said Goethe to Eckermann, " to see such close intercourse between the French, English, and Germans, as we are thus in a position to correct the faults of each other."

[1] F. Metcalfe, *History of German Literature* (1858), p. 425.

2.

As in the case of other abstract terms, Romanticism is described by examples more easily than by definition. Rousseau was a Romantic; Madame de Staël and Byron were Romantics. The French Revolution was a political expression of the Romantic movement, as is also the whole liberal-national movement of the nineteenth century. In literature Romanticism is contrasted with classicism—with the school of thought which attached value to form, rule, precision, symmetry, repose. The Romantic movement represented an intellectual revolt of the younger generation against convention, rigidity, tradition (in spite of their intense attraction to the Middle Ages). It was ' young,' although not until long after the first Romantics did ' Young Germany ' form herself. Sometimes Romanticism degenerated into mere sentimentalism, as in the letters of Bettina von Arnim to Goethe. They were published in 1835 by the Baroness von Arnim, though her surname was not divulged. Goethe was not pleased with the publication; George Ticknor thought the letters disgusting, though " all the rage with multitudes in Germany." Mrs Austin, the celebrated translator from the German, refused to translate Bettina's letters, " which seemed to claim the reputation of an intrigue that undoubtedly never existed." [1]

The Romantics took form as a definite group or school in Berlin in the opening years of the nineteenth century. In the uninterrupted warfare in which France was engaged since 1792 Paris had lost its ascendancy. Although the European war did not completely stop all travelling or dislocate intercourse between the nationals of different countries (as modern grand-scale warfare does), it nevertheless prevented Paris from continuing to be the focus of European culture. The French *noblesse* had, for the most part, emigrated or had been driven into exile. The new rich who battened upon republican Army contracts vulgarized Parisian Society. The *salon* decayed and practically disappeared; at the same time it reappeared elsewhere, and particularly in Prussia, hitherto the Bœotia of cultured Europe, in Berlin.

[1] *The Life of George Ticknor*, i, 500.

Madame de Staël observed that the Germans did not naturally take to " *salon* life " as the French did. For, intellectual as it was, the *salon* was mainly for conversation, for amusement; and the Germans were a little too serious to treat their intellectual intercourse as amusement. The production and development of ideas, for so long directed in Europe by conversation, were among the Germans affairs of quiet, solitary reflection. The *bons mots*, the good things of French conversation, were repeated from one end of Europe to another, and were generally ironical, playful, sometimes spiteful; but the Germans were too loyal to allow themselves this kind of conversation; they took remarks literally. Social ranks were so fixed, so precisely recognized, that free intermingling in a *salon* was less easy in Berlin than in Paris. Good faith, seriousness, reflection, are grand qualities; but in the Prussia of 1800 they were not sure to be found united with elegance and vivacity; and without elegance and vivacity there could be no *salon*. Only clever, charming women could achieve this, and in 1800 Berlin was fortunate in having such women, the best known being of the Jewish race. Such were Rahel Levin, Henriette Herz, Dorothea Veit.

Rahel Levin was born in a well-to-do family. She was poetical, sentimental, romantic, indeed passionate, highly cultured, sociable. Her mother's house became a centre for the literary life of Berlin, particularly after A. W. Schlegel moved thither from Jena. She was unmarried until 1814, when at the age of forty-three she became the wife of Varnhagen von Ense, a Prussian diplomatist, who was twelve years her junior. The marriage proved to be extremely happy, and Rahel maintained her brilliant intellectual circle in his house until her death in 1833. Henriette Herz, *née* de Lemos, was born at Berlin in 1764, the daughter of a Jewish physician. Married at the age of fifteen to Marcus Herz, she gradually formed a circle of friends among the most cultured people of the city. She had a wide knowledge of languages, including Greek, and translated from English into German Mungo Park's *Travels in Internal Districts of Africa* and Isaac Weld's *Travels through North America*. These were

D

published in German in 1799 and 1800. She was a friend of the theologian Schleiermacher; and her *salon* was attended by celebrated early Romantics—the brothers Wilhelm and Alexander Humboldt, Fichte, Börne, Arndt. With these and other friends such as Jean Paul Richter she engaged in correspondence. In 1817 she entered the Christian communion. Much of her time was spent in travelling in Germany and Italy. Her long and useful life ended in 1847.

Dorothea Veit was daughter of the philosopher Moses Mendelssohn, the friend of Lessing. She was born at Berlin in 1763, received a careful education, and married in 1778 a banker, Simon Veit. She was a friend of Rahel Levin and of Henriette Herz, and her drawing-room, like those of her friends, was a place of meeting of the brilliant Romantic writers who visited Berlin or who lived there. Among these were the brothers Schlegel. Friedrich Schlegel first met Dorothea in the *salon* of Henriette Herz, and fell in love. In 1798 a divorce was obtained for Dorothea Veit, and she was married to Friedrich Schlegel in 1799. The marriage caused something of a sensation, not to say scandal, in Berlin Society; and Schlegel's novel *Lucinde*, published in 1799, was undoubtedly meant as a defence of himself and his wife. Next year they left Berlin for Jena. In 1804 Dorothea was received into the Protestant communion. From Jena they removed to Dresden, later to Paris, where Dorothea's Sunday receptions at tea-time were frequented by Romantic authors and scholars. In 1808 Dorothea and her husband were received into the Roman Catholic Church at Cologne. She willingly put her intellectual gifts at his disposal. She was the actual author of the German translation of Madame de Staël's *Corinne* (1808), although only Friedrich was named as translator on the title-page. In 1809 Friedrich Schlegel obtained a position as secretary in the Foreign Office at Vienna, and the Schlegels lived there until Friedrich's death in 1829. Dorothea went to live with one of her sons (by her first marriage), who had also been converted to Roman Catholicism and was director of the municipal Fine Art Institute. She died at Frankfurt in 1839.

August Wilhelm Schlegel was born in Hanover in 1767, was educated at the University of Göttingen, and became a professor of literature and fine art at Jena. In 1802 he moved to Berlin, making a living by giving lectures there, although as yet there was no university. On Goethe's recommendation he became tutor to Madame de Staël's two sons. He was a great friend and admirer of Madame de Staël, and was often one of the brilliant company which made up the house-parties at Coppet. It was from him that Madame de Staël gained much of the information for her book *De l'Allemagne*. In 1813–14 he was secretary to Marshal Bernadotte, Crown Prince of Sweden, during the War of Liberation in Germany. In 1818 he was appointed to be professor of literature at Bonn, and held this position until his death in 1845. The philosopher Schelling married A. W. Schlegel's divorced wife, Caroline Böhmer, a brilliant, restless personality. George Ticknor, who met Schlegel at Paris in 1817, wrote that in consequence of his domestic troubles and of his attendance on Madame de Staël through many countries, " he now looks like a care-worn, wearied courtier, with the manners of a Frenchman of the gayest circles and the habits of a German scholar—a confusion anything but natural or graceful." He was a tremendously hard worker, beginning his studies at 4 A.M., and continuing them until dinner at 6 P.M. From this time until 10 he was a man of fashion and Society, overflowing with amusing conversation, " but at 10 he goes to his study and labours until midnight, when he begins the same course again." Ticknor visited him at Bonn in 1835, and found him, although sixty-eight years old, " fresh and active." Besides carrying on his Sanskrit studies, he lectured every session on Homer, Roman history, and the German language, " lecturing on the first two extemporaneously, in the Latin language, which I am told he does very well." [1] Heine attended his lectures at Bonn in 1819, and has left a vivid description of the famous critic, who was then a vain, elderly gentleman :

He wore kid gloves, and was dressed after the latest Paris fashion. He still had about him the perfume of elegant Society

[1] *The Life of George Ticknor*, i, 127, 129, 453.

and *eau de mille fleurs.* He was the *beau idéal* of elegance and
politeness, and when he spoke of the English Lord of the Treasury
he always began with the words ' my friend.' Beside him stood
his servant, dressed in the livery of the noble house of Schlegel;
his business was to snuff the wax candles in the silver candlesticks
that stood, along with a glass of sugared water, on the desk before
him.[1]

Friedrich Schlegel, brother of August Wilhelm, was born at
Hanover in 1772. Educated at the Universities of Göttingen
and Leipsig, he became, like his brother, a teacher in the
University of Jena, and moved on with him to Berlin in 1801,
with his wife, Dorothea Veit. In 1809 he joined the Austrian
Foreign Office, and was one of Metternich's able corps of
writers of dispatches and proclamations. George Ticknor met
him at Frankfort in 1817, and was first disappointed and then
delighted.

> Never was I more disappointed in the external appearance of any
> man in my life; for, instead of finding one grown spare and dry
> with deep and wearisome study, I found before me a short, thick
> little gentleman, with the ruddy, vulgar health of a full-fed father
> of the Church. On sitting with him an hour, however, I became
> reconciled to this strange discrepancy, or rather entirely forgot
> it, for so fine a flow of rich talk I have rarely heard in Ger-
> many.[2]

Like many of the Romantics, he became a Roman Catholic,
and carried his Catholicism into his writings with the zeal of a
convert.

Already while at Jena the Schlegels had started a literary
journal, the *Athenaeum*, in 1798. It was published at Berlin,
and lasted only two years. Before the Schlegels removed to
Berlin the *Athenaeum* was dead, but it had established a new
school of writers, the Romantics, and in its short life published
notable pieces. Friedrich Schlegel's famous essay on Romanticism and Novalis's *Hymnen an die Nacht* came out in the
Athenaeum.

[1] Heine, *Die Romantische Schule* (*Sämtliche Werke* (1890), v, 279).
[2] *The Life of George Ticknor*, i, 152.

Friedrich Schlegel may have heard Goethe speak about *Welt-literatur* at Jena, which Goethe frequently visited and for long periods. At one period of his life (in 1803) Friedrich Schlegel edited a journal called *Europa* in Paris. His definition of Romantic poetry in the *Athenaeum* presents very powerfully the idea of universality in literature.

Romantic poetry is a progressive, universal poetry. It is not 3. destined merely to bring together again all the different kinds of poetry and to put poetry in touch with philosophy and rhetoric. Its tendency is, and indeed must be, now to combine poetry with prose, inventive genius with criticism, the poetry of art with the poetry of nature, now to weld them together, to make poetry living and social, and life and society poetical, to turn wit into poetry, and to replenish and saturate the forms of art with pure material of every sort, and to give them life by means of flights of humour. It embraces everything so long as it is poetical— from the greatest system of art, which again contains several systems in itself, to the sigh, the kiss, which the poetizing child breathes out in artless song. It can so lose itself in what it represents that one might think its one and only object was to express the character of poetical individuals of every kind ; and yet there is no other form which is so fitted to express completely the spirit of its author—so that many authors who only intended to write a romance have unawares represented themselves. It alone can become like the epic a mirror of the whole world which surrounds it, a picture of the period. And yet, free from all real and ideal interest, it is able above all to hover on the wings of poetical reflection half-way between the thing represented and the one representing it, always reinforcing this reflection and as if multiplying it in an endless series of mirrors. . . .

Romantic poetry is among the arts what wit is in philosophy, and what society, intercourse, friendship, and love are in life. Other forms of poetry are finished and can now be completely analysed. The romantic form is still in the state of growth ; indeed, that is its essential nature, that it for ever grows and can never be completed. It cannot be exhausted by any theory, and only prophetic criticism could venture to give the characteristics of its ideal. It alone is without end, as it alone is free, and acknowledges as its first law that the will of the poet admits of no law superior to itself. The romantic form of poetry is the only one which is more than form and in a manner the art of poetry itself, for in a certain sense all poetry is or should be romantic.

Dante's prophetic poem is the only system of transcendental poetry, still the highest of its kind. Shakespeare's universality is as it were the centre of romantic art. Goethe's purely poetical poetry is the most complete poetry of poetry. That is the great threefold chord of modern poetry, the innermost and holiest circle among all the narrower and wider spheres in a critical selection of classics from the modern art of poetry.[1]

" In no other language," wrote Goethe, " is it possible to read and enjoy the great literary masterpieces of other nations as it is in German." If this judgment is correct, and there is a good deal to say for it, the credit must be given to the Romantic writers. They regarded Shakespeare as the supreme Romantic poet. A. W. Schlegel, who was generally an admirable critic, had a remarkable faculty for appreciating and assimilating the genius of writers of other nations. His sympathetic and vigorous translation of Shakespeare is a German classic; and Tieck, who edited or superintended the completion of the translation, achieved an equal success. A. W. Schlegel also translated Calderon and other foreign writers. Friedrich Schlegel went mainly to Oriental literature, and studied and translated Sanskrit literature.

Ludwig Tieck, like the Schlegels and most of the German Romantic writers, was a native of the country east of the Elbe, and therefore probably had some Slav blood. He was a Berliner, born in 1773, the son of a rope-maker. He had a good education at a *Gymnasium* and at the Universities of Halle, Göttingen, and Erlangen; as a student he was greatly interested in Shakespeare and the other Elizabethan dramatists. At the age of twenty-one he took up his residence at Berlin, to follow the precarious career of a man of letters; and by this, as a matter of fact, he made a sufficiently good living. His first long novel, *William Lovell*, began to appear in 1795. In 1798 Tieck married

[1] F. Schlegel, *Fragmente*. The original passage, in German, is reprinted in K. Breul, *The Romantic Movement in German Literature* (1927), p. 37.

and settled down in Jena, where he became one of the remarkable literary circle of the Schlegels. In 1801 he moved to the
artistic city of Dresden, then to Italy, finally back to Dresden,
where Ticknor later visited him. There he spent many years,
and was literary adviser to the Court Theatre. His last thirteen
years (1841–53) were passed at Berlin; he had a pension from
King Frederick William IV of Prussia. Tieck's daughter
inherited a good deal of his literary ability.

Tieck was a genuine man of letters. He had a strong, flexible
style which is seen at its best in his translation of *Don Quixote*.
He is one of the introducers of the popular fairy-tale into
literature; and he flavours these tales—perhaps some of them
originally were meant to be so flavoured—with satire on contemporary society. He was an excellent critic, appreciated
Shakespeare, and supervised and criticized the latter part of
Schlegel's translation. Like nearly every Romantic writer of
that time, he wrote a long novel which, if not exactly autobiographical, was at any rate a novel of the author's inner self—
an *Ich-Roman*, as the critics call it. *Franz Sternbalds Wanderungen* was published in 1798. The Romantic hero is always a
cosmopolitan. Franz Sternbald wanders through South Germany, Holland, Belgium, Alsace, Northern Italy. He is an
artist of the time of Albrecht Dürer, who is also one of the characters of the book. Conversations, poems, songs, travel scenes,
pleasantly diversify the narrative. It begins with a conversation
outside the gate of Nuremberg. It ends with a song; but Tieck
had then told only a part of the story. It was a work of his
youth. Often in the next forty-six years he took up the pen to
continue the narrative, but could never recapture the ardour
of youth. Finally he added a brief note, indicating how
the plot was meant to develop, and then he laid down the
pen.

William Lovell is, as its name implies, a romance about an
Englishman and English characters. It is composed in letters,
somewhat in the style of *Werther*, though less obviously sentimental. Here, again, Tieck introduces his love of travel—
England, France, Italy. In a Preface he stated that his object

was to combat the rationalism of the eighteenth century by means of nature, art, faith.

The most artistic work of Tieck is his *Novellen*, rather long ' short stories,' after the manner of Boccaccio. Crabb Robinson visited him in 1829 at Dresden, where Tieck lived in a highly cultured circle of friends. Crabb Robinson heard him reading, at which he was famous, at a party. In 1851 Crabb Robinson again visited Tieck, who was now eighty, this time at Berlin, where he had taken up his residence ten years earlier, on the invitation of Frederick William IV. There he died in 1853.

The position of Jean Paul Richter in the literary history of this period is indeterminate. Some accounts of the Romantic writers omit him altogether. Although a man of many and strong friendships, he belonged to no literary school. He neither lived at a literary centre, as Goethe or Tieck did, nor did he hold a university chair, like Wilhelm Schlegel. His literary and intellectual influence was exercised most obviously upon Carlyle, whose abounding mind and spirit, metaphysical, emotional, poetical, and religious, found outlet and ultimately expression through reading Jean Paul's tremendous works.

If the Romantic movement was " the renaissance of the spirit of wonder in poetry and art," Jean Paul was one of its chief men, for nature, and especially the flowers and trees and winds and stars, the common things of life, and the God within them, all were the subjects on which his genius worked. His early life is very like that of Carlyle—each of them sentimental, emotional, thoughtful, puzzled poetic boys, growing up in the country, roaming solitary among the grand manifestations of nature, impressed with the immensity of space and the mystery of the stars. Another man with whom Jean Paul had much in common was certainly Romantic—Jean-Jacques Rousseau; but Jean-Jacques' limpid style is very different from that of Jean Paul Richter, who, besides, had a very impish humour, very like that of the Englishman Sterne.

Jean Paul Richter was born in 1763 at Wunsiedel, a Bavarian village, where his father was schoolmaster. Later the father became Protestant pastor at Joditz. Jean Paul grew up " in the idyllic sabbath life " of the mountain villages of the pine-clad Fichtelgebirge. He was like the scholar (only blessed with a longer life) described at the end of Gray's *Elegy*:

" Oft have we seen him at the peep of dawn
Brushing with hasty steps the dews away
To meet the sun upon the upland lawn."

He was a great reader and walker; he liked the free air, wore his hair long, his shirt open at the neck, despising the wig and cravat. At Leipsig University, where he went in 1781 to study theology, he made no progress in regular studies, and only fell into debt. In 1784, suddenly breaking off his university career, he went home and lived with his mother, who was now a widow, at Hof, in the north of Bavaria.

" To live is better than theory [*Leven is meer dan theorie*]," [1] says a Dutch interpreter of Jean Paul. Jean Paul had no theory of life or of literature; but he had an enormous persistence in reading and writing, and seems not to have been troubled by the apparent purposelessness of his life at Hof. Occasionally his articles or stories were accepted by journals; he began giving lessons to the countrymen's families around Hof, and he gradually worked up a moderate practice as a tutor. In the course of twelve years of this kind of existence he established himself as a writer, particularly with the publication of two novels, *Hesperus* (1795) and *Quintus Fixlein* (1796), and of that curious farrago of nature-prose *Flower, Fruit, and Thorn Pieces* (*Blumen-, Frucht- und Dornenstücke, oder Ehestand, Tod und Hochzeit des Armenadvokaten Siebenkäs*).

After this Jean Paul's life took on a new colour. He became a great social success. Charlotte von Kalb, one of Germany's remarkable group of social-literary ladies of this period, was carried away with enthusiasm for his books, and invited him to Weimar. Jean Paul met Goethe, and did not like him; thought him too classical, correct, self-conscious, dignified, *ohne Accent*. For about five years Jean Paul enjoyed a vivid and varied social

[1] F. H. Fischer, *De Romantiek in Duitschland* (1928), p. 31, essay on " Jean Paul."

life, moving about from place to place; he was made much of wherever he went, idolized by the women, and was celebrated in every city.

Jean Paul married Caroline Meyer, whom he had first met in Berlin, in 1801, and then settled down; really settled down, and not at Berlin or Weimar, but at Bayreuth. The enlightened prince-primate, Dalberg, gave him a pension from the year 1808. The small South German town of Bayreuth, belonging to Prussia, was transferred by Napoleon to Bavaria in 1810. There he lived and talked and wrote. He had a delightful family life with wife and children. Visitors came to the beautiful valley to see the great man. He himself made occasional journeys within Germany. He died in 1825, leaving a fine autobiography, unfinished, which was published in the following year. Richter was a lovable man. He has been called the novelist of friendships, which he makes real in his books, like the vivid friendships of his own life. In this, as in his humour, his tenderness, his high spirits, his love of nature, of country life, and of simple domestic society, he shows the essential humanity of Germany in the Romantic Age.

The Romantic Age could not be otherwise than an age of friendships. The Romantic writers and thinkers were not national, but they were humane; the age was a renaissance, and the representative men were vividly conscious of their community in art, literature, thought. Among the great friendships are those of Goethe and Schiller, Byron and Shelley, Tieck and Novalis. That of Carlyle and Emerson falls later, just outside the period, as does that of Joseph II and the Prince de Ligne before.

Friedrich von Hardenberg was born in 1772 at Wiederstedt, in Prussian Saxony. He had an irregular schooling until he went to the University of Jena, and later to Württemberg. His father was an official in the Salt Directory, and young Hardenberg in 1794 joined a public office at Arnstadt to train himself for the service. It was there that he met and became engaged to Sophie von Kühn, who was only thirteen years of age. Her death two years later plunged Hardenberg, or Novalis, as he called himself in his works, into lasting melancholy. About twelve months afterwards, however, he became engaged again, though his early death prevented the marriage from taking place. Yet, although melancholy was a characteristic, almost a luxury, of the Romantic writers, and though Novalis wrote works of profound melancholy, as a whole, and particularly in his last two or three years, he was cheerful and happy.

The friendship of Novalis with Tieck began in 1800, when he was residing at Freiberg, in Saxony, in order to study mineralogy and to equip himself for an official career in a State mines department. He went over to Jena to visit A. W. Schlegel, and there he met Tieck. Carlyle has translated the passage from Tieck's *Life of Novalis* describing their association :

" In the summer of 1800," says Tieck, " I saw him for the first time while visiting my friend Wilhelm Schlegel; and our acquaintance soon became the most confidential friendship. They were bright days those, which we passed with Schlegel, Schelling, and some other friends. On my return homewards, I visited him in his house, and made acquaintance with his family. Here he read me the *Disciples at Sais* and many of his *Fragments*. He escorted me as far as Halle; and we enjoyed in Giebichenstein, in the Riechardts' house, some other delightful hours. About this time the first thought of his *Ofterdingen* had occurred. At an earlier period certain of his *Spiritual Songs* had been composed : they were to form part of a Christian Hymn book, which he meant to accompany with a collection of Sermons. For the rest he was very diligent in his professional labours; whatever he did was done with the heart; the smallest concern was not insignificant to him."

Embarked on his career as a mining official, Novalis was able to seek out lonely places in the Thuringian hills and to cultivate his poetic feelings in loneliness, varying this, nevertheless, with occasional company and a good deal of tranquil joy with his friends; and he wrote *Heinrich von Ofterdingen*, an unfinished romance of the semi-autobiographical or rather of the *Ich-Roman* variety. If Ofterdingen's character is that of Novalis his adventures are purely imaginary. The novel takes the hero to Greece and other strange places which Novalis knew only in imagination. Before the story was nearly finished Novalis showed signs of consumption. He remained cheerful and interested in his literary work, and spent his last days conversing about literature with F. Schlegel, who had come over to Weissenfels from Jena to visit him. At the end of the week Schlegel came into the room and found Novalis fallen into a quiet sleep from which he never awoke. He was not yet twenty-nine years of age. Tieck describes his friend as tall and slender, with clear eyes and transparent complexion, a man always cheerful and kindly, without striking bearing or conspicuous manner. " He was lost in a crowd," but on closer observation he would be called beautiful. He resembled, says Tieck, the evangelist St John, as represented in Albrecht Dürer's noble picture. Tedium he never felt, even among dull company, for he was interested in people, and always found something to like and to observe. Though he lived on the heights, and in thought and conversation unfolded the deeps of the soul, he was mirthful as a child, " Without vanity, without learned haughtiness, far from every affectation and hypocrisy, he was a genuine, true man, the purest and loveliest embodiment of a high immortal spirit." [1]

The cosmopolitan aspect of German Romanticism is obvious in the writers Friedrich de la Motte Fouqué and Adelbert von Chamisso (correctly Louis-Charles-Adelaide de Chamisso de Boncourt), the first a descendent of Huguenots, the other by birth a Frenchman. The Baron de la Motte Fouqué was a Prussian cavalry officer who served in the campaigns against France in 1794 and 1813. When not in the Army he was on his country estate at Nennhausen or, after the peace, at Paris or at Halle. *Undine*, his masterpiece of fairy romance, was published in 1811. His active literary life went on to the year 1843. Chamisso, born in 1781 in Champagne, became an *émigré* with the rest of his family in the French Revolution. After being a

---

[1] Tieck, Preface to the third edition of *Novalis Schriften* (ed. Tieck and Schlegel), translated by Carlyle (*Essays*, ed. 1899, ii, 21). Mario Praz finds a trace of decadence in Novalis (M. Praz, *The Romantic Agony*, trans. Davidson, 1933, p. 28).

page to Queen Louise he entered the Prussian Army, and served until 1807, leaving the Army at the Peace of Tilsit. Drawn towards France and Prussia in the War of Liberation, he abstained altogether from bearing arms, and wrote, as a sort of outlet to his perplexity, the quaint story of Peter Schlemihl, the man who sold his shadow, written in delightful, simple German prose. He was a good botanist, took part in a voyage of exploration in the South Seas (1815–18), became curator of the botanical gardens at Berlin, married happily, and spent the rest of his life between poetry and his botanical studies and duties. He died in 1838.

The minor personalities of this wonderful German period, all with something of genius in them, are numerous, though mainly forgotten—Friedrich Hölderlin (1770–1843), poet and prose-writer, author of the novel *Hyperion*, whose active career ended with insanity when he was thirty-two; Johann Gaudenz de Salis-Seewis (1762–1834), a native of the Grisons, captain in the Swiss Guard at Versailles, a writer of nature poetry; the poet group of Göttingen (*Göttinger Dichterbund*); Voss, the two brothers Counts Stolberg, Bürger, whose *Lenore* was translated by Scott, and a host of others. It might be said of Germany then, as Dr Johnson said of Pembroke College in his time, " we were a nest of singing-birds." Or it was like England in the age of Elizabeth, with a number of grand geniuses and a host of fine singers whose prose was as good as their poetry. And every pulse beat with the spirit of freedom.

The Romantic writers had other characteristics too. They were inclined to make a god of melancholy and solitariness. Tieck invented the word *Waldeinsamkeit*. Some of them, F. Schlegel and Gutzkow, had unconventional ideas about love and marriage. Gutzkow, for a notorious book called *Wally die Zweiflerin* (*Wally the Sceptic*) (1835), which, in point of fact, he seems to have meant as an attack on Romanticism, not as an explanation of it, was imprisoned by the Baden authorities for three months. Goethe had sternly set his face against this unconventional Romantic tendency, which he considered to be immodest and immoral. Jean Paul Richter would have nothing

to do with it. Every Renaissance has an excess of energy, an
effervescence, an ebullience, and the German Renaissance of
the Romantic Age required correcting in one direction or
another, as, indeed, does every movement. It was, however, in
spite of any faults, fundamentally a humane movement. The
things in which it was interested were the things common to all
mankind. It influenced the other peoples; it was influenced by
them. This was the most international period of German literature and thought.

A Dutch student of this Renaissance has drawn up tables of
corresponding dates—on one side notable events in German
Romantic literature or art, on the other side events in the course
and development of the French Revolution, the Napoleonic
era, and the Restoration period.[1] Thus:

	GERMANY	FRANCE
1789	Mozart: *Cosi fan tutte.*	Estates-General at Versailles.
1790	Kant: *Kritik der Urteils-kraft.*	Constitutional monarchy.
1792	Fichte: *Kritik aller Offenbarung.*	Girondin Ministry. September Massacres.
1793	Jean Paul: *Die unsicht-bare Loge.*	Execution of Louis XVI.
	Herder: *Briefe zur Be-förderung der Huma-nität.*	Reign of Terror. *Levée en masse.*
1795	Goethe: *Wilhelm Meis-ters Lehrjahre.*	Directory.
1796	Jean Paul: *Hesperus* and *Quintus Fixlein.*	Bonaparte's Italian campaign.

And so on: the tables are extended. Schiller's *Wilhelm Tell*
balances Napoleon's becoming Emperor in 1804; Chamisso's
Peter Schlemihl balances the Vienna Congress in 1814.

From one point of view the correspondence means almost
nothing, but from another it means a good deal. There was no
direct connexion between the novel *Quintus Fixlein* and the
battles of Lodi and Arcola. But there is a vital connexion
between literary Romanticism and the political and social
developments in Europe between 1789 and 1815 or later.

[1] Fischer, *op. cit.*, pp. 15–18.

It is true that none of the Romantic writers of Germany were statesmen, nor, except for Chateaubriand and Benjamin Constant, were any of the French. The biggest, the most dynamic, political movement of the Romantic Age was the French Revolution; and the spiritual origins of this were in the teachings of Voltaire, Diderot, and the various other sceptics of the Age of Reason. While, however, ' Voltairism ' was one source, ' Rousseauism ' was another, and particularly Rousseau's appeal from the pageantry of kings and the pedantry of Courts to simple life, to nature, to the wants and aspirations of the common man, to the ' people.' Rousseau was also, undeniably, the chief literary inspirer of Romanticism. The mountains and streams of Switzerland, Rousseau's wandering, sentimental, open-air life, his simple prose and poetic phrases, were the bases of the literary Romantic movement. Rousseauism in literature and in politics was revolutionary. *The Declaration of the Rights of Man,* Schiller's *Wilhelm Tell,* Schlegel's translation of Shakespeare, have the same spiritual source, were a response to the same urgings of man's nature. The Declaration of the Rights of Man (1791), the Reign of Terror (1792–94), the Directory (1795), the Napoleonic Empire (1799–1814), the Liberation (1812–14), the Restoration (1815)—these things form a movement with a rhythm such as can be discerned all through the age in art and literature as in politics.

Not too much, however, should be made of the difference between classicism and Romanticism. The classical culture of the eighteenth century was based ultimately on the ancient Greek culture; for this the Romantics tended to substitute veneration for medieval culture. Such doubtless is the reason, or one of the reasons, for the conversion of many of them to Roman Catholicism. A French critic, M. Émile Deschanel, has written a brilliantly suggestive work on *The Romanticism of the Classical Writers (Le Romantisme des classiques).* " A Romantic writer is simply a classic writer on the road to fame; and, reciprocally, a classic is only a Romantic arrived." These writers, adds M. Deschanel, who have now undisputed fame were at first, each according to his kind, " literary revolutionaries." The argument

cont'd ...

is a little overstrained. It is easy to think of some classical writers or works—for instance, Gray and the *Elegy written in a Country Churchyard*—to which the word revolutionary could only with very careful qualifications be applied. Nevertheless, it is well to bear in mind that the antithesis between classic and Romantic has been made too pronounced in literary history, and that both qualities are found in the best minds and the loftiest spirits.

4 (cont'd)

CHAPTER V

HEROES

FOR good or ill the French Revolution made an end of the eighteenth century. It broke down the Age of Reason; but it did not extinguish ' Wertherism,' the melancholy and sentimentality which are the foes of action. Wertherism is inaction. The philosophers wanted to show that they were men of action, that they were influencing the world.

The potent philosopher of this time, now almost forgotten, was the Swiss Karl Ludwig von Haller, whose *Restauration der Staatswissenschaft* was a kind of political Bible for the Romantics, a cry from the Middle Ages in the language, in the tongue, of a man of affairs.

Hallerism found a friendly echo in every country, not with the Liberals, of course, but with the conservative elements. Walter Scott was a Tory, with the tastes of a country gentleman and a pen that could recall the ordered eighteenth century out of which he himself came and the Middle Ages which he saw with the eye of romance. His first long poem, *The Lay of the Last Minstrel*, a story of the Middle Ages, came out in 1805; *Marmion* in 1808; *The Lady of the Lake* in 1810. About this time he became acquainted with the stories of Miss Edgeworth, " whose Irish characters," he wrote later, " have gone so far to make the English familiar with the character of their gay and light-hearted neighbours of Ireland that she may be truly said to have done more towards completing the Union than perhaps all the legislative enactments by which it has been followed up." [1] Scott thought to do for the Scots what Miss Edgeworth had done for the Irish—to make them familiar to the " sister kingdom." He had begun an eighteenth-century novel of

[1] Preface to the 1829 edition of the *Waverley Novels*.

Scotland a few years earlier, had laid it aside, and then had lost it. Luckily, on searching for some fishing-tackle in a lumber-room at Abbotsford, he came across a writing-desk with the manuscript of the unfinished romance of *Waverley*. The complete story was published in 1814. Although it was a tale of only " Sixty Years Since," it created for the British public, and, indeed, for the whole European public, the romantic past, of which they could admire the quaintness and chivalry in contrast with the sombre present.

More tales of Scotland followed upon *Waverley*, until the author began to fear that by frequent repetition of the same theme he might weary his public. So he turned to English history for a theme, and selected the reign of Richard I, where he could contrast the blunt and homely manners of the depressed Anglo-Saxons with the high spirit and military fame of the Normans, their " personal adventure, and whatever could distinguish them as the Flower of Chivalry." [1] *Ivanhoe* was published in 1819, and Hallerism received a notable reinforcement. The cult of the Middle Ages became fashionable and was a great support to the ultramontane Catholic movement; it strengthened the well-known tendency of the Romantic writers to join the Roman Catholic communion.

Liberalism was making progress too, and had the allegiance of a greater number of men of intellect than had Hallerism; it was the political creed of the rising *bourgeoisie*, as yet unmenaced by Socialism. Yet another theory of society and politics was considered—the theory which much later (1865) Tolstoi put into *War and Peace*. This was to the effect that the plain man, or rather the multitude of plain men, makes history. It is what *they* think that moves states and settles the destiny of principalities and powers. It is not a theory of democracy; it has nothing to do with votes or constitutions. It is simply the theory that the obscure but definite urgings of the common people are the directing forces, although the people themselves are not conscious of this. Carlyle wrote in *Sartor Resartus* (published serially in *Fraser's Magazine* in 1833–34):

[1] Preface to the 1830 edition.

Two men I honour, and no third. First, the toilworn Craftsman that with earth-made Implement laboriously conquers the
Earth, and makes her man's. Venerable to me is the hard Hand;
crooked, coarse; wherein notwithstanding lies a cunning virtue,
indefeasibly royal, as of the Sceptre of this Planet. Venerable
too is the rugged face, all weather-tanned, besoiled, with its rude
intelligence; for it is the face of a Man living manlike. Oh, but
the more venerable for thy rudeness, and even because we must
pity as well as love thee! Hardly-entreated Brother! For us was
thy back so bent, for us were thy straight limbs and fingers so
deformed: thou wert our Conscript, on whom the lot fell, and
fighting our battles wert so marred. . . .

A second man I honour, and still more highly: Him who is
seen toiling for the spiritually indispensable; not daily bread, but
the bread of Life. Is not he too in his duty; endeavouring towards
inward Harmony; revealing this, by act or by word, through all
his outward endeavours, be they high or low? Highest of all,
when his outward and his inward endeavour are one: when we
can name him Artist; not earthly Craftsman only, but inspired
Thinker, who with heaven-made Implement conquers Heaven
for us! [1]

Tolstoi, who was born in 1828 and therefore grew up to full
manhood in the Romantic Age, had no belief in heroes. For
him Alexander, Napoleon, and all the other potentates in the
stirring year 1812 were just puppets, helplessly involved in the
silent forces, the instincts, desires, and judgments, of the
common people, whom the dynasts thought they controlled.
The man who really met, who alone was equal to, the situation
of 1812, the invasion of Russia by Napoleon, was not the
Emperor Alexander, but General Kutusov, old, serene, leth-
argic, who sat silent among his masses of peasant troops and
did nothing, or did according to their unspoken directions.
This is the pervading theme of *War and Peace*.

If Carlyle at one time had an idea of the plain man on the
great stage of history he soon arrived at another theory: the
world was moved by heroes. " Worship of a Hero is tran-
scendent admiration of a Great Man. I say great men are still

[1] *Sartor Resartus*, Book III, Chapter IV.

admirable; I say there is at bottom nothing else admirable. . . . It is at this hour and at all hours the vivifying influence in man's life." Kings and potentates, he wrote to Miss Welsh, were gaudy folk who flaunted about with plumes and ribbons; " but the Miltons, the de Staëls—these *are* the very salt of the earth; they derive their patents of nobility direct from Almighty God, and live in the bosoms of all time men to all ages." [1]

While tutoring the Bullers, and under the *élan*, the buoyancy and optimism of having achieved the " Everlasting No " and the " Everlasting Yea," Carlyle planned a new kind of history, with a more generous view of human nature than Gibbon's. Of course, he admired Gibbon's history: " How gorgeously does it swing across the gloomy and tumultuous chasm of those barbarous centuries: Gibbon is a man whom one never forgets —unless oneself deserving to be forgotten; the perusal of his work forms an epoch in the history of one's mind." Yet Carlyle found Gibbon also to have " a coarse and vulgar heart," worshipping power and splendour and sympathizing little with suffering virtue or with the most heroic devotedness, unless successful and arranged in the pomp and circumstance of outward glory. Carlyle's history was going to be something different from this. He would select the Commonwealth for his theme, not by way of regular narrative, but grouping together the most singular manifestations of mind that occurred then under distinct heads, and selecting some remarkable person as the representative of each class—Laud, Clarendon, Cromwell, Milton, Hampden. [2] This design came to nothing at that time, although some twenty years later, with the curious persistence of literary ideas and purposes, it produced *Cromwell* and *Heroes and Hero-Worship*.

Although his *Past and Present* showed a fine appreciation of medieval monastic life, Carlyle had nothing but contempt for Hallerism and Neo-Catholic veneration of the Middle Ages. Nor was he a liberal, for he distrusted and opposed democracy. His great men were not mighty captains, or, if they were such,

[1] To Miss Welsh, July 1822 (*Letters*, ii, 107).
[2] To Miss Welsh, January 1823 (*Letters*, ii, 170).

were only incidentally so. Their greatness consisted in their vision of truth and justice. It seems to have been through his study of Goethe that he came to this conclusion. At the end of the year 1824 Carlyle established contact by correspondence with the master, Goethe taking the initiative, on the publication of the translation of *Wilhelm Meister*. Carlyle writes to Miss Welsh, December 20, 1824:

> The other twilight, the lackey of one Lord Bentinck came with a lackey's knock to the door, and delivered me a little blue parcel, requiring for it a receipt under my hand. I opened it somewhat eagerly, and found two small pamphlets with ornamental covers, and—a letter from—Goethe. Conceive my satisfaction: it was almost like a message from Fairy Land; I could scarcely think that *this* was the real hand and signature of that mysterious personage, whose name had floated through my fancy, like a sort of spell, since boyhood; whose thoughts had come to me in maturer years with almost the impressiveness of revelations. But what says the letter? Kind nothings, in a simple patriarchal style, extremely to my taste.[1]

Carlyle was not yet thirty years old when the correspondence began; Goethe was seventy-five. The two men never saw each other. On April 14, 1832, Carlyle, at Dumfries, received a letter from William Fraser, proprietor and editor of the *Foreign Magazine*, containing news that Goethe was dead. " Alas! Alas! " writes Carlyle to his brother Alick; " I feel as if I had a second time lost a Father. The world holds not his like within it. But it is appointed for *all* ' once to die.' " Emerson, with whom Carlyle carried on a splendid correspondence for nearly forty years, could not away with Goethe. " Mine," wrote Emerson,

> must be a qualified admiration. It is a singular piece of good-nature in you to apotheosize him. I cannot but regard it as his misfortune, with conspicuous bad influence on his genius, that velvet life he led. What incongruity for genius, whose fit ornaments and reliefs are poverty and hatred, to repose fifty years on chairs of state!

[1] To Miss Welsh, January 1823 (*Letters*, ii, 292).

The American Puritan could not condone, as Carlyle (though also a Puritan) had managed to condone, the " bad morals " of Goethe, a genius " pampered, acknowledged, crowned." [1] Carlyle, of course, had his answer ready.

> I will tell you in a word why I like Goethe: he is the only *healthy* mind, of any extent, that I have discovered in Europe for long generations. It was he that first convincingly proclaimed to me (convincingly, for I saw it *done*): Behold, even in this scandalous Sceptico-Epicurean generation, when all is gone but hunger and cant, it is still possible that Men be Men. [2]

So, in this search for real men within the shams and trappings of degenerate society, Carlyle arrived at his idea of heroism as the moving force of history. His lectures on *Heroes*, delivered in London in May 1840, were well attended and brought in considerable emolument, although, Carlyle wrote to Emerson: " On the whole, I fear I did little but confuse my esteemed audience." He found his men in Odin, Mahomet, Dante, Shakespeare, Luther, Knox, Cromwell, Johnson, Rousseau, Burns, and—rather doubtfully—Napoleon. Later he adopted the great Frederick.

This man mesmerized his generation—mesmerized Joseph II, Mirabeau and (for a time) Voltaire, the Prince de Ligne, and a host of others. And now Carlyle fell under the enchantment of success. Frederick succeeded; his work (in spite of Jena) lasted, and brutality was consecrated for ever. Carlyle sometimes had doubts. When it was all over and the colossal book finished he wrote to Emerson: " I was nearly killed by that hideous Book on Friedrich—twelve years in continuous wrestle with the nightmares and the subterranean hydras." [3] The truth was, he confessed in another letter to Emerson:

> Fritz himself is not sufficiently divine to me, far from it. . . . The insuperable difficulty of *Frederic* is, that he, the genuine little ray of Veritable and Eternal that was in him, lay imbedded in the putrid Eighteenth Century, such an ocean of sordid nothing-

---

[1] *The Correspondence of Thomas Carlyle and Ralph Waldo Emerson, 1834–1872*, edited by C. E. Norton (1883), i, 29–30.
[2] *Ibid.*, i, 40. [3] *Ibid.*, ii, 301.

ness, shams and scandalous hypocrisies, as never weltered in the world before; and that in everything I can find yet written or recorded of him, he still, to all intents and purposes, most tragically *lies THERE.*

The Prussian soldiers, anyhow, impressed Carlyle with admiration: " Truly and really the Prussian Soldiers, with their intelligent *silence*, with touches of effective Spartanism I saw or fancied in them, were the class of people that pleased me best." [1] The Prussian Government offered him the Order of Merit, and Carlyle, who refused an English baronetcy, accepted the Prussian distinction. He had enthroned Frederick, prepared the European mind for the acts of force of Bismarck, and helped on the Prussian tradition of what has been called Prussia's " great mission in world history." [2]

Emerson was enthusiastic about the book, though not on account of its disclosing a hero or discovering Prussia's mission. It was " infinitely the wittiest book that ever was written," he noted in his diary. " . . . Carlyle's *Friedrich* is a great book; opens a new extension to history. How much event, personality, nationality, is there disclosed or hinted at, and will draw multitudes of scholars to its exploring and illustration." This is a good piece of criticism, and certainly does not make too much of Frederick himself as a hero. But it was probably not the impression of most people who read *Frederick the Great.* Carlyle helped to establish a legend of ' greatness ' which was only too readily accepted by the Prussians.

Carlyle was innocent, however, of the Napoleonic legend. Public interest in Napoleon, intense while he was living and active, has continued down to the present day, and shows no sign of diminishing. The two best prose-writers in England during the Romantic Age, Scott and Hazlitt, wrote lives of the great man. Scott's *Life of Bonaparte* was published in 1827. Goethe, who was then seventy-eight years old, was keenly interested, and declared:

[1] *The Correspondence of Thomas Carlyle and Ralph Waldo Emerson, 1834–1872,* edited by C. E. Norton (1883), ii, 225.
[2] General Hermann Goering, *Germany Reborn* (1934), p. 11.

The richest, the easiest, the most celebrated, narrator of the century, undertakes to write the history of his own time. What expectations the announcement of such a work must have excited in me will be understood by anyone who remembers that I, twenty years older than Scott, conversed with Paoli in the twentieth year of my age, and with Napoleon himself in the sixtieth. . . . What could now be more delightful to me than leisurely and calmly to sit down and listen to the discourse of such a man, while clearly, truly, and with all the skill of a great artist he recalls to me the incidents on which through life I have meditated, the influence of which is still daily in operation.[1]

Scott did not make a hero of Napoleon, and his work did not please the believers in the legend that was already in existence. The book, which, " if it had been printed on the original model of his novels, would have filled from thirteen to fourteen volumes," was composed in about twelve months, and it earned, the first and second editions, £18,000—a sum which, Scott's biographer, Lockhart, wrote ten years later, " even now startles me to mention." The *Life* depicts Napoleon not (as Lockhart claims) with " lofty impartiality," but as the conservative Europeans saw him, and probably correctly, a great disturber of Europe and the great egoist. Hazlitt, who was a radical and a revolutionary, brought out his long *Life of Napoleon* next year (1828). Though he took a different view from Scott and idolized Napoleon, he was right in regarding Napoleon as the finisher, the " sword-arm," of the Revolution. Scott's biographer could not resist writing a life of Napoleon too; it was published in 1829. Here, as would be expected from the pen of a conservative *Quarterly Reviewer*, there was no idealization of the Emperor; he was the victim of his good fortune.

The blaze which dazzled other men's eyes had fatal influence on his. He began to believe that there was something super-human in his own faculties, and that he was privileged to deny that any laws were made for him. Obligations by which he ex-pected all besides to be fettered he considered himself entitled

[1] From *Kunst und Alterthum*, quoted by Lockhart, *Life of Scott* (ed. Hope-Scott, 1898), ii, 658.

to snap and trample. He became a deity to himself; and expected mankind not merely to submit to, but to admire and reverence, the actions of a demon.

Yet though, in Lockhart's view, perhaps no man ever passed through life " sympathizing so slightly with mankind," he surpassed all in the intensity of the sway which he exercised over his contemporaries.[1] And the spell has continued long after his death. In an essay in *Blackwood's Magazine* Lockhart wrote:

> Nations yet to come will look back upon his history as to some grand and supernatural romance. The fiery energy of his youthful career and the magnificent progress of his irresistible ambition have invested his character with the mysterious grandeur of some heavenly appearance; and when all the lesser tumults and all the lesser men of our age shall have passed away into the darkness of oblivion history will still inscribe one mighty era with the majestic name of Napoleon.

Heine grew up in Düsseldorf amid the fame and the talk of Bonaparte's achievements. Early in 1813 he saw battered French soldiers passing towards France, remnants of the Grand Army which had been shattered in the retreat from Moscow. The sight of two stalwart men, pathetic in their wounds and weariness, called forth ultimately one of his finest lyrics, *Die Grenadiere*, so effectively set to music by Schubert. The Emperor Napoleon was the hero whom the two grenadiers worshipped blindly, heroically; and Heine felt the spell himself.

Carlyle was exempt from the witchery to which Hazlitt and Heine had succumbed. Napoleon, he thought, compared badly alongside of the great English Puritan.

> His compact, prompt, everyway articulate character is in itself perhaps small compared with our great, chaotic, *in*articulate Cromwell's. . . . Hume's notion of the Fanatic-Hypocrite, with such truth as it has, will apply much better to Napoleon than it did to Cromwell, to Mahomet or the like.

[1] J. G. Lockhart, *The History of Napoleon Buonaparte*, ad fin.

Not that Napoleon was a hypocrite all the time, according to Carlyle's view. For the first ten or twelve years of his active career there was a sort of faith in him.

> That this new enormous Democracy asserting itself here in the French Revolution is an insuppressible fact, which the whole world, with its old forces and institutions, cannot put down; this was a true insight of his, and took his conscience and enthusiasm along with it,—a *faith*.

As he sits with Bourrienne in a Parisian *café* on the terrible day of June 20, 1792, and sees the mob roll by, he " expresses the deepest contempt for persons in authority that they do not restrain this rabble." He knew, too, that democracy could not be an anarchy. As he watches the mob storm the Tuileries, to force their way into the presence of the King and massacre the Swiss Guard, on August 10, 1792, " he wonders why there is no man to command these poor Swiss." Faith in democracy, hatred of anarchy, is what carried Napoleon through his work. " Through his brilliant Italian Campaigns, through Wagrams, Austerlitzes; triumph after triumph—he triumphed so far. There was an eye to see in this man, a soul to dare and do. He rose naturally to be the King."

" But at this point," writes Carlyle, rather vaguely, " the fatal charlatan-element got the upper hand." If this was in 1802, when Bonaparte became Consul *à vie*, or in 1804, when he became Emperor, it was before the " Wagrams and Austerlitzes." He " took to believing in Semblances; strove to connect himself with Austrian Dynasties, Popedoms, with the old false Feudalities," to found his own dynasty. " *Self* and false ambition had now become his god: *self*-deception once yielded to, *all* other deceptions follow naturally more and more. . . ."

This brought Napoleon to his doom.

> The heavier this Napoleon trampled on the world, holding it tyrannously down, the fiercer would the world's recoil against him be, one day. Injustice pays itself with frightful compound-interest. I am not sure but he had better have lost his best park of artillery, or had his best regiment drowned in the sea, than shot that poor German Bookseller, Palm!

When Napoleon's Empire collapsed and he was " flung-out on the rock," on St Helena, he was simply surprised. But the truth was that he had brought this fate upon himself when he " parted with Reality." Yet he was not a small man. " He had to sink there, mournfully as man seldom did; and break his great heart, and die—this poor Napoleon: a great implement too soon wasted, till it was useless: our last Great Man! " [1]

Taine, who wrote later than Carlyle, called Napoleon the third great man of the Renaissance, Dante and Michelangelo being the first and second. Napoleon was their equal, by reason of " the definite contours of his vision, the intensity, the coherence, and inner consistency of his dream, the depth of his meditations, the superhuman greatness of his conception." Carlyle could not see this in Napoleon; but his apotheosis of heroes on the one hand and the Napoleonic legend to which he was not a party on the other helped to produce the Nietzschean theory of the superman. Germany, however, was already prepared for Nietzsche. Fichte had exalted *Heroismus*. But Fichte was national, patriotic, exclusive. Nietzsche regarded the superman as cosmopolitan, universal.

> What I am concerned with—for I see it preparing itself slowly and hesitatingly—is the United Europe. It was the only real work, the one impulse in the soul of all the broadminded and deep-thinking men of this century—the preparation of a new synthesis, the tentative effort to anticipate the future of the European. Only in their weaker moments, when they grew old, did they fall back again into the national narrowness of the Fatherlander.[2]

Few people will be prepared to deny that there are heroes, and that heroism is a grand and admirable quality. Carlyle's message was a message of energy to the people of the Romantic Age; and it proved itself a gospel of energy to the much later post-War age of Hitlerite Germany. It was expressed by Signor Mussolini when he told his people that they must live

[1] The quotations in the above five paragraphs are from Carlyle, *Heroes and Hero-worship*, Lecture VI, *ad fin.*
[2] Quoted by H. J. C. Grierson, *Carlyle and Hitler* (1933), pp. 55–56.

on a plane of " high ideal tension." It leads to the dangerous
infatuation that a people, a nation, has a ' mission,' although,
as Benedetto Croce writes, " nations, like individuals, have no
mission save that of living their lives as human beings—that is,
as idealists." [1]

[1] B. Croce, *A History of Italy*, *1871–1915* (trans. C. M. Ady, 1929),
p. 4.

CHAPTER VI

THE WAY OUT OF "WELTSCHMERZ"

BYRONISM—melancholy, world-weariness, disillusion—was the disease of the Romantic Age. It was not, of course, peculiar to this period, for young men, especially those of the more intellectual kind, are prone to it in every age. Byron, however, was a famous personality in his own lifetime. His poetry was eagerly read, and his attitude towards life was imitated all over Western Europe and even in Russia. His *vogue* was, as it were, a revived Wertherism, for Goethe's hero had already made popular and fashionable melancholy, fantastic waistcoats and neckties, hopeless love, the contemplation of suicide, self-pity, tears. Goethe himself disliked all this. He was horrified at the melting effect which *The Sorrows of Werther* had upon contemporary youth. The troubles and struggles incidental to the Revolutionary and Napoleonic eras obscured Wertherism and made it unfashionable, but Byron revived the cult, and this time it seemed to have come to stay. Heine in Germany, Pushkin in Russia, Béranger in France, admired and themselves expressed Byronic melancholy and contempt for society and convention; Lamartine had the melancholy without the pessimism and bitterness; Leopardi in Italy had the melancholy without the bitterness. The world of fashionable young men became ' dandified.'

German thought in this period was in favour of ' action ' as the end of life. Fichte among philosophers, Jean Paul among men of letters, insisted that an active life must result from the exercise of mind upon the great problems of life. Fichte's objects were eminently practical : he aimed at influencing the political and economic structure of the State. Though Kant never left Königsberg, he was scanning public affairs closely all the time, and he had his plan for the better government of Europe. Goethe's ' Olympian ' attitude towards the world was exceptional in that era, for this was the great age of the ' public counsellor,' the ' publicist,' to use a rather awkward Germanism.

6.

Byron's melancholy, his world weariness and unco-ordinated inner life, made his life aimless and, in a sense, actionless, though filled almost incessantly with tumult. He was still only a young man, thirty-six, when he landed at Missolonghi in January 1824; and now at last he found peace of mind and sustained purposefulness in action, for three and a half months, for the cause of Greece.

These undecided, unsatisfied, pessimistic men of thought of the Romantic Age were in marked contrast with the serene and assured men of the eighteenth century, the Age of Reason; but gradually the Romantic Age too assumed a more tranquil aspect; the men of thought became more assured. They found peace in action, public, philanthropic, educational; after 1832 the great Age of Reform began—the abolition of slavery, Parliamentary reform, labour legislation, Froebel's *Kindergärten* at Burgdorf, in Bern, Free Trade, and the development of Continental liberalism.

Alongside of Byronic pessimism there seemed to exist a kind of political pessimism, expressed in the ' Metternich system.' In Metternich's view all or nearly all the political impulses and aims of the people were bad. The Revolution, although for the time being checked, had doomed Europe to political decline; all that Metternich could do was to " prop up a mouldering edifice." *I am so weary*, he wrote, after thirty years of this effort. Metternich was a man of the eighteenth century. His pessimism was that of one who lived in the memory of a past age of stability, reason, moderation, and who now saw the times completely out of joint.

There was a tendency for the Romantic movement to become pessimist, to degenerate into the cult of corruption, the philosophy of the Marquis de Sade.[1] But it is just times like these—

[1] The Marquis de Sade (1740–1814) wrote romances in which crime was made the source of all happiness (Praz, *op. cit.*, pp. 102 ff.).

of pessimism, disillusion, world weariness, autumnal decline,
and the coming of the end of all things — that are the
opportunity of a prophet. The third decade of the nineteenth
century was an age of prophets; of these the most moving, the
most vehement, was Carlyle. And he found all his inspiration
in German thought, although he did not visit Germany itself
until he was sixty years old.

The philosophy which Carlyle drew from Germany was a
philosophy of action. " Like Plato, he would fain have ruled
men, at least guided them, for that seemed to him the want of
his age." [1] Like most people, he had to arrive at his philosophy
through doubt and internal struggle. Born in 1795, the son of
a Scots stonemason in Dumfriesshire, he was brought up with
a knowledge of the Bible and with Calvinist principles. He
received a good education at the local school. At fourteen he
went to Edinburgh University, with a view to preparing for
the ministry. He read widely and deeply—in classics, history,
mathematics. In the end he did not enter the ministry, and
left the university with his career still unsettled (1814). There
followed years of school-teaching, of translating German, of
working as tutor. It was the life of many scholars in Germany,
some of them the greatest of their time. He was assailed by
doubts, by the devil. What was life? What was the end of
man? Why was he created? Existence, thought, became a
torture to him. At last relief came, and it seems to have come
suddenly, though doubtless he had many struggles to make
after this. The incident happened in Leith Walk in 1822. " I
remember it well," he told Froude years afterwards, " and
could go straight to the place." The incident is described in
Sartor Resartus (Book II, Chapter VII):

" So had it lasted, as in bitter protracted Death-agony, through
long years. The heart within me, unvisited by any heavenly dew-
drop, was smouldering in sulphurous, slow-consuming fire. . . .
" Full of such humour, and perhaps the miserablest man in
the whole French Capital or Suburbs, was I, one sultry Dogday,

---

[1] Grierson, *op. cit.*, p. 63.

after much perambulation, toiling along the dirty little *Rue Saint-Thomas de l'Enfer* . . . when, all at once, there rose a Thought in me, and I asked myself: ' What *art* thou afraid of? ' . . . And as I so thought, there rushed like a stream of fire over my whole soul; and I shook base Fear away from me for ever. I was strong, of unknown strength; a spirit, almost a god. From that time the temper of my misery was changed: not Fear or whining Sorrow was it, but Indignation and grim fire-eyed Defiance.

" Thus had the *Everlasting No* (*das ewige Nein*) pealed authoritatively through all the recesses of my Being, of my Me. . . .

" It is from this hour that I incline to date my Spiritual New-birth."

A philosophy of action, however, can scarcely come directly out of the " Everlasting No." " Was that high moment in the Rue de l'Enfer, then, properly the turning-point of the battle? " There was another decision, gradually arrived at by Teufelsdröckh (Carlyle) in musings in his attic chamber up among the house-tops of Leith Walk.

Beautiful it was to sit there, as in my skyey Tent, musing and meditating; on the high table-land, in front of the Mountains; over me, as roof, the azure Dome, and around me, for walls, four azure-flowing curtains,—namely, of the Four azure winds, on whose bottom-fringes also I have seen gilding. And then to fancy the fair Castles that stood sheltered in these Mountain hollows; with their green flower-lawns, and white dames and damosels, lovely enough; or better still, the straw-roofed Cottages, wherein stood many a Mother baking bread, with her children round her:—all hidden and protectingly folded-up in the valley-folds; yet there and alive, as sure as if I beheld them. Or to see, as well as fancy, the nine Towns and Villages, that lay round my mountain-seat, which, in still weather, were wont to speak to me (by their steeple-bells) with metal tongue; and, in almost all weather, proclaimed their vitality by repeated Smoke-clouds; whereon, as on a culinary horologe, I might read the hour of the day. For it was the smoke of cookery, as kind house-wives at morning, midday, eventide, were boiling their husbands' kettles; and ever a blue pillar rose up into the air, successively or simultaneously, from each of the nine, saying, as plainly as smoke could say: Such and such a meal is getting ready here. Not uninteresting! For you have the whole Borough, with all its love-makings and scandal-mongeries, contentions and contentments, as in miniature, and could cover it all with your hat.— If, in my wide Wayfarings, I had learned to look into the business of the World in its details, here perhaps was the place for combining it into general propositions, and deducing inferences therefrom.

This glimpse of the divine brought Teufelsdröckh to the threshold of pity. " Man, with his so mad Wants and so mean Endeavours, had become the dearer to me; and even for his sufferings and his sins, I now first named him Brother. Thus was I standing in the porch of that ' *Sanctuary of Sorrows.*' " And here the Professor first got an eye on the knot that had been strangling him, and straightway could unfasten it and was free. He saw into the secret of his self-torture: that man's unhappiness comes of his greatness; it is because there is an infinite in him which, with all his cunning, he cannot quite bury under the finite. " Will the whole Finance Ministers and Upholsterers and Confectioners of modern Europe undertake in joint-stock company, to make one Shoeblack Happy? They cannot accomplish it, above an hour or two: for the Shoeblack has a Soul quite other than his Stomach." And the freeing of the soul is not to be found in the quest of happiness:

" I asked myself: What is this that, ever since earliest years, thou has been fretting and fuming, and lamenting and self-tormenting, on account of? Say it in a word: is it not because thou art not happy? Because the Thou (sweet gentleman) is not sufficiently honoured, nourished, soft-bedded, and lovingly cared-for? Foolish soul! What Act of Legislature was there that *thou* shouldst be Happy? A little while ago thou hadst no right to *be* at all. What if thou wert born and predestined not to be Happy, but to be Unhappy! Art thou nothing other than a Vulture, then, that fliest through the Universe seeking after somewhat to *eat*; and shrieking dolefully because carrion enough is not given thee? Close thy *Byron*; open thy *Goethe*."

F

At last Teufelsdröckh was nearing the end of his quest—
that is, he was coming to see the ideal which he would follow :

> " It is only with renunciation that Life, properly speaking, can
> be said to begin. . . . *Es leuchtet mir ein*, I see a glimpse of it;
> there is in man a Higher than Love of Happiness; he can do
> without Happiness, and instead thereof find Blessedness. . . . On
> the roaring billows of Time, thou art not engulfed, but borne
> aloft into the azure of Eternity. Love not Pleasure; love God.
> This is the Everlasting Yea."

Thus, Carlyle's thinking led him to a philosophy of life
which, starting with the idea of renunciation, brought him to
an ideal of action. Something positive lies at the back of the
conception of the " Everlasting Yea." By closing his Byron
and opening his Goethe Carlyle meant the reading of *Wilhelm
Meister*, a novel of action, where he found a practical ethic.
This reading had helped him to both the " No " and the
" Yea," to defiance of Fear and the Devil, and to the assertion
of Purpose and Duty.

> I had at length, after some repulsions, got into the heart of
> *Wilhelm Meister*, and eagerly read it through ;—my sally out, after
> finishing, along the vacant streets of Edinburgh (a windless,
> Scotch-misty Sunday night), is still vivid to me: Grand, surely,
> harmoniously built together, far-seeing, wise and true: when,
> for many years, or almost in my life before, have I read such a
> Book?

This was in 1821, the year before he found the " Everlasting
No " and " Yea." The peace to which he attained was not
unbroken. Those who wrestle with the Devil cannot dispose
of him with one throw. Carlyle had relapses. He was " in the
very midst of Wertherism, the blackness and darkness of death,"
just before he found his deepest peace. This occurred at Hoddam Hill. He had saved some money by tutoring the Buller
family at £200 a year for two years, and so he was able to rent
a farm at Hoddam Hill, in Annandale, his brother Alexander
doing all the practical work, while Carlyle walked about the
countryside or read and wrote indoors. The year was 1825.

He translated one book of *Wilhelm Meisters Wanderjahre*, and gradually and finally achieved his " conversion." " I call that year *idyllic*, in spite of his russet coat," he declared, looking back on it in later life. To a friend he wrote that summer (October 26, 1825): " Few persons in the British Isles have spent an idler summer than I, and it is long since I spent one as happy. . . . We live on our hill-top, enjoying a degree of solitude that might content the great Zimmermann himself." [1]

> This year I found that I had conquered all my scepticisms, agonising doubtings, fearful wrestlings with the foul and vile and soul-murdering Mad-gods of my Epoch . . . and was emerging free in spirit, into the eternal blue of ether. . . . I understood well what the old Christian people meant by their " conversion," by God's Infinite Mercy to them. . . . I then felt, and still feel, endlessly indebted to Goethe in the business; he, in his fashion, I perceived, had travelled the steep rocky road before me—the first of the moderns. [2]

Next year, 1826, Carlyle, now thirty years old, married Jane Welsh, and settled down, at Comely Bank, Edinburgh, later at Mrs Carlyle's property, Craigenputtock, Dumfriesshire, and, finally, at Chelsea, to a long, active life as prophet of the age.

The confidence, assurance, conviction of purpose in life, which came to him, largely, at any rate, through reading Goethe's works, and chiefly *Wilhelm Meister*, was not attained in a flash. But he quickly conceived a profound admiration for Goethe. " This Goethe has as much in him as any ten of them," he writes in a letter of 1823 to Miss Welsh. " Wordsworth and Byron; they are as the Christian Ensign and Captain Bobadil before the Duke of Marlborough." Again: " You make a right distinction about Goethe: he is a great genius and does *not make you cry*." That was what the Lake School of poets was inclined to do. While indulging in some rather feeble

[1] *Early Letters of T. Carlyle* (ed. C. E. Norton, 1886), ii, 328–329. Zimmermann was a Swiss, physician to George III and Frederick the Great. He was the author of *über die Einsamkeit (On Solitude)*, published in 1785.
[2] *Reminiscences* (" Everyman's " edition), pp. 281–282, quoted by C. F. Harrold, *Carlyle and German Thought* (1934), p. 48.

regrets for the past and desires to recall it Carlyle suddenly
checks himself writing: " You observe I am verging to the
Lake School in sentiment? I will leave it then." [1] But although
he was quick to recognize Goethe as a man of " true culture
and unusual genius," he was not so sure at first about *Wilhelm
Meister*. While working on it in the Bullers' house he calls it

> a book which I love not, which am sure will never sell, but which
> I am determined to print and finish. There are touches of the
> very highest, most ethereal genius in it; but diluted with floods
> of insipidity, which even *I* would not have written for the world.
> ... There is poetry in the book, and prose, prose, for ever.
> When I read of players and libidinous actresses and their sorry
> pasteboard apparatus for beautifying and enlivening the ' Moral
> world,' I render it into grammatical English—with a feeling mild
> and charitable as that of a starving hyaena.

He began to see faults even in the personality of the author.
" Goethe is the greatest genius that has lived for a century, and
the greatest ass that has lived for three. I could sometimes fall
down and worship him; at other times I could kick him out
of the room." [2] Meister himself, he writes to Miss Welsh,
was a great blockhead, *ganache*—" perhaps one of the greatest
ganaches that ever was created by quill and ink." The only
particle of *historical* interest in it was connected with Mignon.
The book itself was " bushels of dust and straws and feathers,
with here and there a diamond of the purest water "; at best
a mixed performance, " and, though intellectually good, much
of it is morally bad." All the same, Carlyle finished the translation, published it, received a very good fee (£180), and
found peace.

Every European ' age ' has its novel, or more than one: *Don
Quixote* expresses the late sixteenth century, *Simplicissimus* the
middle seventeenth, *Gil Blas* the age of Louis XIV, *Candide*
and *Werther* the eighteenth century, *Wilhelm Meister* and *Les*

---

[1] To James Johnstone, September 21, 1823 (*Letters*, ii, 221). The two
previous quotations are from letters to Miss Welsh, March 4 and April 6,
1823 (*Ibid.*, pp. 183–184 and 190).

[2] To James Johnstone, September 21, 1823 (*Letters*, ii, 223–224).

Misérables the Romantic Age. The first part of *Wilhelm Meister* (*Lehrjahre*) was published in 1795, the second part (*Wanderjahre*) in 1821, the final part in 1827.[1]

Wilhelm Meister, who, of course, is Goethe, was the son of a well-to-do, rather stolid German merchant in an old commercial town. When he was a boy his romantic nature had been deeply affected by a puppet-show which a young officer of artillery helped him to work. As he grew up he was attracted by the stage. His father complained of his absence, so Wilhelm stayed regularly at home and did his commercial duties by day, but spent his evenings among actors and actresses. He fell in love with a very unworthy actress who lived in the town with a venal, intriguing old maidservant. After a time he became disillusioned with his actress, and thought of abandoning all his ideals and throwing his art to the winds. His friend in the town, Werner, an unimaginative young *bourgeois* of strict common sense, gives him good advice : " I am greatly mistaken if it were not better for thee in some degree to yield to these propensities, than to waste thyself by the contradictions of so hard a piece of self-denial." Wilhelm's family tactfully sent him off on a journey, commissioning him to do some business on the way. Most of the rest of the *Lehrjahre* is a travel-story of Germany ; in the course of the long and varied journey the ineffective, generous, moody youth acquires steadiness and purpose through engaging in useful activity and finding duty to perform.

Wilhelm set off from the old town with an ambition, apparently, to establish a national theatre for Germany. " We now find him on horseback, with his saddlebags behind him, exhilarated by the motion and the free air, approaching the mountains, where he had some affairs to settle." In a little market town he falls in with a cheerful company of travelling players rather down on their luck, and after transacting his

---

[1] There is a still earlier version or portion of *Wilhelm Meister*, called the *Theatralische Sendung*, or *Theatrical Mission*, of Wilhelm. This was begun about 1777, but never completed. The manuscript was discovered in private possession in Zürich, and was published in 1911.

commercial business he joins company with them, as friend, adviser, and occasional actor. They make a chequered progress through the Rhineland and Western Germany, meeting robbers or soldiery when they approach the war zone. The French Revolutionary war was going on, but, except in the actual neighbourhood of a belligerent army, the course of life and society was uninterrupted.

The acting company, like all its kind, had interesting characters. Wilhelm found a congenial spirit in Laertes, a good fencer, a thoughtful, ironical young man, disillusioned. Philine, a generous, extravagant, cheerful, incalculable young woman, was a friend of the woman-hater Laertes, although they professed to be severe critics of each other. Wilhelm was never sure whether he liked Philine or not. At almost their first meeting he was struck by " her lavish generosity, in a style of gaiety reaching to extravagance." When she had spent all her money and all that her companions could spend " she threw her straw hat from a window to a girl, and her neckerchief to an old woman who asked her for alms." Wilhelm Meister rescues a beautiful child, called Mignon, from some rope-walkers and mountebanks who were treating her unmercifully; and he takes her with him in company with the travelling players. The modest, innocent child conceives a deep devotion for Wilhelm, and becomes something like a servant, companion, daughter, to him; and he, in taking care of her and showing himself worthy of her confidence and affection, begins to feel at last happiness—" pure and undescribable felicity." An old harper, who also had attached himself, rather vaguely, to the company, is often drawn towards Mignon and Wilhelm. From time to time Wilhelm, who still occasionally has doubts and uncertainties about himself, is soothed by hearing the soft sounds of the old man's harp before his door. Sometimes the old man sings as he plays on the harp. One of these lyrics—*Kennst du das Land, wo die Zitronen blühn?*—expressing the haunting beauty of sunny Italy, has captured the affection of the whole world.[1]

[1] J. G. Robertson, *The Life and Work of Goethe* (1932), p. 187.

Having helped some of the players out of their difficulties with money, Wilhelm went on with them to a nobleman's castle, where they are to perform a play. They were boorishly treated by the castle servants, and were very indifferently housed, but Wilhelm and Philine made friends with the gentry and had interesting experiences of castle life. Although not so refined as French Society, the German aristocracy was interested in the drama and in literature, and Wilhelm had discussions on Shakespeare with one of the guests, a somewhat mysterious young nobleman, Major Jarno, who enters the story for a time and then vanishes, to appear years later (under the name of Montan) in the *Wanderjahre*. They discourse about Shakespeare, and Wilhelm is inspired to give an interpretation of the character of Hamlet which is a landmark of Shakespearian criticism. It is one of the finest passages in Carlyle's translation:

> He was calm in his temper, artless in his conduct; neither pleased with idleness, nor too violently eager for employment. The routine of a university he seemed to continue when at Court. He possessed more mirth of humour than of heart; he was a good companion, pliant, courteous, discreet, and able to forget and to forgive an injury; yet never able to unite himself with those who overstept the limits of the right, the good, and the becoming.

The Countess, whose husband is lord of the castle, falls in love with Wilhelm, but she suddenly realizes what she is doing, and begs him to leave. The Count (or rather the Countess) sends him a handsome present of money for his acting and management, and Wilhelm departs with the rest of the company.

Wilhelm bought a new travelling kit—a waistcoat, a short mantle, long knitted pantaloons, a silk sash, and lacing boots. " He freed his neck from the tyranny of stocks," and wore instead a ruff, which he made out of a few strips of muslin, and a silk neckerchief. He used some of his money to procure carriages for the company. He and Laertes generally walked. Wilhelm felt exhilarated as never before. " He could now imagine his present company to be a wandering colony, and himself the leader of it."

The tour took the company into the zone of hostilities, where there was always danger from wandering soldiery or bandits. In a forest, while the women were boiling potatoes and setting out the food, the company was suddenly attacked. Wilhelm, fighting hard, received a blow on the head and swooned. When he came to himself his head was on Philine's lap; Mignon tended his wounds. The robbers had gone off, having plundered the company. A party of gentlefolk come riding up; and one of them, a beautiful young lady, takes off her overcoat and puts it over Wilhelm before they ride away. Her face and form remain in Wilhelm's memory. He calls her the ' Amazon.' Wilhelm is taken off to an inn and placed on a couch in the public room. The mean-spirited actors upbraid him for having brought them to such a pass. He receives their gibes meekly, and promises to see that they each shall receive double, treble, of what they have lost. In the thick atmosphere of the inn parlour he raises himself on his couch and stretches out his hand. " I promise," he says. But no one takes his hand. " I promise it again," he cries, sinking back on his pillow. Philine kept on cracking nuts, a stock of which she had discovered in her pocket.

After recovering from his wound Wilhelm pursues his journey, and (still accompanied by Mignon, the Harper, and Philine) joins another, superior acting company, managed by an actor called Serlo, who greatly admires Shakespeare. Wilhelm takes the part of Hamlet, and translates the play, basing his translation on " Wieland's spirited performance." The house in which he and Mignon lodged is burned down by the Harper, who is a little mad; Wilhelm again loses all his effects. He continues acting for some time longer; then leaves the company to deliver a letter of a dying actress to her husband, Lothario, who had deserted her.

Riding through a rather rainy country, Wilhelm arrives at Lothario's castle, an irregular building with turrets and peaked roofs. And there he finds Jarno again. Lothario, sick with pleasure and vacuity, had once gone off to America to fight in the colonial Revolutionary war and to find the promised land.

But after an unsatisfying period of service there he had written
to Jarno: " I will return, and in my house, amid my fields,
among my people, I will say, ' *Here, or nowhere, is America*
[*Hier, oder nirgends, ist Amerika*]! ' " Lothario turns out to be
the brother of the Countess who had fallen in love with Wilhelm
at the first castle. The Count had gone off and joined the
Moravian community at Herrnhut. Lothario was now resolved
to do good and to save his own soul just where he was. " Here,
or nowhere," he said, " is Herrnhut ! " Wilhelm spends a long
time at the castle. Before he departs he receives a home-truth
from Jarno, who says, " You will once for all renounce the
stage, as you have no talent for it." He returns for a few days
to the town, and takes farewell of the players, who have now
obtained good fortune with an opera. He sends Mignon
and the Harper to be cared for and lodged with a friend. Then
he goes back to Lothario's castle. There he finds his old friend
Werner, who has come to represent his bank in carrying through
with Lothario an investment in the purchase of land. Mignon
falls ill while Wilhelm is away, and is taken into the care of a
rich, kind lady, who in her large and artistic house keeps a
school for girls. Wilhelm goes to visit this house, and finds
that this lady is—the ' Amazon ' Natalie, who gave him her
overcoat as he lay wounded when the robbers had plundered
the players. In the end she becomes his wife.

This is not the whole story, but it is a large part of it. Like
all the big novels which are aimed at giving a social picture on
the grand scale, rather than at telling a story, *Wilhelm Meister*
is full of digressions, of characters who come and go frequently
and bewilderingly, as they do in real life, of coincidences, conversations, anecdotes. Goethe obviously brought real men into
his book. The handsome, dignified stranger with the air of a
clergyman who discourses philosophically on mind and body
in Chapter IX of Book II must be Lavater. The inns, the acting companies, the plundering soldiery, the rich aristocracy, are
all real enough. It was still Germany of the Holy Roman
Empire, with woods and bad roads and little commercial
towns ; Germany of the ' Enlightenment ' (for Goethe was

essentially a man of the eighteenth century), but becoming conscious of the ' Romanticism ' which was making a new age.

In *Wilhelm Meisters Wanderjahre* (published partly in 1821 and partly in 1827) Italy, not Germany, is the scene; hills and lakes (particularly Lake Maggiore) are the normal subjects of description, instead of woods and plains and little commercial towns. Wilhelm's character is now settled: he is clear-sighted, purposeful, serene. Restlessness has given way to poise. The novel itself is highly didactic. Goethe discourses on education, obviously influenced by the views of Pestalozzi, who believed that schools should be situated in the countryside, and that agricultural labour helped to bring out the best qualities of the children. To learn a handicraft, to work and to be useful, is held forth by Goethe as the best way of life for a man. At the end of the *Wanderjahre* many of the characters, as in a play, are gathered together. They form a company and decide to emigrate to America. Wilhelm and Friedrich, Philine and Lydin, and the rest, after a period of preparatory training in Switzerland, set forth across the Atlantic. No longer is the word *Here, or nowhere, is America,* but *Wherever I am of use, there is my Fatherland.*

> *Bleibe nicht am Boden heften,*
> *Frisch gewagt und frisch hinaus!*
> *Kopf und Arm mit heitern Kräften,*
> *Ueberall sind sie zu Haus.*

Carlyle translates this:

> Keep not standing fixed and rooted,
> Briskly venture, briskly roam!
> Head and hand, wher'er thou foot it,
> And stout heart are still at home.

" Thus," as Benedetto Croce observes, " Meister, having set out to found the theatre, undergoes varied sentimental and moral experiences, meets many different people, and passes finally from a vague and unsuitable ideal of art to active practical life." [1]

[1] B. Croce, *Goethe* (trans. Ainslie, 1923), p. 89.

Goethe's way, and Carlyle's, was for the intellectuals. Jahn proposed another method. Young Germany was to be saved on the *Turnplatz*, out of doors, on the heath, running, jumping, whirling round the bar, leaping the horse.

Friedrich Ludwig Jahn, in his later years was called the *Turn-vater*, and looked, with his great beard, prominent nose and dark skull-cap, like a Hebrew prophet. He was born at Lanz, in the Prignitz (North-west Brandenburg), on August 11, 1778. His father, a Protestant minister, gave him his early education. As a university student at Halle, Göttingen, and Greifswald his interest was mainly in theology and philology. An active, keen young man, he travelled widely in Germany, partly from love of action, partly to pursue his studies in dialects. In 1810 he became a teacher at the famous Graue Kloster Gymnasium at Berlin. Germany's deep humiliation, moral depression, and laxity after Jena had impressed him, like Fichte and other patriots. Jahn resolved to devote himself to the task of lifting up his people by physical exercises, which should have a bracing effect, not merely physically, but morally. In 1811 he established a kind of open-air school, or rather physical-drill organization, on the Hasenheide at Berlin. In unbleached grey woollen shirts the youth of Berlin and students from all over Germany came to exercise, to train their bodies and minds, in Jahn's athletic grounds and on his gymnastic apparatus. With this ' physical ' revival he associated the revival of ancient folk-lore, to renew the deep feelings of the original German people; and in pursuit of this aim he developed a hatred of strangers—xenophobia—and of Jews.

When the War of Liberation came in 1813 Jahn put aside his exercises and joined the famous Free Corps of Lützow. When the war was over he resumed his mission for establishing *Turnvereine* (' gymnastic clubs ') and sports places. He obtained considerable *vogue* in Berlin as a rousing lecturer on German race and nationality; and he was in touch with perhaps a number of the liberal and politically suspect Jena student *Burschen-schaften*. On account of his liberalism and demagogy his schools were closed by the Prussian Governments about the time of the issue of the Carlsbad Decrees under Metternich's influence in 1819. Karl Sand, the student who murdered Kotzebue for political reasons, was a *Turn* enthusiast, and so brought further suspicion on Jahn's teaching. Jahn himself served six years in prison at Spandau and Küstrin. Released in 1825, he was forbidden to teach in a university or school; but he maintained himself (or partly maintained himself) by writing. But he was a broken man. In 1848, when the great revolution broke out, he was elected to the Frankfurt Parliament, the *Nationalversammlung*, but made no impression. He died on October 15, 1852, at Freyburg, on the Unstrut, where he had fixed his home for his last seventeen years. Jahn was unmarried.

CHAPTER VII

GERMAN "BÜRGERTUM"

THE spirit which grew up among the German people during the Napoleonic ascendancy and in the great rising called the War of Liberation was the beginning of great things. There can be no doubt about the ' defensiveness ' of this war. The French empire was in Germany ; it imposed servitude, in varying degrees, upon the whole people, and the whole thing had to be thrust out. This was accomplished in a grand heroic struggle. All Germans felt as one. Their armies were not a professional soldiery in the hands of autocrats ; they were a people in arms, directing themselves, under guidance of their representative men, to the achievement of freedom.

When the struggle was over the great meeting of the states, the Congress of Vienna, was to confirm the wholesome tendencies and to organize the generous ardours for the good of Germany. The result, perhaps inevitably, did not correspond to the hopes in which the Congress met. Treitschke, the late nineteenth-century historian, who wrote a brilliant, fascinating, almost conversational *History of Germany*, said that with the passing away of " the pitiless veracity of war " the old illusions and the old egotisms returned. " Like worms after rain, the petty talents of the boudoir and the antechamber crawled out of their hiding-places and stretched themselves luxuriously." [1]

These commonplace elements, the courtiers of *salon* and *bureau*, are not the stuff of history. There were considerable men at Vienna—Metternich of Austria, Hardenberg of Prussia, Castlereagh of Great Britain, Alexander I, Tsar of Russia, with his brilliant *corps* of Foreign Office officials. Naturally every-

[1] H. von Treitschke, *History of Germany in the Nineteenth Century* (trans. E. and C. Paul, 1916), ii, 37.

body had not come to Vienna simply in order to work. Social life revived with a bound when the tyranny of war passed away, and when the terrible Corsican was relegated to his island.

> The distinguished world was once more at ease, in full possession of itself. . . . Although pigtails and powder were not revived, the effeminate love of adornment of the eighteenth century was still manifest in the beardless faces, the snuff-boxes, the shoes and the silk stockings, in the deliberate elegance of masculine clothing; and yet the tone of intercourse had already become much freer and less formal.[1]

The absurdities of ancient etiquette were no longer observed, and ambassadors refrained from disputing about their dignity and from splitting hairs over the shape and colour of their chairs. An old custom, which persists to-day in almost every country, was now noticed. Instead of ecclesiastical functions or courtly gatherings, the display of monarchs and Governments now took the form of military parades. Even the " weapon-shy " Emperor Francis of Austria had " sometimes " to appear in uniform.

The winter of 1814–15 passed away at Vienna in " routs " and dances, in a good deal of hard work and a good deal of disputing. After Napoleon escaped from Elba at the end of February 1815 the disputes were compromised and the serious business of treaty-making energetically resumed. The final act was signed on June 9, 1815, nine days before the battle of Waterloo was to end the Napoleonic empire for ever.

The constitution for Germany, framed and adopted in the Congress of Vienna, lasted from 1816 to 1866. It has received a lot of censure, but the truth is that it satisfied everybody fairly well, except the Prussian ruling class, which disliked the pre-eminence of Austria. The Holy Roman Empire, suppressed in 1806, was not revived, because the ruler of Austria had in the meantime made himself hereditary Emperor of Austria. Although the Austrians had for centuries supplied the Holy

---

[1] Treitschke, *op. cit.*, ii, 4.

Roman Emperor, election to this office had remained in the hands of the seven Electoral Princes of Germany. A restored Holy Roman Empire would have to be elective, a system scarcely compatible with the existence of the hereditary Imperial Crown of Austria. So a Germanic Confederation was established in 1815, a league of the thirty-nine independent German states, with a common Diet, or Federal Assembly, at Frankfurt, in which Austria would by law always have the presidency. It was not a bad constitution, though it would have been made better if some representatives of the German people other than simply Congress diplomatists had been on the drafting committee. Its chief fault was the ambiguity (probably deliberate) of the celebrated Article 13, which declared, " There shall be Assemblies of States in all the countries belonging to the Confederation." [*In allen Bundesstaaten wird eine landesständische Verfassung Statt finden.*] Whether this meant representative assemblies of the modern type or assemblies of feudal estates such as most German principalities already possessed was a matter of dispute. Only four sovereigns—Saxe-Weimar, Baden, Bavaria, and Württemberg—had definitely established a representative Parliament by the year 1848; as a matter of fact, the constitutions of these four states were all established by the year 1819; the rest of the period, to 1848, was in German constitutional history almost blank.

Treitschke notes that after a prolonged and intense period of hostilities the spirit of restlessness and brutalization persists for a long time among the masses; but he adds that this spirit did not exist among the pious and sober-minded men who had fought the " holy " War of Liberation.[1] The lofty idealism of the war period, however, could not be completely maintained in the relaxed atmosphere of the peace. It was, nevertheless, preserved and fostered, at any rate to a very considerable extent, in three circles or elements of the German people—in the Prussian officer class, in the university students, and in a large number of public-spirited writers and men of learning.

The first of these circles, the Prussian officer class, cannot be

[1] Treitschke, *op. cit.*, ii, 232.

regarded as a Germanic element. Its outlook, its loyalty and sense of duty, were confined to the Prussian State. The characteristic movement at this time in the German people was undoubtedly liberalism, as expressed in the desire for Parliamentary institutions, constitutional government, and a free union on this basis of the peoples of all the German States. The Prussian officer class contributed nothing to this movement, which, indeed, was repugnant to it. The only aspect of any principle of the War of Liberation which it cherished was the principle of loyalty and devotion to sovereign and State.

The university students were a source of political and social influence all over Germany. Most of them had served as volunteers in the War of Liberation, and had thus become conscious that they had a position and function in the State. They felt that they were making a new Germany, united, national, free —free externally and internally. Then, when the war was over and the period of fruitful peace was inaugurated, a gap between youth and age was revealed. The older men remained in charge of the State, with their old ideals or with none at all. The young men, the fervent, hopeful youths with their visions and their plans, were left outside affairs; and, what is more remarkable, although it has happened again after the World War, they were kept out of office for the next thirty years. Yet, as George Ticknor observed in 1836, Prussia's history since 1806, when Stein's law gave self-government to the towns, had been a training to the whole country for representative government. And Ancillon, chief Minister of State of Prussia, told the same observer in that year that he did not approve of the system of Metternich.[1] Political experience and the fact that the older men were already in office made them indispensable or immovable. The young men felt themselves neglected, thwarted, or deceived. They turned with passion to their own gatherings and to the new doctrine of physical exercise, and they found a prophet in Jahn.

To the young men of this time Jahn was an inspiration. He personified Germany to them, its spiritual unity, its new life. He wore a grey unbleached shirt, open at the neck, with the

---

[1] *The Life of George Ticknor*, i, 497, 502.

shirt collar lying over the collar of the jacket; no waistcoat. There was no dandyism about *him*. His open-air gymnasium (*Turnplatz*) on the Hasenheide at Berlin was the model for gymnasiums all over the country. Jahn's vigorous nationalism, expressed in a torrent of portentous platitudes, largely consisting in hatred and denunciations of the French, were received as a kind of gospel. Nor did he confine his efforts to direct teaching. In holiday-time he would go off with a band of his pupils, staff in hand, to the woods and mountains. They would tramp and talk all day, eating crusts of bread, drinking milk or only water, sitting round camp-fires at night, singing their marching-songs. It all seems wonderfully modern to the present-day reader.

The gymnasium clubs, the *Turnvereine*, the marching and singing, the holiday tramps, the camp-fire circles and talks, were outlets for the energy and patriotism of Young Germany amid the disappointments, the suffocating *régime*, of the German police states. They bred a war legend, of course—that it was the folk, and especially the young volunteers, who had won the war, not the professional soldiers, the officer class, and the brutal sergeants and corporals; and they bred a cult of Germanism, a rather vague conception, but personified in the memory of Martin Luther and in the corporate presence of Jahn. Also the graceful athletic exercises made these young Germans, whose education had the classical tradition, believe that they were continuing the tradition of the Olympic games, that the young Germans were the modern Hellenes.[1]

The gymnasium clubs became a sort of state within a state. The playing-fields or open spaces were the scene of incessant marching and tramping, conducted with enthusiasm that was a kind of religious fervour and recalled the medieval flagellants. School-teachers found their pupils becoming rather unruly. Enthusiasm assumed the repulsive form of political fanaticism. Jahn hated the French, and led a sort of ' Teutonist ' movement against the Francophile tendency which still prevailed—French words, French fashions, and such things. Individuality was crushed in a forced and aggressive ' berserkerdom ' which all

[1] *Cf.* A. Rosenberg, *Der Mythus des XX Jahrhunderts* (1932), pp. 21 ff.

G

the young men had to adopt. Students took up the idea of *Deutschehit* with enthusiasm, sometimes almost with frenzy— ' Germanomania,' its critics called it, lamenting its roughness and brutality. The sentiment of nationality was fanned into a flame. " Germany," declared Jahn, " needs a war that is entirely her own affair to arouse her nationality to the full." [1] He longed for a despot who would make all the people conform to the *Germanism* which the gymnasium clubs zealously inculcated. And somehow this sentiment took on a military aspect. The historian of the movement writes : " In a valiant nation all methodical physical training must subserve warlike ends unless it is to degenerate into solemn foolery." [2] The professional army, however, looked with considerable dislike, perhaps jealousy, on all this amateur soldiering. The patriotic Henrik Steffens, a Norwegian by birth, professor in the University of Breslau, who, like Fichte, fired his students with zeal for service in 1813, now denounced the Breslau *Turnplatz* as a debasing influence. Perhaps, because he was not himself of the German race, " he failed to realize how rarely a genuine Teuton attains virile energy without a full measure of youthful roughness." [3] The Governments, however, were inclined to share Steffens' view, and were not so enamoured of the *vogue* of *Teutonism* as to sacrifice their notions of law and order to it. In 1819 the gymnasium clubs came under the same ban as the *Burschenschaften*, and were suppressed, officially at any rate, by the Prussian Government; they managed to maintain some sort of existence secretly.

The *Burschenschaften* were clubs or societies in the universities. After the War of Liberation the students returned to the lecture-rooms, and the German universities took an immense leap forward in popularity and in energy. It was the best generation of students that the universities had experienced for many years. They were keen young men, well behaved, eager to learn. Jena, under the benevolent, liberal *régime* of Karl August, Grand Duke of Saxe-Weimar, had the most famous university, thronged with 350 students, a considerable

---

[1] Treitschke, *op. cit.*, iii, 13. [2] *Ibid.*, iii, 6.
[3] *Ibid.*, iii, 16.

number for those days. They lived on the best of terms with
their professors. In 1802 Crabb Robinson, who was just an
unknown foreign student, went with other students to supper
with the famous Professor Schelling at Jena, and engaged in a
keen argument with him. At the inn-table where Crabb Robinson supped at Erlangen there were about fifty students. He sat
next to a professor (Abicht) who pronounced for the transcend-
ence of the genius of Shakespeare, Goethe, and Dante.[1] The
Jena students had the sentiment of fatherland, and regarded
their body, drawn from every state in Germany, as representing the whole country. The social and political atmosphere of
Thuringia was favourable to the development of the ' All-Ger-
man ' sentiment. The Thuringian people and country were split
up into an amazing parcel of states and fragments of states. As
states they were politically powerless; as people they were
happy. The arts flourished in the capital of the chief Thuringian duchy, Weimar; and in Jena Thuringia had the most
celebrated, the most vigorous, the most cheerful, university.
Treitschke, of course, labels this condition of Thuringia as contemptible—contemptible, but happy :[2] German civilization owes
enormously to Thuringia, the German State nothing. It was a
Lilliputian world which was not great, but was perhaps sensible.

On May 5, 1816, Grand Duke Karl August issued the Weimar
Fundamental Law (drafted by Christian Wilhelm Schweitzer,
professor of law at Jena and Minister of State), the first constitution to be established in Germany since the inauguration of
the Federal Act. Elections were held, and in 1816 there met
the first representative Parliament (as distinct from the old
feudal assemblies of estates) in German history. Five miles
away, at Jena, the students too were nourishing the plant of
freedom. On June 12, 1815, the Jena *Burschenschaft* had been
founded, with the black-red-gold flag of liberty as its emblem.
Most of the other German universities formed each a similar
club, but the Jena society, of which Heinrich von Gagern was
a member, was the most famous. But the *Burschenschaft* of

---

[1] *The Diary of Henry Crabb Robinson*, i, 65, 69.
[2] Treitschke, *op. cit.*, iii, 20, 26.

Giessen, in Hesse-Cassel, was soon to become notorious. The
Giessen students, though they had joined a free corps, had not
been brought into the fighting-line in the War of Liberation,
and had returned to the university disappointed. The promised
Golden Age did not follow upon the War of Liberation, and the
students became impatient. Three brothers Follen made the
Giessen *Burschenschaft* into a secret revolutionary society. The
eldest of the three, Adolf Follen, was a ruthless, strong-minded,
cold-blooded young man, of the kind that establishes an ascendancy over weak-minded enthusiasts and turns them into assassins. On October 18, 1817, the anniversary of the recent
" Battle of the Nations " at Leipsig (1813) was celebrated all
over Germany. A number of Jena students, members of the
Burschenschaft, along with visiting *Burschen*, mainly from Berlin, made a bonfire on the Wartburg and burned some emblems
of despotism and authority. A famous and detested pamphlet
of Schmalz, rector of Berlin University, a copy of the Prussian
police code, Haller's *Restauration*, Uhlan stays, a Hessian soldier's pigtail and a corporal's cane, were thrown on to the
blazing pile as the students danced around it. The incident
created considerable perturbation in the Austrian Foreign
Office, and was considered worthy of a special report from the
British Minister in Weimar to his Government in London.
Metternich, who until this time seemed rather indifferent to
German affairs, suddenly began to pay great attention to them.
It was clear that the prevailing sentiment among the students
was liberal ; and their noisiness in this respect might bring more
prominently forward what Gentz called " the most embarrass-
ing question for all the great sovereigns, the introduction of the
representative system into all the states of Germany." [1]

In the year following the Wartburg festival delegates from
the *Burschenschaft* of each university which possessed such a
society met at Jena and founded (October 1818) the Universal
German Student Society (Allgemeine Deutsche Burschenschaft). Its object, adopted in its statutes, was to unite all
German youth together in view of " the coming unity of the

[1] F. von Gentz, *Dépêches inédites aux Hospodars de Valachie* (1876), i, 321.

Fatherland." Though the bulk of the student body throughout Germany was orderly enough, there is no doubt that Adolf Follen and his Giessen clique of revolutionaries meant, if they could, to use the Allgemeine Burschenschaft for their revolutionary purposes. Karl Follen in 1818 became a teacher at Jena University. There he had a devoted disciple, a student of theology, Karl Sand.

In 1818, however, it was not the foundation of the Allgemeine Deutsche Burschenschaft which attracted everybody's attention; it was the Congress of Powers at Aix-la-Chapelle. At this congress the French Government made an arrangement for paying all the remaining instalments of the war indemnity, and it was admitted to the ' Concert ' of Powers. People felt that the international politics of Europe had returned to normality. The Emperor of Russia, Alexander I, had military resources and great personal distinction as compared with other contemporary sovereigns; and all this gave him tremendous influence in Europe, an influence hitherto directed to the support of liberal tendencies in public affairs. At Aix-la-Chapelle, however, his behaviour completely reassured the anxious Gentz, who was Secretary-General of the Congress and Metternich's right-hand man. Alexander, wrote Gentz, now preached only " peace, moderation, respect for the conservative principles of social order and submission to legal authority." [1] A gentle and melancholy young Wallachian called Stourdza, who had written, or helped to write, the text of the Holy Alliance, made a tour of German universities and observed with alarm the political liberalism of the students, and wrote a *Memorial concerning the Present State of Affairs in Germany*. This *Denkschrift* was sent to the Emperor of Russia, and communicated by him to the Congress of Aix-la-Chapelle. No one can say whether Metternich was alarmed by the conclusions of the Wallachian, but he was glad to find that the Tsar Alexander was impressed. The *Denkschrift* somehow escaped from the hands of the Congress deputies and was published. Indignant students challenged the author to duels, but Stourdza, himself immensely

[1] Gentz, *op. cit.*, i, 401.

alarmed by the *furore* created by his pamphlet, hastened to quit German soil.

Metternich and Gentz were immensely pleased with the Congress of Aix-la-Chapelle, which extended the good understanding among the four Powers (registered by the Treaty of Paris, November 20, 1815) into a ' concert,' or confederation, among the five Powers—Austria, Russia, Prussia, Great Britain, and France. The Tsar Alexander's ' Holy Alliance ' of the monarchs had been, according to Gentz, only " an incorrect and defective symbol " of the essential union of the Great Powers, the Confederation of Europe, founded at Paris at the end of the War of Liberation and now ratified and completed at Aix-la-Chapelle ; it was *l'ancre de salut pour l'Europe.*

So everything went well—*à merveille,* as Metternich wrote to his wife. Lawrence, at the command of the Prince Regent, came over from London to paint portraits of the sovereigns and statesmen. On November 28 (1818) Metternich was able to leave for home, *via* Cologne, Coblenz (his birthplace), and his new domain at Johannisberg, a present from his Emperor, with its magnificent store of wine in cask. A Rhinelander by birth, he thoroughly enjoyed the trip ; Coblenz, Bonn, and the ancient Imperial city of Aix rearoused the youthful poetry which the great Foreign Minister of Austria (soon to be made Chancellor) nourished beneath his polished and somewhat mocking exterior. The conference at Aix had been a splendid success. Yet within a few months a frightful event occurred.

August von Kotzebue, a well-known writer of plays, was a native of Weimar who held the practically sinecure position of secretary to the Russian Legation there. He was a witty, dissolute, but industrious old gentleman, editing a *Literarisches Wochenblatt* and sending fairly frequent bulletins or letters to St Petersburg for the information of the Tsar ; these letters were, so far as is known, exclusively on literary subjects. Weimar and Jena, since Duke Karl August [1] published his liberal fundamental law in 1815, had become more than ever a place

---

[1] From 1816 the sovereign of Saxe-Weimar bore the title of Grand Duke (*Grossherzog*).

of journalists and men of letters. George Ticknor met Kotzebue
at Weimar. He wrote that poets lived very comfortably there,
and seemed to be unusually well paid. The professors in the
University of Jena took a keen interest in politics, believing that
they and the rest of the professoriate represented in themselves
the essential unity of Germany. Some of the professors edited
journals. Luden was a professor of history whose lectures,
delivered with ease and convincingness, were a delight and
inspiration to the students of Jena for forty years. His journal
Nemesis was outspoken in the liberal interest. Oken, not a professor, edited the *Isis*, a diverting agency of propaganda for
democracy. Lindner, another journalist, edited the *Oppositions-
blatt*, a serious attack upon the forces which opposed political
progress, especially Prussia. Kotzebue's secretary showed to
Lindner one of his master's letters written to the Russian Court.
Lindner published some of it in his journal, and although the
letter was unobjectionable, all the liberal journals attacked Kotzebue, and he was accused of being a Russian informer. The
students came to believe that it was he who had turned the Tsar
Alexander away from liberalism.[1] Karl Sand, a student of theology, who spent his time in the Universities of Erlangen and
Jena, and who was undoubtedly the tool of Karl Follen, made
up his mind to assassinate Kotzebue. Follen paid his travelling
expenses. Sand followed Kotzebue to Mannheim, in Baden,
obtained access to his room, and stabbed him fatally in the neck
(March 23, 1819). He then ran out of the room into the open
air and, falling upon his knees, thanked God for having blessed
his enterprise. Next he tried to commit suicide, but only
wounded himself seriously. Gentz hoped that Sand would die,
so that the trial and execution should not be turned into an
apotheosis; but the miserable invalid was nursed back to life.
Sand was convicted in the Mannheim *Hofgericht*, and decapi-
tated by the sword at Mannheim (May 20, 1820). He showed
no remorse for his dreadful deed, and misguided Heidelberg
students worshipped him as a hero. Treitschke says that he
and they were guilty of the deadly sin of the nineteenth century

[1] Gentz, in Metternich, *Mémoires* (1848), iii, 229.

—megalomania. The scaffold on which Sand was executed, being apparently a perquisite of the executioner, was made by him into a summerhouse, where students from Heidelberg, which is thirteen miles from Mannheim, could meet and drink and commemorate the hero and martyr.

It is no wonder that Metternich and the rest of the German princes or statesmen were alarmed. Clearly politics were demoralizing a considerable number of the German students. A Giessen student tried to emulate Sand by stabbing a high Prussian official of Wiesbaden. As Gentz wrote to Metternich, the truly alarming thing about Sand's atrocity was its obvious connexion with the worst maladies and dangers of the era. Gentz diagnosed the cause of the whole trouble as liberty of the Press, and he urged Metternich to have the Press article of the Federal Act (No. 18, *cet article à jamais regrettable* [1]) abrogated. Also the situation in the universities must be dealt with seriously; but it must not be assumed that the whole student body of Germany was one vast secret society; a harassing inquisition which would bring misfortune to many an honest family must be avoided. Metternich, who was on a visit to Rome at the time of the murder, agreed with Gentz, and wrote to say that the rules which he proposed would concern the discipline of the universities, and not the studies; " we should accomplish nothing by touching them." Adam Müller, one of the Prussian converts to Roman Catholicism attached to the Austrian Foreign Office, ascribed all the trouble among the students to the Reformation. Metternich " did not contest this proposition," but, writing from " the height of the Quirinal," thought that he could obtain good results without attacking Martin Luther in his Saxon citadel. [2]

Gentz wrote urgently to Metternich to say that the problem of the universities must not be treated in isolation from the whole political problem of Germany, and that, with regard to the universities themselves, disciplinary rules would not suffice: there must be a purging of professors. And now was the time

[1] Gentz, in Metternich, *Mémoires* (1848), iii, 229.
[2] Metternich to Gentz, April 23, 1819 (*Mémoires*, iii, 245).

to act. Metternich agreed. *Aujourd'hui les gouvernements ont assez peur pour vouloir agir,* he wrote (this time from Naples) to Gentz. He would not bother much about the students. *L'étudiant, considéré en lui-même, est un enfant.* It was the professors, maladroit conspirators though they were, that he was after. Thus he would stop the making of the students into a generation of revolutionaries; but—*le plus grand mal, le mal qu'il est le plus urgent de combattre aujourd'hui, c'est la presse.*[1] So he was able to convene a congress of German princes and Ministers at Carlsbad and to induce most of them to approve of certain measures to be enforced in their respective states. The Federal Diet, the *Bundestag,* at Frankfurt was too slow to satisfy him, and in any case was not legally competent to enforce the measures that Metternich desired. He preferred to deal directly with the Governments. Just before the Congress of Carlsbad took place Metternich had an interview with Frederick William III of Prussia at Teplitz, and practically secured a promise that the King would not carry out his famous promise of May 22, 1815, to give a constitution to Prussia, a kingdom *qui* (said Metternich to him) *se prête moins que tout autre État à une innovation pareille.*[2]

The Governments represented at Carlsbad in August 1819 were Austria, Prussia, Bavaria, Saxony, Hanover, Württemberg, Baden, Mecklenburg, Nassau, Hesse-Cassel, Saxe-Weimar. The resolutions they took, known as the Carlsbad Decrees, concerned (i) the interpretation of Article 13 of the Federal Act, in a sense contrary to the claim that it promised representative Parliaments for the German states; (ii) measures to be applied to the universities—a Government plenipotentiary or extraordinary curator, to maintain observation and control of professors and students; (iii) a strict censorship of the Press; (iv) a central commission of inquiry, to be established for the whole confederation at Mainz. These ' decrees ' were adopted unanimously by the *Bundestag* at Frankfurt on September 20, 1819, but the execution of the edicts (except the establishing of

---

[1] Metternich to Gentz, June 17, 1819 (*Mémoires,* iii, 262).
[2] Metternich to the Emperor Francis, July 30, 1819 (*Mémoires,* ii, 272).

the commission of inquiry at Mainz) had to be left to each state, which in practice could do as it liked.

The Prussian Government certainly put the Carlsbad Decrees in force with vigour, it might almost be said with enthusiasm. The *Turnplätze* were closed, and instead gymnasium instruction was introduced into the secondary schools. Jahn was arrested and imprisoned, first in Spandau and later in Küstrin. Arndt, Germany's celebrated patriotic poet, was forbidden to lecture in his University of Bonn. Severe Press laws were adopted in every state. Even the Grand Duke of Weimar bent before the blast, and Oken had to abandon his journal *Nemesis* and become a refugee in Paris. It was agreed or understood among the Governments that a professor or editor forbidden to exercise his functions in one state could not be employed in another. The commission established at Mainz, however, failed to confirm the Metternich-Gentz discovery of a " vast association which appears to work ceaselessly not only to disseminate fanatical, subversive, frankly revolutionary, doctrines, but also to prepare the most criminal enterprises." [1] Metternich believed, however, in 1819 that the revolutionaries were definitely challenging society, had *jeté le gant*; and now, " at perhaps one of the most decisive epochs for the safety of all Europe," he had, through the Carlsbad Decrees, saved the situation. Liberalism was given up in high places in Germany; and from Warsaw came approving declarations from the formerly liberal Tsar Alexander of Russia. [2] The assassination on February 13, 1820, at Paris of the Duc de Berri, son of the Comte d'Artois (afterwards King Charles X), naturally confirmed Metternich in his belief that the epoch was revolutionary, and that conspiracy and assassination were universal dangers. The Cato Street Conspiracy, a plot to blow up the whole British Cabinet (February 23, 1820), seemed to be further corroboration; *le libéralisme va son train; il pleut des assassins*, was Metternich's comment. [3] Later in the year there were serious revolutionary movements in Naples and Piedmont.

[1] See Metternich's *Instructions to Buol*, September 1, 1819 (*Mémoires*, iii, 296).　　　[2] *Ibid.*, iii, 305.　　　[3] *Ibid.*, iii, 325.

For the next twenty-eight years the bulk of the German *bour-geoisie* led a quiet existence at home, engrossed in their professional or commercial duties and in their domestic interests. Those who had political ideals and attempted to engage in political activities faced the risks and shared the lot of European liberals under reactionary or conservative *régimes*. Whatever their fate, the *bourgeoisie* did not resign their liberal and universal outlook in this period. They were German and cosmopolitan. They had a conception of their unity in respect of race and culture. They would probably all have agreed with Renan, who wrote (much later): *l'existence d'une nation est un plébiscite de tous les jours.*[1] They regarded themselves, the Germans, as a nation, though they were not national; if they had any conception of race it was as Saxons, Prussians, Bavarians, Suabians, Franconians. They were admirable citizens, of their own country or of the world, like the celebrated scholar-diplomatist Bunsen or Karl Schurz, the 1848 revolutionary and later American statesman—men " who could belong as much to an adopted country as to that in which they were born and educated." [2] Those who thought seriously about European politics were conscious of their solidarity with the other European nations and of the community of their ideals with those of the rest of the European *bourgeoisie*; they were *weltbürgerlich*. Their view has been expressed by a modern scholar who has studied their history closely and philosophically:

A finer view, ever maintained grandly by the representatives of German culture, is this: that the true, the best, German national feeling also includes the cosmopolitan ideal of a supranational humanity, with the understanding that *it is un-German to be only German.*[3]

---

[1] Renan, *Qu'est-ce qu'une nation ?* (1882), p. 27.
[2] R. W. Church " Bunsen," in *Occasional Papers* (1897), iii, 273.
[3] Meinecke, *Weltbürgertum und Nationalstaat*, p. i : *Eine schon feinere und von den Trägern deutscher Bildung immer hochgehaltene Meinung ist die: Dass das wahre, das beste deutsche Nationalgefühl, auch das weltbürgerliche Ideal einer übernationalen Humanität miteinschliesse, dass es " undeutsch sei bloss deutsch zu sein."*

Freytag's *Soll und Haben* was published in 1855.   Entirely *bürgerlich* though it was, it was addressed, in the Preface, to the Duke of Sachsen-Coburg-Gotha.   Liberalism and aristocracy seemed then to be harmonized and, indeed, blended with each other.

Chapter VIII

THE ARISTOCRACY

THE great European revolution which took place between 1789 and 1848 was the overthrow of the aristocracy. This was accomplished in France through the deliberate action of Government and Legislature; elsewhere it was a silent revolution, unperceived, and in some countries only partially achieved, yet amounting to an impressive change.

The aristocracy of the Middle Ages was an aristocracy of land and of the sword; and they did most of the fighting themselves. For the mounted, heavily armoured nobleman medieval warfare was not very dangerous; but the invention and use of gunpowder put him, in respect of danger and of prowess, on a level with the common man. Accordingly the nobility gradually gave up, or were deprived of, practically all their military prerogatives and duties. The enlightened autocrats of the eighteenth century carried the levelling process further by choosing Ministers and public servants irrespective of class, and, indeed, almost irrespective of country. Nevertheless, though it had lost its governmental and military functions, the aristocracy everywhere retained enormous social and important legal privileges.

The Estates-General met at Versailles on May 5, 1789; and on August 4 the noble estate renounced all its privileges. Afterwards the Revolution took a more violent course in France, and transfers of property, forfeitures, forced sales, brought about for a time almost the extinction, or at any rate the complete upsetting, of class distinctions. In the course of the Napoleonic wars the Codes Napoléon were applied in annexed territory, and had influence upon the legal system in Napoleon's client states. Stein's reforms abolished serfdom and established municipal self-government in Prussia. In the territories covered by the Confederation of the Rhine, including the Duchy of Posen, serfdom was likewise abolished. The military conscription levelled classes; and the astonishing strokes of fortune of the Napoleonic adventures, which raised Murat, an innkeeper's son, and Bernadotte, a lawyer's son, to thrones, destroyed for ever the myth of the superiority of noble blood. Except the Archduke Charles of Austria, the aristocrats showed no particular military talent in any country. The War of Liberation was conducted on the part of the Allies as a great popular war, the " great cause " of the peoples, the vindication of the common man.

When the Great War was finished " restoration was naturally the chief aim of the statesmen." It was at this time that Karl Ludwig von Haller's *Restauration der Staatswissenschaft*, idealizing the Middle Ages and feudalism, went the round of Europe. The aristocracy, rather ignored as a class amid the terrible realities of war, seemed to expect that society would resume the old course which the Revolution had interrupted. At the Congress of Vienna in 1814–15 the aristocracies of all Europe seemed to be collected or at least epitomized; and, in a superficial view, the Congress was just a continual round of pleasure. Actually, however, the European aristocracy, both on the Continent and in England, could be regarded in two classes. There were the minority, workers who, with talent and industry supporting birth and social influence, were entitled to be called public servants and statesmen. And, secondly, there were the majority, the men of fashion and pleasure, who consumed their incomes and spent their days in the hunt for happiness, as Stendhal called it. Both classes had one aspect, which was a good one, in common: they maintained the elegances of life in an age when culture, except in the big commercial and industrial cities, had not extended itself to the *bourgeoisie*. The aristocracy in the German capitals, as at St Petersburg, still spoke French, at any rate when they were 'in good company.' But when Count Stroganoff remarked in a Dresden *salon* that he rarely spoke German in good company (meaning that he had

opportunity of speaking it only with the servants) the spirited
Princess Löwenstein replied, " *Mais vous parlez l'Allemand si
parfaitement, Monsieur le Comte, qu'il paraît que vous avez beau-
coup de pratique.*" [1]

The first class, the statesmen, led deeply interesting lives.
The way to high office was open to them, provided that they
had ambition, some industry, and considerable talent, or at
least adroitness. Except England or France, where Parliamentary careers were possible, the way to statesmanship usually
lay through the bureaucracy. A young nobleman, after education at a " noble academy " (usually a royal foundation), a
Jesuit school, or a *lycée*, and perhaps after a few semesters at a
university, would enter a public bureau without examination
(except in Prussia), and would go through the stages until he
became chief of a section or department. From such a position
he might be selected as a royal Minister or Privy Councillor.
Though not all these working aristocrats could be Chancellors
or Ministers-President, they could all be busy and have responsible work. Some, no doubt, were really drones, and were
carried along somehow by the momentum of the office. And
some were proved to be complete failures, like the over-musical
scion of a noble house described in Grillparzer's *Poor Fiddler*
(*Der arme Spielmann*, 1848). But most of them had a certain
zest for the business of public service and a notion of doing
their duty to the State. Alexander Herzen, who, though a
Socialist, was by origin a Russian noble, has described the
happy life of his bureaucrat courtier uncle:

> His whole life was spent in an artificial world, a world of diplo-
> mats and lords-in-waiting, and he never guessed that there was
> a different world which comes nearer to the reality of things. . . .
> He had no time to be bored—always busy with one of his occu-
> pations, perpetually on the way to some engagement, and his
> life rolled along on easy springs in a world of files and official
> envelopes.[2]

[1] *The Life of George Ticknor*, i, 487.
[2] *The Memoirs of Alexander Herzen* (trans. J. D. Duff, 1923), pp. 24–25.

In this ' working class ' of the aristocracies there are few names of great families. It is true that the Habsburg monarchy had for Chancellor a Schwarzenberg and France had a Richelieu; but Metternich, Bismarck, Cavour, Beust, Nesselrode, Palmerston, Wellington, came out of only minor noble families, the *petite noblesse* of Europe. Occasionally a *grand seigneur* proved to be an earnest statesman, like Prince Chlodwig Hohenlohe, but such instances are rare. The working aristocracy, great or little, made the best of their lives. They worked reasonably hard; their day, spent in politics and administration, was interesting; their labour was generally useful; and they did not sacrifice their social pleasures. Their active career, in fact, added to their social pleasures, for in the course of their work they met clever, well-informed people; and receptions and banquets had a basis of political interest which made them more than a mere filling-in of the time. Metternich frequently complained in his letters and State papers of the weight of his responsibilities and the wearisomeness of the relentless daily pressure of work. Yet he undoubtedly enjoyed it all, and when not too hard pressed he would sit down at the conclusion of a conference and write to his wife an account of his rides in the park, his breakfast with a Schwarzenberg, his dinner with the King of Prussia, his disappointment at seeing not one pretty face at the *bal masqué*, his plan of going home by way of his vineyard at Schloss Johannisberg. These people, the ancient and genuine aristocrats, were in many, probably most, instances friendly and simple in manner. The democratic American Professor Ticknor, having started with a suitable letter of introduction, was received into the noblest families in France, Italy, and Spain. " I always dined in company," he wrote from Paris in 1818, " generally either at Count Pastoret's, at the Duc de Duras', at the Count de Ste Aulaire's, or, if I had no special engagement, at the Duc de Broglie's, on whose table I always had a plate." [1] He found society at Holland House, London's great Whig mansion, simple, witty, cultured—" the best I have seen in Europe." Macaulay has described the splendid social

[1] *The Life of George Ticknor*, i, 253.

circle of Lord Holland and the winning frankness of the host in one of his briefest but most beautiful essays.

The working aristocracy, however, was just a minority. Most of the aristocrats and all the rich *bourgeois* young men whom they attracted into their circle led a life of pleasure and boredom. *Ennui* was the bugbear of the dandies. They spent their lives in avoiding it, and they lived almost continuously with it.

Dandy, though originally French (*dandin*, ' a silly fellow '), was a domiciled English word meaning an affected person who gave himself airs and aped the latest fashion, and who even thought that he led it. Thackeray popularized the word ' snob,' and in many cases the snobs and the dandies were the same people. But snobbism is a deep-seated spiritual quality, which makes a person despise other people and fear above all things to be thought of the same clay as them. Dandyism is an external characteristic, which may have a deep source, but on the other hand may be purely superficial—merely a mannerism. The snobs are cut off from the rest of mankind by their self-love and their fear of being discovered to be inferior. The dandy has achieved security, in his own mind and in society, by setting himself a difficult but attainable standard of dress and deportment, and by aiming at nothing more. Chateaubriand describes the dandies as he saw them in the time of his embassy at London in 1822, and again as they were when he compiled his *Memoirs* in 1840:

> In 1822 the man of fashion had to present at first sight the appearance of an unhappy and unhealthy man: he must have something negligent about his person, long nails, the chin partly unshaven, as if the hair had grown in a moment unsuspectedly, through forgetfulness in his absent-minded desperation; his hair tousled by the wind, his looks at once deep, sublime, distracted, and fateful: his lips contracted in scorn of the human race; his heart weary, ' Byronian,' drowned in the dissatisfaction and mystery of life.
>
> To-day it is different: the dandy must have a conquering, light, insolent air: he must be careful of his toilet, wear moustaches,

H

or a beard cut in a round like a ruffle of Queen Elizabeth, or like the luminous disc of the sun; he displays the proud independence of his character by keeping his hat on his head, lolling on the sofa, sticking out his boots under the very noses of admiring ladies who are seated on chairs opposite to him; when riding he carries a cane as if it were a church candle, and sits his horse unconcernedly, as if he were on it by accident. His health must be perfect and his spirits always overflowing with five or six enjoyments. Some radical dandies, those that are ultra-modern, have a pipe.[1]

Pushkin, the Russian Byron, in his *Evgeny Onegin* (published 1827), describes his hero, "like a London dandy dizened"; and he rhetorically asks:

> How paint to your imagination
> That room retired in colours true,
> Where the prize pupil of the Fashion
> Is drest—undrest—then drest anew?[2]

It was to dandyism that the idle aristocrats—those who did not enter politics or the Government service—gave themselves over in the general relaxation of mind and spirit which followed upon the close of the Great War. The aristocrats, as a whole, had not taken a prominent part in the war or suffered severely from it. Military service as a profession was in the tradition of certain families. In the Austrian effort against Napoleon in 1809, in the Russian defence against Napoleon's Moscow expedition in 1812, and in the German War of Liberation in 1813 all sorts of gentry had taken service, whether they were in the military tradition or not. Otherwise they had not been active in the wars. Nevertheless, war conditions imposed a mental and moral strain upon everybody; and when peace came there was a feeling of relief from tension. It was then that dandyism came into its own.

According to Chateaubriand, the dandy's day was very strenuous. At six in the morning he was riding out to an early break-

---

[1] *Mémoires d'outre-tombe* (ed. Biré), iv, 246.
[2] A. Pushkin, *Evgeny Onegin*, Canto I (trans. Oliver Elton, in *The Slavonic Review*, January 1936, pp. 250, 256).

fast-party in the country. He came back to lunch in London.
Then he changed his clothes for the afternoon promenade in
Bond Street or Hyde Park; changed again for dinner at half-
past seven; changed once more for the opera. At midnight he
changed his dress for a *soirée* or a *raout*. " What an enchanting
life ! " adds Chateaubriand. " I would prefer the galleys a
hundred times." [1] Prince Pückler-Muskau, who travelled in
England in 1826–28, on a visit in a country house at New-
market noted a dandy in the drawing-room ignoring the whole
company.

> Sunk into a large easy-chair, he had laid his elegantly shod
> right foot over his left knee, and in that attitude became appar-
> ently so absorbed in Madame de Staël's *Allemagne* that he took
> not the slightest notice of anyone present.

At dinner, however, this dandy talked a great deal about
Goethe and " *Fost*." Pückler-Muskau also heard a story in
England of a dandy, known to be a powerful swimmer, who was
walking with a lady where a man fell into water and was drowning. The lady adjured the dandy to lend help, but he only
raised his lorgnette, looked at the drowning man, and replied,
" It is impossible, madam; I never was introduced to that
gentleman." [2]

With the Romantic movement English ways became popular
on the Continent, so that French historians wrote seriously
about ' Anglomania.' *Quelle drôle de vie mènent les Country-
Esquires*, writes Sainte-Beuve from Oxford, August 26, 1828:
Chasse, pêche, dîners, promenades à cheval. He adds that they
also preached on Sunday, for " most of them are *curés* of their
parish." [3] Apart from this overstatement, his description is
not bad. English clothes, horses and carriages, the English
Constitution, clubs and country houses, Walter Scott's novels
and Byron's poetry—in fact, every characteristic feature of the

---

[1] *Mémoires d'outre-tombe*, iv, 250.

[2] *A Tour in Germany, Holland, and England in the Years 1826, 1827, 1828*
by a German Prince (Pückler-Muskau) (trans. 1843), iii, 87, 381.

[3] Sainte-Beuve, *Correspondance*, i, 104.

English people, except its cooking—became wildly popular with the Continental gentry. 'Anglomania' was the fashion not only in Paris, where it was particularly strong, but in all the other European capitals and the prominent provincial towns, which were still a kind of local capital, with their own Society and self-conscious social life. Hungarian noblemen bought their horses from England; St Petersburg High Society had its English club; Byron was a hero in Venice, Landor in Florence. The Italians had excellent, contemporary translations of the poems of Byron and Shelley.

To admire and copy English sport, country life, politics, and literature was well enough and could harm nobody. But 'Anglomania' in the idle rich became affectation, foppery, dandyism. Beau Brummell was the perfect expression of vacuous High Society.

George Brummell was not of noble birth, but sprung from the *bourgeoisie*, whose socially aspiring members all hung on to the skirts of the aristocracy. His father made money as secretary to Lord North. George, who was born in 1778, was sent to school in 1790 at Eton; there, and afterwards at Oriel College, Oxford (where he resided for less than a year), he displayed enormous skill and industry in leading the fashion in dress and manners. He was the incomparable snob, recognized as his equals only people in the first social rank, and was studiously offensive to all others. In his imperturbable coolness he surpassed Talleyrand, who said, *bouche riante, et front d'airain, et vous passez partout*. The Regent George, whose notice Brummell had attracted at Windsor, made him an officer in a hussar regiment. The Beau pretended to be unable to recognize his own squadron. He resigned from the Army when his regiment was due to leave London for Manchester. This was in 1798, when he was twenty years old. He never showed any inclination to go to the wars which went on for the next fifteen years; there was no social pressure put on anyone to go to the wars. Brummell about this time came into a fortune of £30,000; with this as a basis for contracting enormous debts he was able to live the fashionable life of London at No. 4 Chesterfield

Street for another sixteen or seventeen years. He studied, with industry that almost amounted to passion, the elegancies of apparel. Dressing himself, with the help of a valet, was an effort of prolonged and severe artistry. But a capital of £30,000 could not carry a grand dandy through the extravagances of High Society; and in 1816 Brummell had to flee from his creditors to Calais. After this he lived meagrely enough on the doles of his friends. In 1830 they procured for him the sine-cure post of consul at Caen, but two years later Palmerston suppressed the post; and Brummell was imprisoned for debt. People in London still remembered him, and raised a subscription to pay his pressing debts and get him out of prison. The miserable old bachelor stayed on at Caen, sponging on impressionable travellers for a dinner and a glass of champagne. He died in a pauper asylum, imbecile, in 1840.

The mantle of Beau Brummell was not taken up until 1821, when a young and handsome Count Alfred d'Orsay, who had some independent fortune, but not very much, came to live in London. " It was the time," writes the Comte d'Antioche, " of the greatest coming and going between French and English High Society." [1] Chateaubriand, coming to London as ambassador shortly afterwards, did not like the French fop, who none the less proved to be very congenial to London Society and who became quite the rage. " You should be content with writing in your own language, like Grammont; and succeeding in London as nobody has succeeded since the days of Charles II," Byron wrote to him. [2] Chateaubriand thought so too, but did not think this a credit to him. " Nothing succeeded at London like insolence; witness d'Orsay," wrote Chateaubriand later in his memoirs. [3] D'Orsay's reign was different from that of Brummell. He was, like Brummell, elegant, and he invented a garment, the *paletot*, which for a time every man had to wear when riding in Hyde Park; but he had much more *esprit* than

---

[1] Comte d'Antioche, *Chateaubriand, ambassadeur à Londres* (1912), p. 280.
[2] *Letters and Journals of Lord Byron* (ed. Prothero, 1904), vi, 194 (April 22, 1823).
[3] *Mémoires d'outre-tombe*, iv, 247.

Brummell; he was witty and amusing. High life, however, requires money; and d'Orsay would have had to go back to France and draw pay as an Army officer in garrison; but he was rescued from this fate by the Blessingtons.

The Earl of Blessington was a rich Irish landowner who had married a talented and handsome though penniless Irishwoman, Marguerite Power, widow of Captain St Leger Farmer. She had separated from her first husband, and had been living with Lord Blessington for two years before the captain providentially disposed of himself by falling out of the window of the King's Bench prison. She was then able to marry Lord Blessington in 1818. They lived in London, at first in Manchester Square and later at 11 St James's Square, and it was there, or in some other grand house, that they met Count Alfred d'Orsay and established a lifelong friendship with him. When they set forth with three big carriages and a number of servants for a great tour to Italy they met d'Orsay on the way, in his garrison town at Valence, and took him off to Italy with them. It was a case of the *cicisbey* over again, just when, Leigh Hunt was told, this curious feature of married life was disappearing from Italian Society.[1] D'Orsay lived on the Blessingtons' means, marrying their daughter, though he soon separated from her.

The Blessingtons and d'Orsay spent some months (1823) at Genoa, where Byron and the Countess Guiccioli were then living. Byron liked d'Orsay, who was then twenty-five and " has all the air of a *Cupidon déchaîné*, and is one of the few specimens I have ever seen of our ideal of a Frenchman *before* the Revolution." [2]

From Venice the Blessingtons and d'Orsay passed on to Naples and Rome; Byron went to Greece to fight for freedom. After six years spent in Italy the Blessington party returned to Paris, with their fortune considerably diminished, and set up house in the mansion where Marshal Ney had lived. Lord

---

[1] *Autobiography of Leigh Hunt* (ed. Ingpen, 1903), ii, 178.
[2] Byron to Moore, April 2, 1823, in *Letters and Journals of Lord Byron*, vi, 180.

Blessington had an apoplectic fit and died in the Hôtel Ney in
1829. Lady Blessington stayed on, and, with the help of
d'Orsay, created quite a *salon* of celebrated people; but after
the Revolution of July 1830 she returned to London with her
fortune sadly reduced. There the indomitable woman doubled
her income by publishing *Conversations with Lord Byron*,
various novels, ' keep-sake ' books, and travel books. D'Orsay,
who was a good draughtsman, published books of pictures and
portraits; they were very popular among the snobs who figured
in the books.[1] He drew Thomas Carlyle's portrait—dashed it
off in twenty minutes. Carlyle wrote to Emerson from Chelsea,
April 1, 1840:

> Count d'Orsay, the emperor of European Dandies, portraying
> the Prophet of Spiritual Sansculottism! He came rolling hither
> one day, many months ago, in his sun-chariot, to the bedazzle-
> ment of all bystanders; found me in dusty grey-plaid dressing-
> gown, grim as the spirit of Presbyterianism (my wife said), and
> contrived to get along well enough with me. I found him a man
> worth talking to . . . ; a dashing man who might, some twenty
> years sooner born, have become one of Bonaparte's Marshals and
> *is*—Count d'Orsay![2]

Lady Blessington maintained a great establishment in Gore
House, Kensington. D'Orsay lived in the house, and helped
to do the honours of the *salon*, which was attended by the Duke
of Wellington, Bulwer Lytton (who made d'Orsay the hero of
Pelham), Thomas Moore, Robert Browning, the young Disraeli, and many distinguished foreign visitors, including Louis
Napoleon Bonaparte, who became an intimate friend of d'Orsay.
Very few ladies were ever seen at the Blessington *salon*. The
count, though growing older, was still considered to be the
handsomest man in London, and the best dressed. B. R.
Haydon described him coming into his studio when the
artist was engaged upon an equestrian picture of the Duke of
Wellington.

[1] Jacques Boulenger, *Les Dandys* (1907), p. 80.
[2] *The Correspondence of Thomas Carlyle and Ralph Waldo Emerson*, i,
273–274.

He took my brush in his dandy gloves, which made my heart
ache, and lowered the hindquarters by bringing over a bit of the
sky. Such a dress! White great coat, blue satin cravat, hair oiled
and curling, hat of the primest curve and purest water, gloves
scented with eau de Cologne or eau de jasmin, primrose in tint,
skin in tightness. In this prime of dandyism he took up a nasty,
oily, dirty hogtool and immortalized Copenhagen (the charger)
by touching the sky.[1]

In 1849 Count d'Orsay had to flee from his creditors to
Paris, where Louis Napoleon Bonaparte was now Prince President, soon to be dictator and Émperor. Lady Blessington,
who also had heavy debts, followed d'Orsay to Paris and hired
an *appartement* in the rue du Cercle, but she died in two months.
D'Orsay eked out a living by sculpture; one of his works, a
bronze bust of Lamartine, is in the Galerie des Bustes of Versailles. At last Louis Napoleon made him Directeur des Beaux-
Arts, but shortly after taking up this post he died, August 4,
1852, and was buried at Chambourcy, a property of his relatives,
the Grammonts, by the side of Lady Blessington.

Before 1830 the Palais Royal, the vast mansion, with its great
central court or garden, of the Dukes of Orleans, had been the
chief place of concourse for all sorts of people, including the
dandies. Philippe Égalité had let out the arcades for shops,
cafés, gaming-houses, and other places of amusement, from
which he obtained an enormous revenue. His respectable son,
Louis Philippe, was still living in the Palais Royal when Pückler-
Muskau visited Paris in 1829—the only instance, wrote Pückler,
of a prince living under the same roof with shopkeepers and
more dubious persons and deriving a revenue from them. Louis
Philippe, however, replaced the old wooden gallery with an
elegant covered way or arcade, installed gas-lamps in it, and,
as soon as his accession to the throne gave him power, closed all
the gaming-houses.[2] He must have lost enormously in money

---

[1] T. Taylor, *Life of B. R. Haydon* (1853), iii, 115, quoted by Prothero,
Letters and Journals of Lord Byron, vi, 184.
[2] *A Tour in England, Ireland, and France in the Years 1828 and 1829*,
by a German Prince (Pückler-Muskau).

by this policy; the crowds in the Palais Royal were reduced, and the dandies and men of pleasure all went to the boulevards, which were being improved by the demolition of mean or obstructive houses and by the introduction of omnibuses for the relief of foot-passengers. Even revolution did not quench the " gaiety of the Champs Élysées," which Crabb Robinson found " quite exhilarating." [1] Art was not absolutely neglected. Pückler-Muskau visited the Louvre in 1829, and saw " a beautiful Venus, discovered a few years since in Milo, and presented to the King (Charles X) by the Duc de Rivière." He met a Napoleonic general in the gallery, and had interesting talk with him there. About the same time, between 1827 and 1834, horse-racing, an English sport, was becoming fashionable in Paris; and club life was beginning slowly to be popular in the world of fashionable men, who found their ' circles ' in the Café de Paris or other restaurants not sufficiently private or exclusive. The first club of this kind was the Cercle de l'Union, which was cosmopolitan, aristocratic, and somewhat grave; diplomatists belonged to it, after the manner of the St James's Club in London. The Jockey Club, founded in 1834, at the corner of the rue Helder and Boulevard des Italiens, was meant to be equally exclusive and luxurious, though less solemn and, of course, more definitely sportive. The English Lord Henry Seymour was the first president of the Jockey Club from 1834 to 1836.

Lord Henry Seymour was one of those eccentric characters, almost monstrosities, which heredity, a lax upbringing, and great wealth sometimes combine to produce. He was born at Paris on January 18, 1805, and was the reputed second son of Lord Yarmouth (later third Marquis of Hertford), who was a prisoner at Verdun, and Lady Yarmouth, who resided at Paris. M. Boulenger is of opinion that Seymour was, in fact, the son of Lady Yarmouth and the Comte de Montrond, one of the most vicious men of Talleyrand's vicious circle.[2] She was the daughter of an Italian actress called Fagniani, and her father was either

[1] *The Diary of Henry Crabb Robinson*, ii, 316 (visit of 1850 to Paris).
[2] Boulenger, *op. cit.*, pp. 237–238.

George Selwyn or his friend, the Duke of Queensberry, both of whom left her their fortunes. It was from his mother that Lord Henry Seymour had his great wealth. His mother and he lived at Paris, though inhabiting different houses. She had also living with her a so-called nephew, Richard Wallace, who was probably another illegitimate son of hers. Her husband, Lord Yarmouth, who succeeded to the title of Marquis of Hertford in 1822, fabulously rich, likewise lived in Paris, in his own house, letting his London mansion, Hertford House, Manchester Square, to the French Government for their embassy. The Marquis formed in his Paris house a magnificent collection of pictures, which he bequeathed to Richard Wallace and which is now public property, in the Wallace Collection, Manchester Square. Montrond, the probable father of Lord Henry Seymour, lived to a great age in Paris, the complete *roué* and cynic, relating, like another Casanova, his innumerable intrigues and gallantries. He died in 1843. Lord Henry Seymour, who never married, but had many mistresses, died in 1859. The selfishness, luxury, and extravagance of the Paris Seymours is typical of the idle (as distinct from the political or working) aristocracy which was passing out of date in that vigorous nineteenth-century world, the promised land of the vigorous, growing *bourgeoisie*. Yet Lord Henry Seymour left funds bringing in a revenue of £36,000 a year to the Paris hospitals. Richard Wallace was extremely public-spirited, and is said to have spent two and a half million francs in aiding the inhabitants of Paris during the Siege of 1870–71, at which he was present.

There was in France, as in all the civilized countries of Europe, a cultivation of sport and of outdoor recreations which is natural to all country gentlemen. But Lord Henry Seymour and the dandies who copied him were not interested in country life. It was horse-racing, betting, boxing, fencing, that were their idea of sport. Seymour was proud of his muscularity, of his big biceps, of the weights which he could lift. This, indeed, was not natural to the dandies of the period, with their wasp-like waists and their effeminate manners. Seymour resigned from the Jockey Club two years after its foundation because

he found that its members were going in more for dining than
for racing. He was fond enough himself of dining and of wine.
He was largely responsible for making smoking popular among
the gentry of Paris, and his cigars were famous. But his abid-
ing passion was muscularity. The dandies' rage for English
sport died down after the mid-century, and was not resumed
again until the twentieth century, when the young Frenchmen
took up football and rowing.

The life of the frivolous, as distinct from the working, aristocracy was much the same everywhere. It was passed, not in
the countryside, but at any rate for considerable periods of
each year, in the great capitals—London, Paris, Vienna,
Moscow and St Petersburg, Rome, Milan, Madrid, Munich
and Berlin.

Everywhere were to be found English people, but particularly in Italy. "The English women," wrote Chateaubriand
at Rome in 1828,

> have the air of performers engaged to dance for the winter at
> Paris, Milan, Rome, Naples, returning to London at the expiry
> of their engagements, with spring. The leapings upon the ruins
> of the Capitol, the uniform manners which *grand* Society exhibits
> everywhere, are very strange things. . . . What is truly deplor-
> able here, and out of keeping with the nature of the places and
> scenes, is this multitude of insipid English women and of frivo-
> lous dandies, holding each other linked by the arm like bats
> clinging together by their wings, parading their eccentricity,
> their boredom, and their insolence in your fêtes, and settling down
> among you as if at an inn. This Great Britain, vagabonding and
> ungainly, leaps into your best places at your public celebrations
> and fights with you to drive you from them. Every day it eats
> up in haste pictures and ruins, and, to do you honour, comes
> to eat up the cakes and ices at your evening parties. I do not
> know how an ambassador can bear these coarse guests and not
> have them shown to the door.[1]

The British, of course, were not the only travellers. In
every capital there was a cosmopolitan, if somewhat fluid,

[1] *Mémoires d'outre-tombe*, v, 63.

society. When Chateaubriand was received into the Accademia Tiburina, *toute l'Europe, à Rome, était là avec Rome*.[1] The *salon*, where feminine influence was dominant, was weakened by the growing fashion, especially after 1830, of smoking; cigars, still more pipes, were not suitable to the drawing-room. After 1837 or 1840 the railways opened up the capitals to easy visits from the provincials, from the *bourgeoisie* of the small towns. The access of the provincials drove the idle aristocracy off the boulevards. Therefore they took to passing their time in clubs, rather than in the *salon* or on the boulevard or in the restaurants and *cafés*; and in the clubs they were probably just as dissipated as they had been elsewhere. It was from about 1830 that the age of clubs may be dated. The coffee-houses, so influential in the eighteenth century, went on now only as the gathering-places of the smaller *bourgeoisie*. The aristocracy preserved their exclusiveness in the clubs of St James's and Pall Mall, in the *cercles* of Paris, in the English Club of St Petersburg. The 'officer class' in every big city, having a strong corporate sense and a belief in the military value of social exclusiveness, developed the club habit very strongly.

It would appear that in the long run the aristocracy as a socially defined class could not survive the French Revolution. Titles of nobility, it is true, were granted by Napoleon I, and a hereditary peerage was re-established by Louis XVIII. The tenacity of the sense of birth and wealth is proved by the quasi-legal recognition of titles of nobility in contemporary republican France. But the Constitution of the United States, adopted in 1788, prohibited titles of nobility there, and its example was followed in the other American republics. In Europe the Balkan territories, when the nineteenth century opened, were still under the levelling despotism of the Turk, and titles of nobility have never since then been instituted there. The Norwegian Constitution of 1814 prohibited royal grants of noble title, and in 1821 all titles of nobility were suppressed in Norway. In Great Britain and in Russia the legal process was in a contrary direction to this policy of prohibition; titles were

[1] *Op. cit.*, v, 99.

distributed so freely as to prevent a caste prestige of the aristocracies. In Russia superior Civil Servants were regularly ennobled. In Great Britain the younger Pitt, in the last part of
the eighteenth century, brought large numbers of squires into
the House of Lords, and made a beginning with the ennobling
of bankers and commercial men. The Reform Bill of 1832,
which destroyed ' pocket boroughs,' and the institution of
open competitive examinations for the Civil Service in 1855
removed two powerful supports of the political influence of
the aristocracy.

In Prussia, to a lesser extent in the other German states,
including Austria, and in Hungary noble political privilege
successfully resisted the tide of democracy. This was achieved
through the monarchical system in these countries, which
enabled the nobles to keep the posts of officers in the Army
and the higher positions in the Civil Services almost exclusively
to themselves. Everywhere else in Central and Western Europe
the *bourgeoisie* (sometimes called the professional and commercial classes), and particularly the big industrialists, were
gaining political power. With the destruction of feudalism, with
the recognition of equality of all citizens before the law, with
the growth of industry, the roots of the aristocracies withered
away. Nevertheless, the conservatism characteristic of modern
societies and the permanence of large landed estates or capital
funds in the possession of noble families maintained these
families and their titles amid democracy, even in egalitarian
France. The World War, however, completely ruined them as
a class. Agrarian legislation in many countries distributed their
land among the peasantry, and inflation of currency reduced the
value of their monetary compensation. Where they manage to
retain part of their wealth and social status they are inevitably
being assimilated with the *haute bourgeoisie*.

In the first half of the nineteenth century, however, the aristocracy still seemed vigorous and, if not dominant, at any rate
contesting upon favourable terms the control of the State with
the liberal professors, students, journalists, lawyers, and industrialists. The Congress of Vienna, the base of the European

system of the nineteenth century, was the affair of the high
aristocracy. Its round of balls and other amusements may have
been, as Treitschke says,[1] just " colossal insipidity," and the
important subject discussed at Talleyrand's table may have been
the supremacy of Brie among cheeses. Yet with the defeat of
" the Revolution " in the person of Napoleon the aristocracy
felt that they had re-entered into their own domain. Never,
wrote Niebuhr, had they shown themselves more haughty and
contemptuous than in the generation after the Congress of
Vienna.

The only justification for the continued existence of the class
was the working section, the bees among the drones. Of the
workers Metternich is the grand type. As the years went on
and the Revolution, beaten back and suppressed, was always
bursting forth somewhere, he might complain that he was " so
weary," yet he manfully went on. His way of life has been
sympathetically, perhaps too sympathetically, described in
Mazade's *Un Chancelier d'ancien régime* : he was courtly, orderly,
serious, witty, a regular reader of the Bible ; full of reflections
and wise observation.

The curious and interesting career of one dandy who adopted
a very vigorous and wholesome way of life in his later years
has been put on record. This was a " Colonel C.," an
Englishman, whom the observant Prince Pückler-Muskau met
in London in 1828. Colonel C. was then a middle-aged man.
He had been one of the most admired *beaux* of the metropolis,
and had run through all his fortune, except a few thousand
pounds. Happening once to look at the map of America, he
conceived the idea of becoming a backwoodsman, and (merely
by study of the map) he fixed upon Lake Erie. So, marrying
his valet to a pretty young woman, he took them both out to
Canada. There, in the region of Lake Erie, he lived a hard
life, until, with the help of some of the neighbouring settlers,
he was able to build a log-house for himself. He lived on the
best of terms with the settlers, encouraged them in their labours,
and brightened their life by showing them how to cook good

---

[1] *Op. cit.*, ii, 10.

dishes, instead of the half-raw meat which they usually ate. When Pückler-Muskau met him the Colonel appears only to have been on a visit to England, and thoroughly content with his Canadian life.

Colonel C. was an exception among dandies. Nevertheless, a more vigorous way of life was opening for some of them. The secrets of "Darkest Africa" were soon to begin to be revealed. Exploration and big-game shooting expelled dandyism from popular estimation.

CHAPTER IX

AUSTRIAN ITALY

IN 1814 Italy was, for the most part, returned by the Allies to its old masters. Murat was left as King of Naples; but he joined Napoleon in the Hundred Days, was captured by the Austrians, and shot. The Bourbon dynasty was restored in Naples. Monarchy was still fashionable and republics out of date. Napoleon Bonaparte had suppressed the republics of Genoa and Venice. Genoa was allotted in 1814 to the kingdom of Sardinia, and Venice to Austria. Lombardy, along with Venice, formed the " Lombardo-Venetian Kingdom " of the Habsburg emperors. Thenceforth for forty-five years the Austrians dominated Italy, as the Spaniards had done in the seventeenth century. Except the King of Sardinia, the Italian monarchs were bound to Austria by treaties of alliance and dependence.

Of the many routes into Italy perhaps the Simplon was the most popular after the Great War, for Napoleon had enormously improved it. Byron came that way in 1816, writing in his perverse manner to his sister: " The Simplon, as you know, is the most superb of all possible routes, so I shall not describe it." [1] Superb, but not altogether safe. Before Byron crossed a " chain of English carriages " had been stopped near Cesto and plundered. Having descended into Italy, Byron " navigated the Lago Maggiore " and went over the Borromean Islands, which he found to be " fine, but too artificial." Then, by way of Milan and Verona (whence he carried away four fragments from the tomb of Juliet), he went to Venice. He stayed there for a whole winter, and is said to have chosen Venice because, " as nobody walks there, his not having the power is not so remark-

---

[1] *Letters and Journals of Lord Byron*, iv, 2.

able." [1] But Byron declares in his letters more than once that Venice was one of the dreams of his youth: " It has always been (next to the East) the greenest island of my imagination." [2] Many people have felt something like this too. Henry Crabb Robinson, coming to Italy in 1831, wrote: " From Vienna I proceeded, through Styria and Carniola, to Trieste . . . and entered Italy at Venice, the rich, but *I* say the romantic."

Byron stayed at a draper's house in the Frezzeria, a narrow street of high houses on the left-hand side going from the Ascensione to the Caffè dei Lazzaroni, and there he had a long and disgraceful intrigue with the draper's wife. He also studied Armenian at the Mekhitarist convent [3] on the island of St Lazzaro, as amid the languors of Venice he found that his mind " wanted something craggy to break upon." He meditated on the plan of *Manfred* in the convent garden, but did not write a great deal, for he preferred to describe scenes not on the spot, but after a considerable interval, when the impressions had settled down in his mind. He wrote, in Canto 4 of *Childe Harold*:

> I stood in Venice on the " Bridge of Sighs ";
> A Palace and a prison on each hand:
> I saw from out the wave her structures rise
> As from the stroke of the Enchanter's wand:
> A thousand Years their cloudy wings expand
> Around me, and a dying Glory smiles
> O'er the far times, when many a subject land
> Looked to the winged Lion's marble piles,
> When Venice sat in state, throned on her hundred isles!
>
> . . . .
>
> In Venice Tasso's echoes are no more,
> And silent rows the songless Gondolier;

---

[1] T. Moore, *Memoirs of Byron*, iii, 93, quoted by Prothero, *op. cit.*, iv, 7, *n.* 2.

[2] To T. Moore, November 17, 1816 (*Letters and Journals of Lord Byron*, iv, 7). For the following quotation see *The Diary of Henry Crabb Robinson*, ii, 85.

[3] Mekhitar was an Armenian monk who was received into the Roman Church in 1700, and founded an order for bringing other Armenians into the Church.

I

> Her palaces are crumbling to the shore,
> And Music meets not always now the ear:
> Those days are gone—but Beauty still is here.
> States fall, Arts fade—but Nature does not die,
> Nor yet forget how Venice once was dear,
> The pleasant place of all festivity,
> The revel of the earth—the Masque of Italy!

George Ticknor's remark (in 1818) was: "As in all Italian cities, so in Venice, there is little society." The famous Carnival of Venice still took place every year, but it never regained the *vogue* which it had in the eighteenth century. Venice had not recovered from the Napoleonic war, and did not show signs of recovery until about the year 1840.[1] When the carnival began on December 26 " every mouth was put in motion. There was nothing but fiddling and playing on the virginals, and all kinds of conceits and divertissements, on every canal of this aquatic city."[2] When the carnival was over and Passion Week began there was an " eternal churching, as in all Catholic countries "; but the people were " not so bigoted as they seem to be in Spain." Everybody has some idea of the appearance of Venice without having been there. Byron wrote:

> It is one of those places which I know before I see them, and has always haunted me the most after the East. I like the gloomy gaiety of their gondolas, and the silence of their canals. I do not even dislike the evident decay of the city, though I regret the singularity of its vanished costume.

The French dominion had ended a couple of years before Byron came to Venice. The city and province were now under Austria. The Venetians seemed to reck little of these changes at this time. The Austrian Governor, Count Gretz, did not make the foreign occupation too obvious. His wife was " a very amiable and pleasing woman, with remarkably good manners, as many of the German women have." There was

---

[1] See Murray's *Handbook for Northern Italy* (1842), p. 328. The Ticknor quotation is from *The Life of George Ticknor*, i, 164.

[2] To John Murray, December 26, 1816 (*Letters and Journals of Lord Byron*, iv, 34).

not a great number of foreign residents. " There are no English here," wrote Byron, " except birds of passage, who stay a day and then go on to Florence or Rome." The city, though in decline, was full of life and bustle, at any rate in the evening. The *cafés* remained open until five o'clock in the morning, and, in summer at any rate, the Giudecca and Grand Canal were covered with gondolas. Metternich visited Venice in June 1817, and was charmed with its liveliness and gaiety. *Je suis promené hier dans Venise comme dans une ville des Mille et une Nuits*, he wrote to his wife.[1] Byron, about the same time, wrote : " St Mark's, and, indeed, Venice, is most alive at night. The theatres are not open until *nine*, and the society is proportionately late." This suited Byron very well, but the English visitors in general regretted the absence of the rattle of hackney-coaches, without which they could not sleep.[2] Yet English ways, or what were supposed to be English ways, were fashionable in Venice. At the ' routs ' in High Society, while the ladies sat in a circle round the hostess and the men stood about the room, stiff rum-punch was drunk, because it was thought to be English, instead of the former lemonade, and ices. There were numerous theatres, among them the Fenice, which Byron said was the finest he had ever seen, and grander than those of Milan and Brescia.

Byron liked Venice so much that, though he left it for Rome in the spring of 1817, he came back again in June, not stopping to rest anywhere, except on the river Clitumnus, where he caught some " famous trout." He now kept four horses in Venice on the little island called the Lido. Almost every day he would go over there with his friend John Cam Hobhouse in a gondola and ride with him along the shore. He rented the Palazzo Mocenigo on the Canal' Grande, and a country villa on the Brenta, among the Euganean hills, as a summer residence. He kept very bad hours, rose at midday or three in the afternoon, and so missed seeing a fellow-countryman, Captain Basil Hall, R.N., the traveller, although he called

[1] Metternich, *Mémoires*, iii, 23.
[2] Byron to John Murray, November 25, 1816.

several times on Hall, and Hall on him; one or the other was always in bed.[1] In one of his last letters from Venice Byron gives an account at once of his life there and of the place itself:

Venice is not an expensive residence (unless a man chooses it). It has theatres, society, and profligacy rather more than enough. I keep four horses on one of the islands, where there is a beach of some miles along the Adriatic, so that I have daily exercise. I have my gondola and about fourteen servants, including the nurse for a little girl (a natural daughter of mine), and I reside in one of the Mocenigo palaces on the Grand Canal; the rent of the whole house, which is very large and furnished with linen, etc., etc., inclusive, is two hundred a year (and I gave more than I need have done). In the two years I have been at Venice I have spent about *five* thousand pounds, and I need not have spent a *third* of this, had it not been that I have a passion for women which is expensive in its variety everywhere, but less so in Venice than in other cities. You may suppose that in *two years*, with a large establishment, horses, house, box at the opera, gondola, journeys, women, and charity (for I have not laid out all on my pleasures, but have bought occasionally a shilling's worth of salvation), villas in the country, another carriage and horses purchased for the country, books bought, etc., etc.,—in short everything I wanted, and *more* than I ought to have wanted, that the sum of five thousand pounds Sterling is no great deal, particularly when I tell you that more than half was laid out on the Sex;—to be sure I have had plenty for the money, that's certain. . . . If you are disposed to come this way you might live very comfortably, and even splendidly, for less than a thousand a year, and find a palace for the rent of one hundred—that is to say, an Italian palace; you know that all houses with a particular front are called so—in short, an enormous house. But, as I said, I do not think you would like it, or rather that Lady Frances would not; it is not so gay as it has been, and there is a monotony to many people in its canals and the comparative silence of its streets. To one who has been always passionate for Venice, and delights in the dialect and *naïveté* of the people and the romance of its old history and

[1] *Letters and Journals of Lord Byron*, iv, 252 *n*. Hall was ill with ague at the time.

institutions and appearance, all its disadvantages are more than compensated by the sight of a single gondola. The view of the Rialto, of the Piazza, and the Chaunt of Tasso (though less frequent than of old), are to me worth all the cities on earth, save Rome and Athens.[1]

The boundary between Venetia and Lombardy was the Mincio. Each province, though combined to form the Lombardo-Venetian Kingdom under Austria, had a separate administration and a separate congregation, or elected council but only a consultative assembly. Opinion varied about the quality of the government. The white tunics of the Austrian soldiers and their black and yellow sentry-boxes made the foreign domination obvious; as did also the great fortresses, the ' Quadrilateral ' of Mantua, Verona, Legnago, and Peschiera. There was no political liberty. Byron wrote from Venice in 1818: " An English newspaper here would be a prodigy, and an opposition one a monster; and, except some extracts *from* extracts in the vile, garbled Paris gazettes, nothing of the kind reaches the Veneto-Lombard public, who are, perhaps, the most oppressed in Europe." [2] On the other hand, the *Handbook of Northern Italy* of 1842 put it on record, for all visitors to test the statement: " The natives are entirely in possession of all the offices of administration, except the highest, and enjoy an incalculably greater degree of independence than when under the baneful and corrupting influence of France." The Prussian historian Friedrich Ludwig von Raumer declared (1840) that Lombardy had never been so well governed as under the sceptre of Austria, nor so free, because the liberty of the former Italian republics was nothing but a sham. The truth probably is that the administration was technically of a high quality, for the Austrians had a uniform legal system and efficient, if rather slow, bureaucratic methods. " Of Lombardy I ought to say," wrote Henry Crabb Robinson in his tour of 1837 with Wordsworth, " that the nearly entire absence of

---

[1] *Letters and Journals of Lord Byron*, iv, 255–256.

[2] To T. Moore, September 17, 1818 (*Letters and Journals of Lord Byron*, iv, 257).

beggars, except very old people, speaks well for the Austrian Government." [1]

There is no doubt that the countryside of Lombardo-Venetia was prosperous. The land was cultivated with great care, and the landowners invested much capital in it. New routes were opened up and roads constructed, like that by which Crabb Robinson and Wordsworth travelled from Venice by way of Lengarone and Sillian to Salzburg in 1837. With the rise of national feeling the Austrians became unpopular. "The desire to see Italy united," wrote Henry Crabb Robinson from Florence in 1831,

> was the fond wish of most Italian politicians. One of the most respectable of them, Mayer—not to mention any I was at that time unacquainted with—used to say that he would gladly see all Italy under one absolute sovereign, national independence being the first of blessings.

At this time the popular plan was for a federation of nine states, including the Austrian provinces of Lombardy and Venice. "To purchase the consent of France to this arrangement," wrote Crabb Robinson from Florence in 1831, "many Italians were willing to sacrifice Savoy and Nice." [2] The national sentiment was not very obvious until the late forties, although Count Alessandro Manzoni's *I promessi sposi*, a novel about the Spanish dominion of the seventeenth century, published in 1825–27, did something to arouse it earlier. The book achieved an almost inconceivable popularity in Italy. Frescoes of its scenes were painted in the Pitti Palace of the Grand Duke of Tuscany, and chintzes on the sofas and chairs of taverns bore pictures of the story. Feeling was roused against Austria by the publication of Silvio Pellico's *Le mie prigioni* in 1832. Pellico, a native and subject of the kingdom of Sardinia, earning his living at Milan as a teacher and playwright, was arrested by the Austrian authorities and kept in the Spielberg. He was released in 1830, and lived thereafter at Turin. Ticknor met

---

[1] *The Diary of Henry Crabb Robinson*, ii, 187; *cf.* p. 113.
[2] *Ibid.*, pp. 113–114.

him there in 1836, " a small, commonplace-looking man, about
fifty years old, gentle, modest, and quiet in his manners, his
health still feeble, but not bad, from his long confinement." [1]
He died in 1854.

The Lombardy plain is rather dull for the traveller. Byron
wrote in 1816 to his sister: " Lombardy is not a beautiful
country—at least in autumn, excepting, however, the Lago di
Garda and its outlines which are mountainous on one side:
and it is a fine, stormy lake throughout—never quiet." The
crown of Lombardy was, of course, Milan, which still had the
air of a great capital. When John Ruskin first visited Milan
in 1833 he saw the Milanese aristocracy driving in the Corso,
" happy and proud as ours in their park." It was a beautiful
sight. No railway station yet blocked the view, and the " whole
chain of the Alps " could be seen from the Corso.[2] Milan, in
contrast with Venice, is not now a quiet city; but it was in
1833. Ruskin remembered how it appeared.

> The beautiful city with its dominant, frost-crystalline Duomo.
> . . . Then the drive home in the open carriage through the quiet
> twilight up the long streets, and round the base of the Duomo,
> the smooth pavement under the wheels adding with its silentness
> to the sense of dream wonder in it all—the perfect air in abso-
> lute calm, the just seen majesty of encompassing Alps, the per-
> fectness—so it seemed to me—and purity, of the sweet, stainless
> marble against the sky.

The superb series, or " forest," of pinnacles on the roof of
Milan Cathedral was not yet finished, but was steadily being
completed in the fifty years after the Napoleonic wars. The
Austrian viceroy of the Lombardo-Venetian Kingdom occupied the Palazzo Imperiale-Reale for six months each year,
being for the other six months in the Palazzo San Marco of
Venice.

Stendhal has depicted life in Milan as he saw it in the early
part of the century. Gautier, George Sand, and other French

[1] *The Life of George Ticknor*, ii, 39. The reference above to *I promessi
sposi*, the palace frescoes and tavern chintzes, is ii, 86.
[2] Ruskin, *Præterita* (1899), i, 168.

writers describe it in the middle period of the century. The most numerous cosmopolitan Society was always in Rome, but practically every other large city had a European Society.

The Milanese were the most cultured among the large and rather impoverished class of Italian aristocracy. In Lombardy, as elsewhere, the French occupation had practically put an end to feudalism, which in any case had been milder there than in the rest of Italy. They took great care over the cultivation of their properties, which were conducted on a system of " high farming." Their main interests were economic and social, for though the Austrian Army and administration were open to them they took little part in these services. Agricultural societies flourished, and the doctrines of Adam Smith were in the ascendant, as indeed, in all North Italy, for Tuscany had a free port at Leghorn, and even the Austrians maintained a free port at Venice. The nobles were gradually becoming assimilated to the rising *haute bourgeoisie*. Count Alessandro Manzoni is typical of many of them, except for his genius. He was born at Milan in 1784, the son of a count with a small fortune. His mother was the daughter of the celebrated philanthropist and prison reformer the Marquis Beccaria. After completing his studies at Milan and Pavia, he went to Paris in 1805 (the year in which his father died), and was introduced into the brilliant society of Cabanis and Madame de Condorcet at Auteuil, which continued the tradition of wit and of literary and philosophical discussion of the *salons* of the eighteenth century. Manzoni, however, was not for long an eighteenth-century rationalist, but became a devout Catholic, with a romantic historical sense. His great friend in this Paris period was the eminent literary critic Claude Fauriel. In 1808 Manzoni married and settled down on his estate at Brusuglio, near Milan. Fauriel became godfather to his first-born. Manzoni's hymns are characteristic of the religious piety of the Romantic period, of Lamartine and Hugo. His tragedy *Carmagnola* was begun in 1816. He revisited Paris for some months in 1819–20, and renewed intercourse with Fauriel, and formed a friendship with Augustin Thierry, the historian, and Victor Cousin, the philo-

sopher. *Carmagnola*, published in 1820, received warm praise
from Goethe, though severely criticized in the *Quarterly Review*.
His great novel, *I promessi sposi*, was partly the result of his
reading of Walter Scott's historical romances, partly of conversations with Fauriel, who for two years (1823–25) stayed
with him or lived near him at Milan. *Promessi sposi* was published in 1825–27. Though the result of prolonged historical
researches, there is little historical incident in it. Rather it is
a picture of the times and of Society, of Milanese and Lombard
life in the seventeenth century. Its vividness, its historical
truthfulness, its warm romantic and devout religious outlook,
its sympathy with the common people, its conception of high
nobility, made its publication an epoch in the history of the
Italian *Risorgimento*. He lived to see the union of Italy, and
died in 1873.

The frontier between Piedmont (the kingdom of Sardinia)
and Lombardy was at the river Ticino. Here free Italy began.
The King of Sardinia, who retained nothing but his island
during the Napoleonic occupation, came back to his main-
land territory in 1814 and decreed that everything should be
restored to the legal condition of *novant-ott* (1798). In practice,
however, it was found that the past could not be undone;
and French forms of administration were maintained or re-
established. Victor Emmanuel I, however, refused to grant a
constitution. A revolution in 1820 was suppressed by intervention of an Austrian army. It was in this year that Silvio
Pellico, who was resident in Milan, was sent to prison by
the Austrians. The young Mazzini, a Genoese, was shocked
by the wretched appearance of refugees from the disturbed
area, driven from their homes by the soldiery because they
had aspired to freedom. Later (1829) he joined the secret
political society the Carbonari, was betrayed, imprisoned,
banished.

Nevertheless, in spite of incessant and meticulous police
supervision, liberalism spread. It was to find a sane and
powerful champion in the Conte di Cavour. George Ticknor
met in Madrid a young man called Cesare Balbo whose father

was Sardinian ambassador there (1818). The young Balbo, later famous as author of the *Speranze d'Italia*, was, says Ticknor, consumed with passion for the unity and greatness of Italy and with sorrow for its present condition. He took for his motto Dante's sad lines *Ahi, serva Italia, di dolore ostello.* His passion for Italy preyed upon his health.[1]

Nice was still in the kingdom of Savoy (until 1860); Savona, the next place of note along the Riviera, was " nicely paved with flagstones," and, as Wordsworth and Crabb Robinson found in 1837, was " agreeable to walk in, having a sort of college air about it." But the chief port now was Genoa, incorporated in the kingdom by the treaties of 1814–15. Leigh Hunt, who stayed there in 1822, agreed, as the Genoese claimed, that it was *Genova la superba*, especially as seen from the sea.

> Imagine a glorious amphitheatre of white houses, with mountains on each side and at the back. The base is composed of the city with its churches and shipping; the other houses are country-seats, looking out, one above the other, up the hill. To the left are the Alps with their snowy tops; to the right and from the back, are the Apennines. This is Genoa.[2]

The great quay was well paved and clean. There were many churches, quiet, cool, and rich. The streets were many, the houses spacious and high and painted on the outside, the ground floors in many cases occupied by shops. The city was large and increasing; it had about 100,000 inhabitants. Turin, the capital, situated almost at the gate of the Alps, suffered greatly under the French occupation down to 1814. Its population declined, but was still large—65,000 at the Restoration; after this it grew rapidly, and was 165,000 in 1840. The city had been mathematically laid out with squares and straight streets in the seventeenth century; its ground-plan remained like that of a modern American city. It had a vigorous Royal University.

South of Piedmont and Lombardy were the ' duchies '—

---

[1] *The Life of George Ticknor*, i, 209–210.
[2] Leigh Hunt, *Autobiography* (1903), ii, 130.

Parma, Modena, and the Grand Duchy of Tuscany, all three
' enfeoffed ' to Austria by treaties of alliance. Down to 1846
Parma (and its conjoined duchy Piacenza) was under Marie
Louise, widow of Napoleon. During her lifetime Lucca was
maintained as a duchy for the family of the old ducal dynasty
of Parma; it was under Duke Carlo Ludovico, who was to
succeed to Parma on the death of Marie Louise.

Metternich travelled in 1817 from Venice to Bologna by
way of Padua and Ferrara, and from Bologna by the regular
post-road through Covigliaio. At Florence he was simply
overwhelmed with delight at the city, the picture-galleries, the
countryside. The galleries had been improved by the Grand
Duke Leopold (the Emperor Leopold II), and the pictures
and statues which the French had carried off to Paris were
now in their proper place again. The countryside, though not
naturally very fertile, was rendered highly productive by good
cultivation, and supported a large population. Metternich
wrote that between Florence and Pistoia, which he could see
from his window, twenty-one miles away, there were four
thousand country houses and farmhouses.[1] When Ruskin first
visited Florence in 1840 it was still largely unchanged.

> An avenue of magnificent cypress and laurel ascended, un-
> broken, from the Porta Romana to Bellosguardo, from whose
> height one could then wander round through lanes of olive, or
> through small rural vineyards, to San Miniato, which stood
> deserted, but not ruinous, with a narrow lawn of scented herbage
> before it, and sweet wild weeds about its steps, all shut in by a
> hedge of roses. The long ascending causeway between smaller
> cypresses than those of the Porta Romana gave every conceivably
> loveliest view of the Duomo, and Cascine forest, and passing
> away of Arno towards the Sunset.[2]

When Leigh Hunt went to Florence in 1823 he made the
acquaintance of Walter Savage Landor, who resided there for
twenty years. Hazlitt came on a short visit. Charles Armitage
Brown, a friend of Keats and (wrote Hunt) " the best com-
mentator on Shakespeare's Sonnets," was living at Florence, as

[1] *Mémoires*, iii, 26.   [2] *Præterita*, ii, 182.

were also Seymour Kirkup, an artist, and Viscount Dillon a
" cavalier of the old school " turned radical. Italy, and particularly Florence, was becoming a home for romantic, cosmopolitan Englishmen. There were many ' Landors,' though
without his genius and extravagant tendencies.

Walter Savage Landor was born in 1775. Educated at Rugby
and Trinity College, Oxford, and expelled from both places for
insubordination, he made a home in Bath. In 1808 he fought,
at his own expense, as a volunteer in the Peninsular War. In
1809 he purchased Llanthony, an estate in Wales, and lived
there until 1814. Finding life at last impossible there because of
his perpetual quarrelling with neighbours and tenants, he went
abroad, first to Tours, then to Florence. When Crabb Robinson
visited him there in 1830 he was living with his wife and three
sons in a villa at Fiesole, near the famous villa " where Boccaccio's hundred tales were told." Crabb Robinson describes him
as " a man of florid complexion, with large, full eyes, and
altogether a *leonine* man, and with a fierceness of tone well
suited to his name." [1] Though Landor meant to live and die in
Italy (as he did, after a second residence at Bath, occasionally at
Clifton, from 1835 to 1858), he did not like the Italians, who,
on their part, said, " Every one is afraid of him." Yet he was
universally respected in Florence for his downright honesty and
for his generosity. The Government of the Grand Duke (the
only efficient and well-liked Italian Government) had to expel
him from Tuscany on account of his insolence.

> He asked for leave to return for a few days on business. The
> Minister said a passport could not be given him, but that instruc-
> tions would be given at the frontiers to admit him, and his con-
> tinuance would be overlooked if he wished it. He has remained
> unmolested ever since.

He died at Florence in 1864.

" Tuscany," wrote Queen Hortense (wife of Louis, ex-King
of Holland), referring to the year 1831, " was the happiest
country of Italy. The sovereign [Leopold II, of the younger

---

[1] *The Diary of Henry Crabb Robinson*, ii, 101 (August 16, 1830).

branch of the Habsburg family] was beloved. The only thing which people wanted from him was a constitution which—so it was said—the Ministers had ready." When the July Revolution broke out in Paris Metternich said, " *Does anyone believe that we were afraid of granting constitutions?* " It looked as if Metternich were going to grant one straightway. But afterwards he said no more about this.[1]

Metternich, in his 1817 tour, went from Florence down the Arno to Pisa. According to his view, there was a general fear of " Jacobins "; and the good party—" which is immense "—came flocking around him, as if expecting safety only from him.[2] Pisa was becoming quite a literary centre—for English writers. In 1822 Leigh Hunt was in Pisa, along with Byron, and Shelley, who had arrived from Lerici, near Spezia. One afternoon (July 8, 1822) Shelley and his friend Williams went off to Lerici, on the Gulf of Spezia. Ten days later Shelley's body, unrecognizable, was cast up by the sea near Viareggio. The last volume of Keats' poems, lent by Leigh Hunt to Shelley, was found open in the pocket of the jacket; it was " doubled back, as if the reader, in the act of reading, had hastily thrust it away." [3] The body was burned on a pyre on the sandy beach in the presence of Byron, Hunt, and Edward John Trelawny, and the ashes were sent to Rome for burial in the Protestant cemetery there. Hunt stayed in Pisa with Byron until September (1822). Pisa was beautiful and quiet; all its seaborne trade had been captured by Leghorn. Hunt described the famous group of buildings which are the heart of Pisa :

Let the reader imagine a broad grass-walk, standing in the solitary part of a country-town. Let him suppose at the end of this walk the Leaning Tower, with a row of small but elegant houses right under the inclination, and looking down the grass-plot; the Baptistry, a rotunda, standing by itself at the opposite end; the public hospital, an extremely neat and quiet building, occupying the principal length of the road which borders the

[1] *Mémoires de la reine Hortense* (ed. Hanoteau, 1927), iii, 186.
[2] Metternich, *Mémoires*, iii, 27.
[3] E. J. Trelawny, *Records of Shelley, Byron, and the Author* (1878), i, 190.

grass-plot on one side; on the other side, and on the grass itself, the Cathedral, stretching between the Leaning Tower and the Baptistry; and lastly, at the back of the Cathedral, and visible between the openings of its two ends, the Campo Santo (Holy Field) or burial-ground walled in with marble cloisters full of the oldest paintings in Italy. All these buildings are detached; they all stand in a free, open situation; they all look as if they were built but a year ago; they are all of marble; the whole place is kept extremely clean—the very grass in a state of greenness not common to turf in the south; and there are trees looking upon it over a wall next the Baptistry. Let the reader add to this scene a few boys playing about, all ready to answer your questions in pure Tuscan—women occasionally passing with veils or bare heads, or now and then a couple of friars; and though finer individual sights may be found in the world, it will be difficult to come upon an assemblage of objects more rich in their combination.[1]

All this has changed very little. At this time, 1823, Leigh Hunt and Mrs Hunt were living at Pisa with Byron, who had taken the ground floor of the Casa Lanfranchini, on the Arno; the river flows through the city. The Countess Guiccioli, the last of his mistresses (the best character of them all), was also with him, and the Countess's brother. Byron was writing *Don Juan* during the greater part of every night, with the help of gin and water. He rose late, breakfasted, read, lounged about singing an air, generally from an opera of Rossini; then he took a bath and dressed. He came downstairs; he was heard still singing in the courtyard at the back of the house, out of which a few steps ascended into the garden. Hunt had a little room for a study in a corner of the villa, with an orange-tree at the window. Byron would shout, " Leontius! " a nickname for Hunt invented by Shelley. He generally wore a nankeen jacket, white waistcoat and trousers, and a linen or velvet peaked cap. He carried a small tobacco-box in his hand, and put a morsel in his mouth from time to time, to keep him from becoming too fat; for he was growing very corpulent. After a little La Guiccioli, " with her sleek tresses," having made her toilet,

[1] Leigh Hunt, *Autobiography*, ii, 112.

would join Byron and Hunt in the garden. She was about twenty years old, handsome and lady-like, with a soft, gentle voice. After Pisa the friends moved to Genoa. It was from this city that in July 1823 Byron, having pledged all he had in the world to charter and fit out a ship, set forth on his last journey, to the Greek War of Independence.

The Papal Government in the legations of Ferrara, Bologna, and Romagna, in the marches of Ancona and Spoleto, in Umbria, and in Rome itself, existed only " by the sufferance of the great Catholic Powers." [1] It could hold the allegiance of the idle population of Rome, because, through the concourse of visitors and pilgrims, it afforded them subsistence. But in the Papal dominions outside Rome and the Campagna there was a serious revolt in 1831, in which the two Bonaparte princes (one of them the future Napoleon III) took part. Rome was left without troops, the Government without revenue. For weeks everybody lived in expectation of approach by the rebels.

> The truth is that but for the intervention of Austria the Italian Governments (with the exception of Tuscany) had contrived to render themselves so odious to the people that any rebellion, supported by the slightest force, was sure to succeed. A single Austrian regiment, however, was enough to disperse all the revolutionists in the peninsula the moment they found that the French would not make war in their behalf.[2]

Naples, or the ' Kingdom of the Two Sicilies,' had been restored to its Bourbon king, Ferdinand IV(I), in 1815. He died in 1825. His successor was his son, Francis I, who died in 1830. To Francis I there succeeded Ferdinand II, later called " Bomba," because he bombarded his capital in the revolution of 1848. In the ' eighteen-forties,' and, indeed, ever since the restoration of 1815, the condition of Neapolitan politics had been terrible. Liberals who claimed the fulfilment of royal promises of a constitution were confined in pestilential dungeons, chained to common felons. Mr Gladstone visited the political prisoners in their prisons at Naples in 1850, and saw

---

[1] *The Diary of Henry Crabb Robinson*, ii, 108.   [2] *Ibid.*

" scenes fitter for hell than earth." He watched the political trials, saturated with corruption and perjury. In his celebrated *Letters to Lord Aberdeen* he called the Bourbon *régime* " the negation of God erected into a system of government." But it required a man of Gladstone's type, with a passion for justice and liberty, to penetrate below the shining surface of Neapolitan life, which had a pleasant and attractive side. *Vedi Napoli e muore* was a common saying. Henry Crabb Robinson felt inclined to agree with this when he visited Naples and Sicily in 1830. Vesuvius, " the lurid light of the burning mountain," seen at night, gave the Englishman the impression of a *paradisiacal hell*. The city of Naples itself was " the seat of voluptuous enjoyment "; as Wordsworth happily designated it, *Soft Parthenope*. " The affluent seem to have nothing to do but saunter about, sip ices, and be gallant." [1] The *lazzaroni*, the idlers who lounged about the squares and down at the harbour, were a cheerful crowd. Crabb Robinson saw a lot of them on the Mole, listening to a half-naked fellow who was reading verses from a tattered and unimaginably dirty manuscript; it was Tasso, and the *lazzaroni* were listening with grave interest. " Certainly," writes Crabb Robinson, " I saw nothing to make me think ill of the *lazzaroni*. If offended they are ferocious, but they are affectionate, and are said to be honest to an exemplary degree." [2]

In 1832, the last year of his life (which was also the last year of Goethe's life), Sir Walter Scott visited Italy. He was then in his sixty-second year, prematurely old and failing in health, owing to his tremendous labours of writing. The British Government had put a frigate at his disposal, in order that he might have a holiday and find health in the Mediterranean. He had sailed from Portsmouth on H.M. *Barham* on October 29, 1831. The ship arrived at Malta on November 22. On December 14 it weighed anchor again, and on December 17 was at Naples. There Scott left the ship. He remained at Naples for four months, treated like a king, welcomed everywhere, given every opportunity of using the intellectual and artistic re-

[1] *The Diary of Henry Crabb Robinson*, ii, 91.　　[2] *Ibid.*, ii, 92.

sources, as well as the resources of scenery, climate, society, in that sunny and joyous city. He could not, however, in his weak and depressed state of health, make much use of them. At Pompeii alone did his thoughts seem to be wholly commanded by the realities before him. There he had himself carried from house to house, and examined everything leisurely; but said little, except ever and anon in an audible whisper, " The city of the dead! The city of the dead! " The excavating of Pompeii had been begun in the middle of the eighteenth century in the reign of the enlightened Bourbon King of Naples, Charles III.

From Naples Scott went by carriage to Rome (April 1832), and was cheered by the delightful society there, both Italian and English. Scott was a Tory and a Jacobite. The beautiful monument by Canova, erected at the inspiration and expense of King George IV to the Stuart princes, magnificently called James III and Charles III, greatly pleased him. But he was anxious now to return home. Goethe had died at Weimar on March 22; one of the things which had brought Scott to the Continent had been the desire to meet Goethe, with whom he had corresponded, but whom he had never seen. He left Rome on May 11 (1832), travelling by carriage—he had a son and daughter with him—by way of Florence, Bologna, Ferrara, and Venice; thence onward by Innsbruck, Munich, Ulm, Heidelberg, Frankfurt, Cologne—" the immortal panorama of Childe Harold." His was a familiar name in every city, from Naples and Rome northward. An Englishman resident at that time said that at Rome " the stalls are filled with translations of his novels in the cheapest forms; and some of the most popular plays and operas have been founded upon them." Donizetti's *Lucia di Lammermoor* took Naples by storm in 1835. In remote villages of Tuscany people would accost an English traveller, eagerly inquiring after the health of his illustrious countryman.[1]

[1] Lockhart, *Life of Scott*, Chapter XVII, *ad fin.*

K

CHAPTER X

ETERNAL ROME

A GREAT problem, of deep and lasting interest to the whole of Europe and of Christendom, has for some time been in process of solution in the Roman, or Papal, States," wrote Mr Gladstone in 1851 in the Preface to his translation of Farini's *Lo Stato Romano*. The indefatigable statesman had been on holiday in Naples in the previous year, had made himself conversant with the terrible condition of affairs in that kingdom, had (of course) interested himself in the Roman problem, and had found time and energy to translate a large portion of the four volumes of Farini's *Roman State*. On his return home, besides writing the now celebrated letters to Lord Aberdeen, he completed the translation of Farini's monumental work. " Some things I have learned in Italy that I did not know before," wrote Gladstone to Henry Edward Manning (later Cardinal), " one in particular. The temporal power of the Pope, that great, wonderful, and ancient erection, is *gone*." The Roman problem, however, was not so nearly settled in 1851 as Mr Gladstone seemed to suppose; for, as Farini wrote: " It is the peculiar nature of the Roman Court that it can acquiesce upon occasion, but never bends in mind before either violence or adverse fortune, and never forgets her claims through length of time." [1]

The restoration of the old order of things was more nearly complete in Rome than anywhere else, except the kingdom of Sardinia. Pius VII either could not or would not, like Victor Emmanuel I of Sardinia, decree that everything should be put back to the legal condition of *novant-ott*, of 1798. Much water had flowed under the bridges of the Tiber, or, as Chateaubriand wrote when he went on embassy there in 1829, " the great trans-

[1] L. C. Farini, *The Roman State, 1815–50* (trans. Gladstone, 1851), i, 4.

formation has above all been effected by our double occupation of Rome "—in 1797, when the French ' Directory ' established a short-lived Roman Republic, and from 1808 to 1814, when Rome was in the Napoleonic Empire. " The French, in traversing Rome, have left their principles there . . . Bonaparte, by taking the sons from their mothers, by forcing the Italian nobility to quit their palaces and to bear arms, hastened the transformation of the national spirit." [1]

Chateaubriand was right in detecting national spirit among the unpolitical peoples of Italy, even in the Papal State and in changeless Rome herself; but it would scarcely be obvious to a casual observer. When Pius VII returned to Rome from his imprisonment at Fontainebleau the French administration had vanished. The Papal Court, with all the ancient and elaborate hierarchy—cardinals, councils, holy office, congregations, picturesquely named officials and picturesquely uniformed guards—was restored, along with the Society of Jesus, which had been dissolved in 1774. Farini, who was himself a citizen (and in time an official) in the Papal State (from 1812 to 1848), says that Pius VII returned from his exile with enormously enhanced prestige, and with a great opportunity of establishing some moderate constitutional *régime* which might have solved the Roman problem. The Pope might even have assumed the leadership of Italy, and have been head of an Italian federation, [2] thus solving the Italian question in a manner often later, but vainly, proposed. But the old influences, particularly the Society of Jesus, made any such solution impossible.

Fundamentally the city and citizens changed very little during the period of the French occupation. Rome looked just the same as when Madame de Staël described it in 1805, and made Corinne and Oswald walk on foot across the bridge of Sant' Angelo and conscientiously visit all the monuments. [3] In the streets, under the French domination, military uniforms had become more prominent and priestly dress rather less prominent. With Pius VII the old aspect, as well as the old order, was

---

[1] *Mémoires d'outre-tombe*, v, 53, 54.   [2] *Ibid.*, v, 116.
[3] Madame de Staël, *Corinne* (1807), Chapters IV–V.

restored. Black-coated priests dominated the religious city; the military uniform was obvious only among the Papal Guard in the Vatican, although, as a matter of fact, an efficient, though small, army was soon organized, commanded by former Napoleonic officers who entered the Papal service.[1] The city retained its changeless appearance—the majestic ruins of the ancient world, the wall of Aurelius, medieval fortresses, Renaissance palaces, colossal churches, and vast open spaces, waste lands, cypresses, and gardens. The minds of visitors were impressed by scenes of greenery and tumbling masonry, broken columns and desolate palaces. And such visitors were so numerous, so distinguished, so sociable, that, according to George Ticknor, Society at Rome was foreign. They flocked to Rome more than ever after the peace, men of all European races, English, Germans, French, Russians, Americans, politicians, artists, men of letters and men of leisure, with their wives and children. They spent the winter in Rome, departing, with the coming of spring, for the " mists of the North," for the trivialities of politics and the agonies of ambition. In Rome they had not thought of politics; the majesty of Time reduced all else to insignificance.

> Oh, Rome! my Country! City of the Soul!
> The orphans of the heart must turn to thee,
> Lone Mother of dead Empires! and control
> In their shut breasts their petty misery.
> What are our woes and sufferance? Come and see
> The cypress—hear the owl—and plod your way
> O'er steps of broken thrones and temples—Ye!
> Whose agonies are evils of a day——
> A world is at our feet as fragile as our clay.[2]

Nostalgia, wrote Chauteaubriand, is regret for one's native land; and on the banks of the Tiber one has the *mal du pays*— but of an opposite kind from what is usual. One is seized with the love of solitude and with distaste for one's own country. The spell is repeated at each visit. On arriving for the second time Chateaubriand experienced a certain displeasure, and for a moment believed that things had changed; " but little by little

---

[1] Farini, *op. cit.*, i, 5.   [2] Byron, *Childe Harold's Pilgrimage*, iv, 78.

the *fever of ruins* gains me, and I finish . . . like a thousand other visitors, by adoring what at first had left me cold [*ce qui m'avait laissé froid d'abord*]." [1]

The gentle old Pope settled down in the Vatican, and brought back the old inefficient administration, the multitude of officials and taxes, the police and informers, and most of the well-known abuses of the ancient Papal State. When he received the Protestant George Ticknor in 1818 he was dressed " with characteristic simplicity and humility as a friar," without the slightest ornament to distinguish his rank. He was very pleasant, and said to Ticknor that persuasion was the only means of promoting piety, though violence might promote hypocrisy. The Pope was kind and merciful, and showed no repugnance to receiving his former enemies. Chateaubriand called Rome a refuge of fallen potentates (*un asile aux puissances tombées*). Queen Hortense called Rome " the country of all the great unfortunates."

The image of human vicissitudes presents itself there on every side; and if these vast ruins, which seize our admiration, show us that all greatness is transitory, these pious monuments raised beside them recall at the same time to our hearts the only consolations whose source is immortal. [2]

Most of the Bonapartes, except the prisoner of St Helena, his son at the Court of Austria, and his brother Joseph, lived there happily for years; later most of them moved to Florence. Joseph, ex-King of Spain, lived on his estate in America (Point Breeze, New Jersey) until 1832, and spent his later years at Florence. Jerome, ex-King of Westphalia, however, came to Rome in 1823. Louis, King of Holland, who lived apart from his wife, took up his residence at Rome in 1814; he preserved, wrote George Ticknor (1818), " the character for good-nature and honesty which he did not lose even in Holland when acting under the orders of a cruel despotism." [3] And there was Queen

---

[1] *Mémoires d'outre-tombe*, v, 3.
[2] *Mémoires de la reine Hortense*, iii, 214.
[3] *The Life of George Ticknor*, i, 181.

Hortense, his wife, who came to Rome only when King Louis
was absent; Pauline, the great Napoleon's sister, wife of
Camillo, Prince Borghese, witty, clever, reckless, " the most
consummate coquette I ever saw," reported Ticknor; and,
finally, Madame Mère, the best of the whole clan, who lived,
contented, crippled, and blind, with her half-brother Cardinal
Fesch in the Palazzo Rinuccini until her death in 1836. Compared with these fallen grandeurs, the Countess of Albany, wife
of Prince Charles Edward Stuart, attracted only moderate attention. She died in 1824, before Chateaubriand's second visit
to Rome. He had seen her, however, in Florence in her old age.
He thought that if the women in Rubens' pictures ever grew
old the Countess of Albany looked like one of them. Her great
passion had been, not Charles Edward Stuart, but the poet and
dramatist Alfieri. Yet she set up house with a French painter,
François-Xavier Fabre. Chateaubriand felt rather angry that
this tender heart had felt the need of another supporter. After
all, notwithstanding her interesting history, she looked common :
la Comtesse d'Albany avait l'air commun.[1] Lamartine, who saw
her years earlier, thought so too : *ni la reine d'un empire, ni la
reine d'un cœur.* George Ticknor, however, found her to have a
good knowledge of literature, and thought her one of the best
women he saw on the Continent. The last of the Stuart princes,
Henry, Cardinal of York, Bishop of Frascati, had died at Rome
in 1807. The Countess of Albany lived on. " The Stuarts con-
soled themselves with the view of Rome. They were only one
more small accident in its vast *débris.*"[2] They fell, and the
fatality of the Stuart race dragged other thrones down. They
saw the fall of old Europe, in Eternal Rome.

Like everything else in Rome, the nobility, though half
ruined and conspicuous by an air of past magnificence, seemed
to have the quality of permanence. " Whatever be the changes
of manners and people in Italy from century to century," wrote
Chateaubriand in 1828, " one notices there a habit of grandeur
which we others, shabby barbarians, do not approach [*une
habitude de grandeur, dont nous autres, mesquins barbares, n'ap-*

---

[1] *Mémoires d'outre-tombe,* v, 47.   [2] *Ibid.,* v, 49.

prochons pas]. There still remains at Rome Roman blood and
traditions of the masters of the world." [1] They had been ruined
by the Revolution, which, starting at Versailles on May 5, 1789,
had spread to Paris, Brussels, Milan, Florence, Naples, Rome.
They still lived in their palaces (or in part of a palace, letting
the rest to wealthy strangers), shut off from the world, making
such economies as they could, and acting as their own men
of business.

When you have the good fortune (which is very rare) to be
admitted to their home some evening, you pass through vast
rooms without furniture, dimly lit. Along the walls antique
statues show up white in the dense shadow, like phantoms or
exhumed corpses. At the end of this succession of rooms the
tattered lackey who is conducting you introduces you into a sort
of *gynēcēum*. . . . Round the table are seated three or four old
ladies or badly dressed young girls, who are working at small
tasks by the light of a lamp. They exchange a few words with
a father or brother or husband, who can scarcely be distinguished
as they half recline on shabby sofas in the obscurity behind.
There is, however, something fine, something commanding, which
has come down from their lofty ancestors in this family group
intrenched behind these masterpieces, and which one thought at
first sight was a witches' midnight meeting. The race of the
cicisbèi is ended, although there are still some *abbés* who fetch and
carry your shawl or your footwarmer; here and there a cardinal
still establishes himself for good in a lady's house, like a sofa. [2]

When, comparing it with all this, you see the foreign visitors
crowded in little new houses at the Porta del Popolo or lodged
in palaces which have been divided into apartments and fitted
up with fireplaces you seem to see rats scratching at the foot of
monuments of Apollodorus and Michelangelo, and making, by
sheer gnawing, holes in the pyramids. [3]

They were rather cold holes too, as Crabb Robinson found
when he had lodgings in Rome in the winter of 1829.

Yet even this medieval Roman aristocracy had to admit into

---

[1] *Mémoires d'outre-tombe*, v, 55.   [2] *Ibid.*, v, 56.
[3] *Ibid., loc. cit.*

its circle a representative of the capitalist era that was now beginning. Torlonia, Duke of Bracciano, was a broker and commission agent in Rome in the time of the French Revolution.
Hugon de Basseville, the deputy at Rome of the French Government, murdered in 1793, had deposited his official funds with
Torlonia, who administered them wisely and returned them in
due course to the French Government. The circumstances of
his rise to power and fortune are not unlike those of the house
of Rothschild. He was financial agent in Rome for the French
Government throughout the Napoleonic period, and for the
Roman aristocracy and the now wealthy Bonaparte family and
other royal families. Pius VII, one of his clients, ennobled
Torlonia as Duke of Bracciano and Roman prince. Chateaubriand went to a ball in Torlonia's palace in November 1828.
" I met all the English people in the world there; I believed
myself to be once more ambassador at London." Four months
later Prince Torlonia was dead.

Besides the rich and transitory strangers, there was another
class of foreign people, of moderate means, making no parade,
but almost permanent. These were the artists, who came from
almost every part of Europe, and who, as a social class, had been
settled there since the Renaissance, and were now more numerous than ever. But what a contrast in their circumstances since
the Renaissance, when artists were the guests and friends of
kings, planned the defences of cities and castles, built churches,
palaces, and ramparts, gave and received great strokes of the
sword, intrigued with women, took refuge in cloisters, were
absolved by Popes and saved by princes! Now, in Rome, the
artists lived poor and secluded. The promising young sculptor
dwells in some grotto under the green oaks of the Villa Medicis,
where he completes his child in marble or gives a serpent to
drink from a shell. The painter inhabits some tumbling-down
house in a waste place, where you may see him any day looking
through his open window at some view of the Roman landscape.
Chateaubriand knew many of them—Overbeck, the German,
converted to Roman Catholicism; Schmetz, another German;
Thorwaldsen, the Dane; Léopold Robert, Swiss, who com-

mitted suicide out of hopeless love for Princess Charlotte Bonaparte; Pierre Guérin, just retired from the directorship of the École (or Académie) de France, like a sick dove, to a pavilion of the Villa Medicis; Horace Vernet, who succeeded Guérin as director of the École; Camuccini, inspector-general of Papal museums and conservator of the collections of the Vatican. Only Thorwaldsen and Camuccini were in affluent circumstances. They were " the two princes of the poor artists of Rome." [1] Horace Vernet gave rather fine *soirées* in the palace of the French Academy on the Pincian Hill. And besides these were a crowd of writers and scholars: Bunsen, who was also Prussian Minister to the Vatican, lived in the Palazzo Caffarelli, and gave occasional lectures at the Archæological Academy; Niebuhr, professor at Bonn, formerly Prussian ambassador at the Papal Court, and still an occasional visitor, engaged upon his Roman history; the young Ranke; and, for longer or shorter intervals, Stendhal, Byron, Keats, Flaxman, Arnold, Newman, Lamennais, Lacordaire, Montalembert; Keats is buried there. Severn lived at Rome and wrote Keats' life. The reflective Crabb Robinson lived with great contentment in Rome in the winter of 1829, like another John Inglesant. " It is the city of tombs and ruins. The environs are a pestiferous marsh," he wrote. Yet he was impressed by " the great unity of effect produced by Rome," and repeated Goethe's remark (which probably every visitor makes), " When shall I be able to come here again? " " I was never more busy in my life," Crabb Robinson noted in his diary on December 17. " I have Rome as well as Italian to learn. Every fine day I visit one or more of the curiosities of this wonderful city. It is a little world in itself." The word ' little ' perhaps seems unnecessary here. February 23, 1830, the last day of the carnival, Crabb Robinson tried his hand at a description of the Roman scene, surveyed from a balcony, as Goethe had once done. Here it is—all done in a few minutes:

A fellow with a wig of paper shavings; another all paper, save his old hat, which had candles, soon to be lighted; a rich devil,

[1] *Mémoires d'outre-tombe*, v, 33–35.

with a crimson tail; a Turkish coachman; lawyers with paper
frills and collars; a conjurer; a bear; a man covered with bells;
a postilion with a huge whip—several carrying men pickaback,
one with a machine which on a jerk opens like a ladder and,
rising to the first floor, conveys flowers to the ladies.[1]

One of the British "King's Messengers," who carried the
diplomatic mail-bag, said to Robinson, referring to the Eternal
City: "Rome is more like Wapping than any place I know."
"That man is no fool," said Flaxman when Robinson told
him this remark. The Russian ambassador, Prince Gargarin,
entertained magnificently. His great dining-room was lit by
eighty-nine wax lights. At dinner a servant stood behind each
couple of guests. You named any wine you liked, and drank
it out of a large tumbler.[2]

The most distinguished *salons* were those of certain foreigners,
and of these *salons* the most eminent was Bunsen's in the Palazzo
Caffarelli. The period covered by the reign of Frederick William III of Prussia was the great time for Germans in Rome—
men of letters, painters, sculptors, classical scholars, historians.
Politics were scholarly. Niebuhr was Prussian ambassador at
Rome from 1816 to 1823. On Niebuhr's recommendation a
distinguished German scholar (pupil of the great Heyne at
Göttingen) who was studying at Rome, Christian Bunsen, was
appointed *Secretary of Embassy* in 1818. After Niebuhr retired
in 1823 Frederick William III made Bunsen ambassador. The
Chevalier Bunsen (later made Baron) was married to a wealthy
Englishwoman, Frances Waddington. They received their
friends regularly twice a week, Germans on one evening, English on the other—a distinction rendered necessary by the difference of language. Crabb Robinson, who spoke English and
German equally well, was invited to both evenings. Bunsen
was already a great admirer of English institutions, and had
determined to make his eldest son an Englishman. He remained
ambassador at Rome until 1838. Curiously, at this time his
Hanoverian colleague, Minister to the Vatican, was the Chevalier Kestner, son of Albert and Charlotte, the characters in

---

[1] *The Diary of Henry Crabb Robinson*, ii, 90.   [2] *Ibid.*

Goethe's *Sorrows of Werther*.[1] After certain other missions Bunsen was appointed to the London Embassy in 1842, and remained there until the Crimean War (1854). An active and successful diplomatist, he was all the time engaged in high scholarship, in classical, Christian, and Egyptian antiquities, on which he published many volumes.

Outside the nobility was the populace—*grasso*, or prosperous, and *minuto*, or poor. Chateaubriand saw little of the *popolo minuto*. The diplomatic world is a world by itself. Queen Hortense was more sympathetic. In Italy more than anywhere else the people on holidays throw aside care and are just happy, noisy, good-natured children.

> The innocent, gay, and simple pleasures of the people have always given me a feeling of contentment mingled with emotion. It is they that endure all suffering and hardships of life; others enjoy the fruit of their labour. On them fall the burden of taxation, of war, of dearth. Glory is for others, and scorn is too often all they receive for their splendid courage. Their pleasures have always done me good. The Romans are delightful at those popular *fêtes* where they dress up as counts and marquisses and imitate their appearance and manners and come to show you their gallant behaviour, their wit and gentle gaiety. I always enjoy following the Corso in the midst of this jolly *fête*, during those eight days of the carnival which are so brilliant at Rome.[2]

Nobility and populace and foreign visitors and classic ruins did not compose all Rome; the Church, the Vatican, the priesthood, the Temporal Power, gave it a peculiar air.

When Pius VII returned to Rome three parties soon formed themselves at the Vatican. The first appears to have had no special name, but might be called the Moderates. Their chief was Cardinal Oppizoni, Archbishop of Bologna, who had shared the exile of Pius VII and had been one of his firmest supporters. The Moderates aimed at marching with the times. The second group were the Zelanti, " who wish to go back [*qui tentent de rétrograder*]." Their chief was Cardinal Odescalchi, but another

---

[1] *The Life of George Ticknor*, ii, 72.
[2] *Mémoires de la reine Hortense*, iii, 204.

was Cardinal Annibale della Genga, who became Pope Leo XII in 1823. The third faction had no name, but might be called the Immovables. They desired neither to go forward nor back. Their chief was Cardinal Vidoni, an unconventional man, a planter of trees. The populace called him *madama Vidoni*. " When I left Rome," wrote Chateaubriand in 1829, " he bought my carriage, and did me the honour of dying in it on his way to the Ponte Mole."

During the Napoleonic period about 1808 a secret society, called the Carbonari, had been formed in the Abruzzi mountains. Its original aim was to overthrow the French rule; ultimately it aimed at the freedom and unity of Italy. After the Restoration it spread into the States of the Church. The Papal Government outlawed it in 1817, condemning many of its members to severe penalties. Against the Carbonari, the Papal Government gave its support to the Sanfedisti, a theocratic, absolutist, and ' Guelphic '—that is, ' anti-Imperial '—society, which had been established in 1815.

Pius VII's pontificate after the Restoration passed tranquilly away. He died in 1823. The new Pope, Leo XII, though one of the Zelanti, proved to be a moderate and conciliatory pontiff, in spite of the ascendancy of the Jesuits at Rome. Leo was sixty-three years old at his election, and was a tall, noble-looking man, with an air both serene and sad. He wore usually a simple white cassock, ate only a little *polenta*, and lived with his cat in a small, scantily furnished room. He was liable to hæmorrhage, and knew that he might die any day. Nevertheless he was by no means inactive, and was a good administrator. He braced the discipline of the Papal troops with Napoleonic ex-officers; set police on the roads to protect them from bandits, whom he punished, when caught, with severity; cleared off beggars from the streets; improved the hospitals, roads, and bridges of Rome; and, for his own amusement, had a little shooting in the parks and glades of the Vatican. He was not very popular. At the time of his election the cardinals would have chosen Cardinal Severoli, but the Austrian Government interposed a veto through Cardinal Albani. Chateaubriand said that they chose Annibale della Genga because he was delicate and likely soon to die; but he lived for about six years more. Also he chose officials and other Ministers from among the monks; the cardinals disliked this practice. His Secretary of State was Cardinal Bernetti, not a priest, who believed that he would live to see the end of the Temporal Power. Liberty and tyranny had both perished. Leo's reign looked like a sunset of the Papacy; but actually a powerful revival was in progress, though not obvious in Rome.

During Leo XII's last illness no letters were permitted to be sent out of Rome. Ambassadors' couriers were kept back. The Vatican courier must be the first to take the news of the death of the Pope to the outer world. The cardinals seemed to believe that they were still living in the age of the Guelphs and Ghibellines, and that the news of the Pope's death, arriving an hour earlier or later, might bring an Imperial army into Italy. As soon as the Pope expired and the Papal courier set off Chateaubriand sent the Embassy courier off post-haste to Lyons, whence the news, dispatched in the evening by the signal-telegraph, would on the following morning reach Paris [1]; and thus the Papal courier would be outdistanced. Chateaubriand was present at the burial in St Peter's of Leo XII—a mixture of grandeur and indecency. The singing of the choir was interrupted by the noise of hammers driving nails into the coffin, which subsequently was drawn up by a pulley into the light of ruddy torches and pale moonbeams before being lowered into the sarcophagus lately occupied by the coffin of Pius VII. After the funeral the defunct Pope's cat was brought to Chateaubriand. It was grey and gentle, " like an old teacher." [2]

The election had now to take place. Three things no longer made Popes—the intrigues of women, the procedures of the ambassadors, and the power of the Courts. Nor, on the other hand (so Chateaubriand told his Government), was the election decided by the general interest of society, but by the particular interest of the individuals or families who sought in the election of the head of the Church places and money. Chateaubriand's

[1] *Mémoires d'outre-tombe*, v, 158.   [2] *Ibid.*, v, 132–133.

statements must be taken seriously. He was a convinced and
strong Catholic, and saw his idea of Christianity, of which he
wrote so eloquently, in the Church of Rome.

Now was an opportunity for a *pape éclairé*, who would unite
the dissident sects and restore the strength of European society.
A Pope who could enter into the spirit of the age would " re-
juvenate the Papacy [*faire rajeunir la papauté*]."

> But these ideas cannot enter into the old heads of the Sacred
> College. The Cardinals, having arrived at the end of their life,
> pass on an elective royalty which soon expires with them. Seated
> on the double ruins of Rome, the Popes have the appearance
> of being impressed only with the potency of death.[1]

Old cardinals elected an old man for Pope, and he, as Pope,
elected old men for cardinals. " Revolving in this vicious
circle, the enervated supreme power is always on the brink of
the grave. The prince does not occupy the throne long enough
to execute the plans for improvements which he has conceived."
Even Leo XII's good administration had not time to show good
results, and when he died there was discontent, misery, and
misgovernment in the provinces. The only means of escape
from the vicious circle that Chateaubriand could see would be
if a Pope should show sufficient resolution to make a numerous
promotion of young cardinals, so as to assure the election of a
young pontiff.

There is always some interest and excitement in an election,
and particularly in the election to the world's greatest throne.
The ambassadors were all on the alert, and yet Chateaubriand
confessed that all the ambassadors on earth could do nothing
in the election of a Pope; *nous sommes d'une parfaite inutilité
à Rome.* Few foreign cardinals could come to Rome in time;
this was in the days before railways. Out of a total number
of fifty-eight only some forty-eight or forty-nine would be
present. The Italian cardinals controlled the situation. During
the Conclave the cardinals were literally immured, the outer
windows of their chambers and of the hall of election being

[1] *Mémoires d'outre-tombe*, v, 134.

walled up with plaster. Chateaubriand said that the first thing which a cardinal did on coming into his room was to scratch a hole in the newly plastered window, so as to be able to pass written notes through it. Crabb Robinson, who was present in Rome at a later Conclave (1831, when Gregory XVI was elected), wrote, " The day before their [the cardinals'] imprisonment I went to look at their miserable little lodgings : very few have fireplaces, and some not even stoves." [1]

The obsequies of Leo XII were finished on February 22, 1829, and on the following day the Conclave began. Each cardinal places a voting-paper with the name of his chosen candidate in an urn. The papers are then counted, and burned if one candidate has not two-thirds of the total number of votes. Every evening Chateaubriand and " all Europe at Rome," as well as everybody else, went out to see if the smoke was ascending; *le jour où il n'y aura pas la fumée, le pape sera nommé*.[2]

Although Chateaubriand maintained in his letters and dispatches that ambassadors could do nothing in a Papal election, he had, in fact, notified to the Cardinal Clermont-Tonnerre the *exclusion* (or veto) of the French Government against the Cardinal Albani, whom it was known that the Austrian Government desired as Pope; and he was able to procure for transmission to the French Government a copy of the official and secret journal of the Conclave.[3] Nevertheless he complained of the difficulties which he had in dealing with a lot of immured and perverse old cardinals.

> I have to act upon an unvisible *corps* shut up in a prison with every approach strictly guarded. I have no money to give, nor places to promise. The failing passions of some fifty old men give me nothing to take hold of. I have to contend with stupidity in some, with ignorance of the world in others; with fanaticism in one group, with astuteness and duplicity in another; and in

[1] *The Diary of Henry Crabb Robinson*, ii, 106.
[2] *Mémoires d'outre-tombe*, v, 156.
[3] *Ibid.*, v, 182–183, and Appendix III. Extracts from the Conclave journal, as contained in the translation sent by Chateaubriand to the Ministère des Affaires Étrangères, were published by Boyer d'Agen in *Revue des revues*, January 1 and 15, 1896.

almost every one with ambition, private interests, political hatreds. And I am separated by walls and by mysteries of the assembly where so many elements of division ferment. The scene changes at every moment; every quarter of an hour contradictory reports plunge me into new perplexities.[1]

At last, however, the French ambassador was able to write (March 31, 1829):

> Victory! I have one of the Popes whom I had put on my list: it is Castiglione, he whom I supported for the Papacy in 1823, when I was Minister of Foreign Affairs, and who responded to me recently in the Conclave with *strong praises*. Castiglione is moderate, and devoted to France; it is a complete triumph. The Conclave, before separating, has given orders for writing to the nuncio at Paris, telling him to express to the King the satisfaction which the Sacred College has experienced of my conduct.

So much for the complete detachment and independence of the Conclave. Castiglione, who was sixty-eight years of age, was partly paralysed on one side. Chateaubriand was present at the service of *Tenebræ* in the Sistine Chapel after the election of Pius VIII.

> One felt oneself overcome by the great mystery of a God dying to wipe out the crimes of mankind. The Catholic inheritor on his seven hills was there with all his memories; but instead of those powerful pontiffs, of those cardinals who denied precedence to monarchs, a poor old paralytic Pope, without family, without support, and princes of the Church without renown were proclaiming the end of a Power which civilized the modern world.[2]

Pius VIII lived as Pope for only twenty months; and a new Conclave took seven weeks to elect another Pope. This was a Camaldolese monk, Dom Mauro Capellari, Abbot of San Gregorio in Rome. He took the name of Gregory XVI (February 1831). As soon as elected he had to face a rebellion in the Papal States, and Rome itself was insecure for the Pope. With the help of Austrian troops, however, the revolt was suppressed. Thereafter Gregory XVI enjoyed a quiet, unprogressive reign

---

[1] *Mémoires d'outre-tombe*, v, 166.   [2] *Ibid.*, v, 168.

until his death at the age of eighty in 1846. Crabb Robinson was at Rome just after the election of Gregory XVI, and wrote on leaving:

Goethe says, in his *Italian Journey*, that every one who leaves Rome asks himself, " When shall I be able to come here again? " There is a great unity of effect produced by Rome. It is the city of tombs and ruins. The environs are a pestiferous marsh, and on all sides you have images of death. What aged nobleman was it who preferred his dead son to any living son in Christendom? Who is there who does not prefer the ruins of Rome to the new buildings of London and Paris?[1]

[1] *The Diary of Henry Crabb Robinson*, ii, 110.

L

CHAPTER XI

THE FOUNDATIONS OF BELIEF

CHATEAUBRIAND, writing memoirs in his later years, passed in review various ages of history. " After Alexander the Roman power began; after Cæsar Christianity changed the world; after Charlemagne feudal night engendered a new Society." Then he continued:

> After Napoleon nothing. [*Après Napoléon néant.*] One sees come neither empire, nor religion, nor barbarians. Civilization mounted to its highest point, but it is material, infertile civilization, which can produce nothing, because no one can give life except by morality; one only succeeds in creating peoples along heaven-ways; railways will only lead us all the more swiftly to the abyss.[1]

The age was, however, not so worldly as Chateaubriand declares. There was a strong current of religious emotion. And as Chateaubriand was not a particularly modest man it is remarkable that in this passage he did not draw attention to his own share in producing this emotion.[2]

Most, if not all, the intellectual and spiritual movements of the early nineteenth century seem to be connected with that obscure book Haller's *Restauration*. Haller created the prestige of medievalism. This appealed to the Romantics. The fall of the Napoleonic Empire and the restoration of a modified *ancien régime*, particularly in Italy, seemed almost to be a restoration of the ages of faith. Chateaubriand's *Génie du Christianisme* (1802), with its magical style, helped on this movement. The constancy of Pius VII in adversity, his humility and merciful-

---

[1] *Mémoires d'outre-tombe*, v, 68.

[2] He gave himself, however, full credit for this in the Preface to the 1822 edition of the *Génie du Christianisme*.

ness in triumph, the dignity and charm, the religious and classical interest, of the Eternal City, visited by all cultured Europeans, re-erected faith upon its pinnacle. Pope Gregory XVI (1831–46), a monk and canonist, seemed as if he had known no other world than the medieval. One by one Protestant Romantics felt themselves drawn into the faith of Rome. Heine said that this happened because they were all Pantheists, and Roman Catholicism was really Pantheism. Haller himself, Friedrich von Schlegel, Adam Müller, Görres, Dorothea Veit, are among the Romantic Protestants of this age who became Catholics; but no converts were made of the few great men of the period, unless Newman, who was received into the Roman Catholic Church in 1845, is reckoned great.

The Reformed communion was influenced by this restoration of faith. Eighteenth-century rationalism had affected the members of the Reformed communion rather less than it had the Roman Catholic communion, which in France, for instance, had many ' enlightened ' abbés, frequenters of sceptical salons; there Voltaire had made l'incrédulité à la mode.[1] Nevertheless, Protestantism too required bracing, as John Wesley braced it in Great Britain; Wesley died in 1791. The Pietist movement in Germany had an effect comparable to that of Wesley in England. It was Schleiermacher, however, not a Pietist, who was the great bracing influence in German Protestantism after the close of the Age of Reason.

German Protestantism had passed through stages which can be definitely discerned. Luther began it by his revolt against the penitential system which was the core of the late medieval Catholicism. Most of North Germany adopted Lutheranism, but the Counter-Reformation of the late sixteenth and early seventeenth centuries kept South Germany for Roman Catholicism. The work of Copernicus, however, which received Papal authorization in 1540 (the year of the Bull recognizing the Jesuit Order, a leading date in Counter-Reformation history), gradually destroyed people's belief in their world as the centre of the universe. The divine system of things, as hitherto taken

---

[1] Chateaubriand, Génie du Christianisme, Introduction.

for granted, was shattered in men's minds, and they fell back upon their own intellect and their own reason. At the same time the infinite universe, which they now began vaguely to realize, became itself in their eyes divine. Thus are found together in practically every country of eighteenth-century Europe the beliefs in those various attitudes towards life called Reason, Deism, Pantheism, and (as a reaction from a now rather formal Lutheran orthodoxy) Pietism. Towards the end of the eighteenth century Kant conquered the mind of religious Germany with his famous paradox, " I have, therefore, found it necessary to deny *knowledge* of God, freedom, and immortality, in order to find a place for *faith*." The Revolutionary period and the War of Liberation, the lectures of Fichte and Hegel, gave German thought a turn towards ' idealism ' which was not wholly favourable to orthodox religion. Most of the German idealist philosophers were Protestant, but if it had been left to them German Protestantism of the nineteenth century would have differed little from eighteenth-century Deism.

Friedrich Ernst Daniel Schleiermacher was born at Breslau in 1768, the son of a Prussian Army chaplain of the Reformed (Calvinist) faith. His mother was the daughter of a clergyman —a *Hofprediger*. Educated at Moravian schools (Gnadenfreude, Niesky, Brüderunität, and Barby), he imbibed their sound classical learning and had his mind strengthened by their intellectual discipline; but he could not accept their formal dogmatic theology; and in 1787, after painful discussion with his father, he left Barby (which, he says, was the " Herrnhut University ") and entered the neighbouring university of Halle, where there were liberal schools of philosophy and theology. There he studied deeply in the works of Plato and Aristotle, in Spinoza and Leibniz, and in Kant; in later years he studied and was influenced by the Transcendentalism of Schelling. In 1790 he passed the examination in theology, and became qualified for the ministry. From 1790 to 1793 he was tutor in the family of Graf Dohna at Schlobitten, and formed a life friendship with the eldest son, Alexander Dohna, later Prussian statesman. In 1794–96 he was minister at Landsberg, on the

Warthe, and in 1796 became minister at the church called the
Charité, a church shared by the Reformed and Lutheran com-
munions, and which therefore had two pastors independent of
each other.

Schleiermacher was at Berlin for six years, in the period of
the early brilliance of the Prussian capital. He frequented the
literary circle of Henriette Herz, Dorothea Veit, Rahel Levin,
Friedrich Schlegel, and Alexander and Wilhelm von Humboldt.
He was much influenced by the Romantic movement, though
preserved from the emotionalism and waywardness of many
of the Romantics by his deep religious conviction and personal
piety. Schleiermacher's first literary work was an article contributed to the *Athenaeum*, the Romantic journal which the
Schlegels edited. Owing to an unhappy love affair, Schleiermacher left Berlin in 1802 and became minister at Stolpe. In
1804 he was called to be professor of theology at Halle, where
he formed a friendship with another professor, Steffens, later
more famous as professor at Breslau. Napoleon occupied Halle
and closed the university after the battle of Jena. Schleiermacher accordingly removed to Berlin and occupied himself
largely with translating Plato. He was there in the circle of
Stein, Fichte, and the Humboldts, and took part with them
in the great work of regenerating Prussia from the moral collapse which followed upon the defeat of Jena. With these men
Schleiermacher was one of the founders of the University of
Berlin, and in 1810 he became professor in it. In the previous
year he had married Henrietta von Willich, the widow of one
of his closest friends, to whom many of his letters about theology
were written. Schleiermacher was then forty-one years of age.

For twenty-four years, to his death in 1834, Schleiermacher
was professor in the University of Berlin. He was also a regular
preacher, and an indefatigable thinker and writer on theology.
He was an active member of the Poor Law Directory of Berlin.
He had a great circle of friends and a large correspondence.
His married life was happy. He had children; and his house
was filled with company, including Henriette Herz, whose
literary *salon* had been the feature of Schleiermacher's early

Berlin life. He is said rarely to have refused an invitation; and
in his wife's crowded drawing-room he would draw aside for
a quarter of an hour to take up some train of thought.[1] Although
one of the greatest theological writers of the nineteenth century,
his preaching, according to Wilhelm von Humboldt, was incom-
parably greater. He was the chief instrument, under the King,
in bringing about, so far as it went, the union of the Reformed
and Lutheran Churches in Prussia in 1817.

Schleiermacher is considered to have done for theology what
Kant did for philosophy: he gave it a new start, on lines which
were approved by the conscience and reason of his own and
later generations. He critically analysed religion, to discover
what was its essence; and he was prepared to subject every
part of the Bible to the most rigorous historical examination.
But he posited the fact of revelation and experience as fundamentals of religious faith. His theology was explained in his
*Christliche Glaube nach den Grundsätzen der evangelischen Kirche
in Zusammenhang dargestellt* (1821).

Personally, Schleiermacher was a small man, slightly deformed. He was lovable, sociable, full of kindness, charity,
and sweet temper. His enormous correspondence with friends
contains wisdom and charm. His last letter, written on January
31, 1834, to his son, describes a child playing with a watch and
early efforts of another child at standing and speaking, and
ends by saying that he had gone out to christen a child and to
give a lecture, which " went off very badly." [2] Next day he
became acutely ill, for twelve days before he died. Through
this last illness, his wife wrote, he was " friendly and patient,
though serious, and as if his thoughts were turned inwardly."
Shortly before he died he declared, " I have never clung to
the dead letter, and we have the atoning death of Jesus Christ,
His body and blood. I have ever believed, and still believe,
that the Lord Jesus gave the Communion in water and wine."
He then administered the sacrament to his family, and partook
himself, repeating the prayer of consecration. He added, " On

---

[1] *Life of Schleiermacher* (trans. F. M. Rowan, 1850), ii, 199.
[2] *Ibid.*, ii, 334-335.

these words of the Scripture I rely; they are the foundation of my faith." To his wife he said, " In this love and communion we are, and ever will remain, united." A heavenly rapture was on his face. A few minutes later he was dead (February 12, 1834).

Schleiermacher was severely critical, and directed his powerful mind to an examination of the origin and development of the Christian religion; yet he recognized revelation and experience as fundamental facts, as the final elements of faith—a faith " independent of all historical reports of miraculous events." He was followed, however, by two other bold thinkers who refused to recognize a religious residuum which criticism could not analyse. Strauss and Renan submitted every aspect of the Christian religion that they could discern to the strictest tests of history and philology. In this they differed from the rationalists of the eighteenth century, like Voltaire, or the agnostics of the nineteenth, like Huxley; they did not consider whether, intellectually envisaged, an alleged fact could have happened, but whether actually there was historical or philological evidence that it did happen. The effects of this handling of the Christian tradition were very diverse.

Of all the people who read the books of Strauss and Renan or who learned about them from the reviews some remained impervious to the criticism, and kept entire the faith with which they started; some were shocked and fled to an even more secure orthodoxy than they already possessed; some lost their faith altogether and became complete sceptics or unbelievers; and some, admitting most or all of the conclusions of Strauss and Renan, were strengthened. They felt that the few facts which were left as incontrovertible in the history of the Christian Church were sufficient for a " religion of all good men."

David Friedrich Strauss was born at Ludwigsburg, in Württemberg, in 1808. Brought up in the Protestant faith, he chose the career of a Lutheran pastor. He was trained in the famous theological faculty of Tübingen, and in 1830 became minister in a parish near Ludwigsburg, but he held this position for only nine months. After a year as teacher in a theological seminary at Maulbronn and six months' study at Berlin, where he attended Schleiermacher's lectures, Strauss became a teacher of theology and philosophy at Tübingen. All this time he was working hard on his *Life of Jesus* (*Das Leben Jesu*), which was ultimately published at Tübingen in 1835. It was an absolutely uncompromising piece of work. Strauss applied to the Gospel narratives the same methods of criticism and research as Niebuhr and the classical scholars applied to the narrative of Livy; like Niebuhr and the classical scholars, he started his criticism with the presumption that alleged supernatural events had never occurred. His object was to disengage from the Gospel narratives, which, according to his tests, appeared as largely a collection of myths, the incontrovertible historical Jesus who was born and lived and died. It will probably be judged by readers to be rather a brutal book, though enormously learned and the result of patient research and rigorous reasoning. It is unsympathetic and destructive; and out of the alleged facts of the Gospels leaves little except the birth of Jesus (placed at Nazareth) and the Crucifixion as absolutely proved. Most of the rest was " myth." There is practically no attempt to appreciate the character or message of Jesus; the book is without poetry, imagination, or religion. It is simply dry reasoning, painful collection and comparison of texts, unsympathetic criticism. Strauss maintained in the last lines of his book that he was freely declaring what could no longer, in spite of the efforts of obscurantists, be concealed—" and time will show whether by the one party or the other the Church, Mankind, and Truth are best served." [1] Strauss was hated because he proved people to be ignorant about things in the Gospel narratives which they had simply, without trouble and without criticism, accepted as certain.

The *Leben Jesu*, naturally, created an enormous stir in philosophical and theological circles, and also among scientists and men of letters. The year 1835 was the time of the Oxford

---

[1] *The Life of Jesus Critically Examined* (trans. George Eliot, ed. 1892), p. 784.

Movement in England and of the conferences of Lacordaire at Notre-Dame in Paris; it was the middle year of the publication of Comte's series of volumes *Philosophie positive*; and it was the year after the publication of Lamennais' *Paroles d'un croyant*, which, however impassioned the faith therein expressed, were not the words of an orthodox Catholic believer. Strauss's work, though it shocked a great many people (who probably never read it), had, by reason of his intellectual boldness and his uncompromising intellectual honesty, an immense effect upon the progress of liberalism in Europe and America. It was a liberating force, an exposition of scientific method applied to mankind's most cherished beliefs, as nearly as possible without prejudice, prepossession, or subservience to custom or desire. For a time the intellectual appeal of Strauss's method and conclusions was going to capture all the most thoughtful men, and Unitarianism, or even a simple Deism, would be for a period the religion of most, if not all, liberal circles. George Eliot translated the *Leben Jesu* (1846) with enormous industry and care. The English Unitarians, an old established group, and the French Positivists, who were adopting Comte's religion of humanity, as well as liberal, though not ' unorthodox,' Protestant theologians, were all influenced by the Tübingen pastor. Equally he is responsible for the *Leben Jesu Christi* of Neander, published in 1837, which was a direct reply to Strauss's book, and which met it, point by point, with patience, accuracy, research, and fairmindedness. Neander, a converted Jew whose original name was David Mendel, was professor in the University of Berlin from 1813 to 1850, and was the most learned contemporary historian of the origins of Christianity.

Strauss's *Leben* was too much even for the liberal authorities of the University of Tübingen, and it cost him his chair. The Government of the canton of Zürich appointed him to a chair, but, on account of public outcry, had to revoke the appointment and pension him off. Strauss, in retirement at Stuttgart, pursued his literary and theological labours, and took an interest in liberal politics. He failed to secure election to the German National Assembly of Frankfurt in 1848, but he represented his native town, Ludwigsburg, in the Württemberg Diet. His literary talent became better and better as time went on, reaching a high point in his life of the famous Reformer Ulrich von Hutten (published in 1858). Unlike most intellectual pioneers, age only found him more daring than ever; and his latest work, *Der alte und der neue Glaube* (1872), abandoned anything that he had formerly admitted of positive Christianity, and prepared the way for a new religion based on appreciation of art and knowledge of nature. Strauss, who had long been separated from his wife, the opera-singer Agnese Schebest, died at Ludwigsburg in 1874.

In the eighteenth century it appeared as if the Christian religion was being destroyed by the Age of Reason. Even the Roman Catholic Church made little defence of it, and sank into formalism. The persecution of the Church by the French Revolution, however, produced a reaction in favour of the old religion; and when Napoleon " restored the altars " religious sentiment re-entered into an ascendancy. But in the second and third decades of the nineteenth century the spirit of criticism, often destructive, again subjected the Christian religion to persistent and searching examination which seemed likely to drive it from, at any rate, Protestant circles; and even the Roman Catholic Church was by no means exempt from criticism and revolt. Lamennais, who was ordained a Roman Catholic priest in 1816, was regarded by orthodox Christians as an enemy after 1834 (when he published *Paroles d'un croyant*), and when he died, in 1854, he was buried without religious rites. When Ernest Renan abandoned the clerical profession in 1845, though his action made no stir at the time, a spirit of criticism escaped into free air, and within ten years was charming and persuading the intellectuals of half the world; for Renan in a unique way united literary grace, learning, and critical acumen.

Like Chateaubriand and Lacordaire, Renan was a Breton. He was born at Tréguier in 1823, a quiet little seaport which had a restored monastic community. His father, a naval officer, died and left two sons and one daughter to be brought up, with little money, by the mother. Renan was educated until the age of fifteen at the local school, which was kept by priests. Later, on looking back to his youth and education, this reputed enemy of the Christian faith wrote with deep appreciation and kindness about his schools and schoolmasters, and also about the young men he knew as candidates for the priesthood. Tréguier was a place with no *bourgeoisie aisée*; everybody lived very simply. The clergy were " serious, disinterested, honest." They were entirely unworldly; *j'ai eu le bonheur de connaître la vertu absolue*, he wrote.[1] The Tréguier school was really " a great school of faith and respect." The people of the town were old-fashioned and devout. When members of the Congregation (an aristocratic " home-mission " society) came round to Tréguier in the reign of Charles X and preached there the people, like the Florentines in the time of Savonarola, brought out their worldly books and burned them. Nevertheless, one poor old man, the ' Spinoza ' of the village, who had attended the Feast of the Supreme Being at Paris in 1794, kept his books, and died among them in 1830; then the careful priests had them bought up cheaply and burned. They kept the Tréguier school free from all contact with the intellectual currents which were circulating in France. *On ne vit jamais un isolement plus complet de l'air ambiant.*[2] The French Revolution seemed not to have occurred. The priests lived up to their profession. Renan, who knew them well not only at school, but later in seminaries, and writing towards the end of his long life, mostly spent in conflict with the Church, declared that he had never known any but good priests: *je n'ai connu que de bons prêtres.* Stories against clerical morals are without foundation.[3]

At the age of fifteen and a half Renan, following the natural course of a youth destined for the priesthood, went up to Paris during " the brilliant Renaissance of lettered and worldly clericalism which took place between 1830 and 1840." Monseigneur de Quélen—*parfait évêque de l'ancien régime*—was Archbishop of Paris. The Abbé Félix-Antoine Dupanloup, whom Renan

---

[1] E. Renan, *Souvenirs d'enfance (Œuvres complètes)*, pp. 41–42.
[2] *Ibid.*, pp. 134–135.   [3] *Ibid.*, p. 139.

calls " a bold young Ultramontane " (though he was later very critical of Ultramontanism and Papal Infallibility), had recently taken over the charge of the Little Seminary of St Nicolas du Chardonnet. This very energetic and attractive priest had been tutor to the sons of Louis Philippe, and was called in to administer the last sacrament to Talleyrand in 1838. He had been appointed by Monseigneur de Quélen to the headship of St Nicolas du Chardonnet in 1837, and he aspired, with success, to make it a brilliant school for aspirants to the clergy; and he awarded one of the scholarships, or *bourses*, to Renan, whose people were unable to pay the fees. There were some two hundred pupils in the seminary, boarded and taught along original lines for the priesthood. Discipline was maintained without any punishments. The world was not shut out. The pupils were given works of Lamartine, Michelet, and Victor Hugo to read.

In fact, education at St Nicolas du Chardonnet under the Abbé Dupanloup was more liberal than in the State schools, for Renan avows that Dupanloup was an educator without equal. St Sulpice, however, the Great Seminary for priests, did not approve. Nevertheless, many brilliant careers began in St Nicolas du Chardonnet, and they would have been more brilliant still " if the *seize mai* had succeeded "—that is, if Monarchy had ousted the Third Republic in 1877.

After finishing with rhetoric at St Nicolas du Chardonnet Renan went to Issy, which was the philosophy college attached to St Sulpice; and from Issy he went on to St Sulpice itself. Renan's experience continued to be invariably of good, conscientious priests. The teaching at St Sulpice was *tout à fait honnête*. It lacked, however, the habit of the criticism of truth: *elle manquait l'habitude de la critique de la vérité*; it was " the rule of systematic mediocrity." The St Sulpicians were virtuous; the seminary was " a school of virtue." And there was much freedom; nobody was forced to study. Renan both studied and thought: organized mediocrity could not satisfy him.

For months when faced with dogmatic assertions or doubtful

passages in Scripture or ancient writings a thought forced itself upon his mind like the clang of a bell: the thought was, *Cela n'est pas vrai*. This could not be put aside. The young seminarist had become critical, and determined to see only the truth, to accept nothing as certain that did not satisfy every test of truth that he could suggest. The insistence of the idea with the bell-like note, *cela n'est pas vrai*, left him no choice. On October 6, 1845, the young seminarist left St Sulpice with two hundred francs, given him by his sister—the foundation of his independence and dignity. A long and fruitful literary and scholastic career followed, with universal attention from all the world, a university chair, a *fauteuil* in the *Académie Française*—a long and happy life devoted to truth, unembittered by the mental contest which he had gone through at St Sulpice, and retaining the genuine respect for the priests whom he has described so lovingly in *Souvenirs d'enfance*. The *Vie de Jésus*, which was published in 1863, shows a long distance traversed since St Sulpice, but its seed was planted there. It shows the same intellectual integrity as forced the young seminarist to the conclusion, *cela n'est pas vrai*; and, more positively, it shows a determination to sift every detail of the Gospel story and to establish incontrovertible facts of history. The opening words of the *Vie de Jésus* are: " The capital event of the history of the world is the revolution by which the more noble portions of humanity have passed from the ancient religions comprised under the vague name of paganism to a religion founded on the divine unity, the Trinity, the incarnation of the Son of God." [1] And if Renan begins his narrative with " *Jesus was born at Nazareth*," and declares that for historians the Life ends with His last sigh on the Cross, he calls Jesus " the corner stone of humanity, so that to take away Thy name from this world would be to shake it to its foundation." [2]

The great merit of Renan's book is that, contrary to Strauss's *Leben*, it is a sympathetic and enthusiastic effort at a positive contribution. Naturally, Renan rejects all alleged facts that do not satisfy his canons of evidence; but rejection or destruction

---

[1] Renan, *Vie de Jésus* (*Œuvres complètes*, p. 449).   [2] *Ibid.*, p. 441.

is not his aim. His labour is positive, constructive. His religious feeling, his wide sympathy, his poetic imagination, his profound learning (lightly borne, as is the French way), and his glowing genius have made a vivid narrative which vibrates in the soul of the reader. The historic Jesus is presented with a vividness to which no reader can fail to respond. The magic of Renan's style, his interpretation—religious, philosophic, psychological—of Christ's character, his interpretation of Christ's mission, make the book a far grander work than Strauss's *Leben* of 1835. In the year which followed the publication of Renan's *Vie de Jésus* Strauss, as it were conscious of the deficiency of his earlier, negative work, published a revised or new version of the *Leben* (1864)—an effort positively to construct a ' Life of Jesus.' Thus the attacks on the foundations of belief, the result of Strauss's " mythical " point of view in 1835 and of Renan's realization in 1840 that certain things (to his mind) were " not true," must be traced down to 1864 before something like a new stability in theology can be considered to have been reached. As Strauss wrote in the Preface to his *Leben* in 1835: " The essence of the Christian faith is perfectly independent of this criticism "; but it took people many years to realize this truth.

With the fierce light of historical criticism beating upon the Gospel story many people felt drawn to the Church which just denies or ignores all this, which confidently asserts that it *knows*, and that it has a complete answer to every religious problem. The Papacy, which declined in power and influence through the eighteenth century, steadily revived throughout the first half of the nineteenth. This revival was not the work of the Popes from 1815 to the middle of the century—Pius VII, Leo XII, Pius VIII, Gregory XVI, Pius IX—though these were all men of note. It was the work largely of writers who expressed the innate desire of the common man and woman for certainty, security, and membership of an age-long community. Joseph de Maistre, Chateaubriand, Montalembert, and a host of able Jesuit preachers and teachers led the multitude in its re-entry into the old faith.

In the eighteen-twenties and eighteen-thirties the romantic spirit of intellectual Frenchmen looked for peace, to find it in the Church of Rome. Montalembert may have found it; " he loved freedom more than all the world, and the Catholic religion more than freedom." Lacordaire, on the other hand, found no peace in the orthodox Catholic system, nor did Lamennais, nor did Sainte-Beuve, who soon gave up looking for peace there.

Félicité-Robert de Lamennais was a Breton of noble family, born at Saint-Malo in 1782. As a boy he already had a passion for solitary study, for meditation, devotion, during long periods spent alone with his brother, who was a priest, on the family estate, La Chesnaie, near Dinan. Not until 1816, after the Hundred Days, was he ordained priest, at the age of thirty-three. Soon he was in the van of the Paris liberal Catholic movement, and after the Revolution of July 1830, when political and ecclesiastical reaction was believed to have been defeated, he joined with the young nobleman Montalembert, with the eloquent priest Jean-Baptiste Lacordaire, and with the Abbé Gerbet in founding a liberal Catholic journal, to be called L'Avenir (September 1830). It was too liberal for the French episcopate. Sainte-Beuve, who was a friend of Lamennais', wrote to Victor Pavie, a member of his literary circle (November 13, 1831):

> L'Avenir has just ceased to appear; the bishops forbid their curés to read it or subscribe to it. M. de Lamennais leaves for Rome with Lacordaire and Montalembert to try and induce the Pope to explain this and to obtain permission to restart it. He is sublime both in his resolution and his faith. He wished to take me with him; alas! why? Rome is no longer in Rome, and I shall never cry Italiam! [1]

The journey of the three believers to Rome was fruitless, and L'Avenir was never revived.

---

[1] Sainte-Beuve, Correspondance, i, 270. By Je ne m'écrierai jamais: Italiam Sainte-Beuve is alluding to the last lines of Montesquieu's De l'Esprit des lois, and also to Aeneid, iii, 523-524, where the crew of Æneas's ship see Italy afar off and shout, " Italiam! "

Joseph-Marie, Comte de Maistre, was born in 1754 at
Chambéry, in Savoy, which was then part of the kingdom of
Sardinia. By age, environment, training, he was a man of the
eighteenth century. His defence of the Pope as the supreme
authority of the world is not the sentimentalism of a nineteenth-
century Romantic; it is the cold rationalism of an eighteenth-
century thinker whose thinking led him to an opposite conclusion from that of the Voltairean philosophers. De Maistre's
family belonged to the hereditary magistracy. His father was
President of the Senate of Savoy. The son, educated in school
at Chambéry, in the university at Turin, was trained for the
magistracy, and entered into the profession. The French
Revolution, however, broke his judicial career; his country
was annexed to France (1792), and de Maistre went into exile
at Lausanne. There he wrote *Considérations sur la France*.
Later he was made ambassador of the kingdom of Sardinia to
the Court of Russia, where he wrote *Soirées de Saint-Pétersbourg*.
He lived with extreme simplicity, refusing to accept any salary
from his impoverished sovereign, although he appears to have
had a small allowance for expenses. His country was restored
to its ancient rule after 1814; de Maistre returned to it in 1817,
and was in the Government service at Turin until his death in
1821, two years after the publication of *Du Pape* at Lyons.

It has been said that the eighteenth century destroyed two
things—the sense of the supernatural and the sense of tradition.[1]
With the decay of these two things the foundations of the
majestic edifice of the Roman Catholic Church were being removed. De Maistre, a devout son of the Church, who regarded
the French Revolution, its liberty and democracy, as evil consequences of a Godless eighteenth century, naturally based his
system on the supernatural and on tradition, these fundamentals
of the Roman Church. Yet he was not a mystic: *raisonneurs
acharnés* is what he and his contemporary de Bonald, have been
called.[2] His *Soirées* and *Pape* leave no room in his system for
democracy and tolerance, and little for mercy.

[1] E. Faguet, *Politiques et moralistes du dix-neuvième siècle*, p. vii.
[2] *Ibid.*, p. xiii.

Ferocious absolutist, outraged theocrat [*théocrate outragé*], intransigent legitimist, apostle of a monstrous Trinity composed of Pope, king, and executioner, partisan in everything of the harshest, the narrowest, the most inflexible dogmas, sombre representative of the Middle Age—the age of the doctor, inquisitor, lawyer—this is the man that the reader imagines to himself, at times, after reading his works.[1]

Such is the Joseph de Maistre of the books published in his lifetime. Private letters and diplomatic correspondence published some thirty years after his death give a different picture—the suave diplomatist, the tender husband, the wise and humorous father. There is nothing really strange in all this. The inflexible Roman Catholic system can comprehend within its limits all the tenderness of the human heart. De Maistre was a tireless worker. He is said regularly to have been at his desk, or rather work-table, for fifteen hours a day. The work-table revolved, so that a servant could place lunch or dinner on a clear portion of it; he would then make the table revolve until the dishes were opposite his master, who would partake of the meal and, when finished, make the table revolve again, and so would resume his work. Throughout all his life he never went for a walk. The unflinching opponent of Voltaireanism, he nevertheless frequently amused himself by reading Voltaire simply for pleasure. In spite of his tremendous industry and economy of time, he had no objection to being interrupted, and was always genial and good-natured. In the last year of his life, however, he became rather pessimist, and said, " *Je finis avec l'Europe ; c'est s'en aller en bonne compagnie.*"

De Maistre's exposition of the necessity of the Pope as the ultimate authority for a civilized world amounts to the assertion—the proof in his own view—of two needs—unity and continuity. The spirit of man yearns after an always, a *toujours*; and a dynasty or an institution to be sure of universal respect must have its origin in the mist of antiquity, " in the night of legends." Christianity, the Papacy, have this element of *always*:

[1] Faguet, *op. cit.*, p. 2.

M

Paganism itself was a kind of Christianity waiting for the coming of Christ. The Church is the repository of truth. Kings and princes are responsible to truth, and therefore to the Church, of which the head upon earth is the Pope. The Pope is authority and continuity and, finally, unity—at any rate, the principle of unity over and above the evil disunities of mankind. De Maistre accepts equally the absolutism of the king and the infallibility of the Pope. It is a curious thing that this Papalist, this protagonist of the Middle Age, should be so essentially un-Romantic, so rational in his method—a *Voltaire retourné*.[1] Sainte-Beuve justly observes that nobody after de Maistre wrote of the Papacy as they had done before him.

The Vicomte de Bonald, the second great literary champion of the Papacy, was, like de Maistre, a man of the eighteenth century, though his long life lasted until 1840. He was born in 1753 at Monna, in Aveyron, was an *émigré* after the Revolution, returned to France under the amnesty of the Year V, and became Minister of Public Instruction for Napoleon in 1808. He made his peace with Louis XVIII at the time of the Restoration, and was raised to the peerage by that monarch in 1823. He died at the age of eighty-six at Monna, his birthplace, to which he had retired after the accession of Charles X. His *Théorie du pouvoir politique et religieux dans la société civile* was published during the Emigration, at Constance in 1796, and was supplemented by various other of his philosophical writings after his return to France. His theory has been explained as a system of logic—cause, means, effect. God is cause, Christ is means, the world is effect. The king is cause, the gentry are means, the conservation of the people is effect.[2] The Pope, as Christ's vicar, is the universal means, the mediator between God and man, and therefore is the ultimate authority. De Maistre and de Bonald corresponded with each other, and rightly regarded themselves as champions of the same thing, though not using the same weapons. De Bonald has been called " the last of the Scholastics." [3] His religious and political views

---

[1] Faguet, *op. cit.*, p. 66, quoting Scherer. [2] *Ibid.*, p. 76.
[3] *Ibid.*, p. 70.

had some influence under the restored Bourbons, but three years after his death Sainte-Beuve could write (1843), *On ne lit plus Bonald*.[1]

Alongside of de Maistre and de Bonald, these rationalists and logicians, Chateaubriand stands forth as the complete Romantic. A Breton of Saint-Malo, born in 1768, nursed to the sound of the sea-waves, growing up in a lonely old castle in desolate, marshy country, he became, and remained, romantic, solitary, poetic, introspective, yet observant. He held a commission in a royal regiment before the Revolution, made a long tour in the ' backwoods ' of the United States, fought (not that he had any heart in this business) in the *émigré* army against the Revolution, began writing *Le Génie du Christianisme* in London, returned to Paris under the amnesty of 1802, and published the *Génie* in the same year, at precisely the time at which the Napoleonic Concordat with the Pope entered into force. Since the breach between the Revolution and Rome in 1790 people had been sighing in France for a restoration of the altars. Now at last it had come. The church bells pealed, and the good priests returned to their public ministrations, and just at this moment the poetic, glowing, coloured words of Chateaubriand expressed the religious emotions of a whole people. In his Introduction he explains:

> When the *Genius of Christianity* appeared France was emerging from the chaos of the revolution; all the elements of society were in confusion; the dread hand which was beginning to separate them had not yet accomplished its task; order had not yet emerged from despotism and glory.
>
> So it was, as it were, in the midst of the ruins of our temples that I published the *Genius of Christianity* in order to call to mind the great ceremonies of ritual in the temples and the servants of the altars. Saint-Denis was disused: the moment had not yet come when Bonaparte would have to remember that he would require a tomb; it would have been difficult for him to guess where Providence had ordained his to be. Everywhere were to be seen the remains of churches and monasteries that were

---

[1] Sainte-Beuve, *Portraits littéraires*, ii, 448 (essay on J. de Maistre).

half demolished; it was even a kind of amusement to go and walk
about among these ruins.

The faithful believed themselves to be saved by the appearance of a book which answered so well to their inward state of
feeling; there was a need for faith, a desire for religious consolation, which came from the very lack of that consolation for so
many years. How much strength from heaven was called for by
the sufferers of so many adversities! How many mutilated families had to seek from the Father of mankind the children whom
they had lost! How many broken hearts, how many souls made
lonely, were calling for the divine hand to cure them? People
hurried to the house of God, just as they would to the doctor's
house in the time of plague. The victims of our troubles (and
what a variety of victims!) rushed to the altar, just as shipwrecked
men cling to the rock on which they hope for safety.

The Roman Catholic Church can always count upon the
receptivity of mankind. Men and women yearn for the comforts
of religion, for communion with each other, for world-wide co-
operation with God and the infinite. The Church supplies all
this, ministering to the spiritual needs of man, meeting all their
questions with an answer, all their doubts or fears with assurance. The strength of the Church is the innate yearnings of all
the people. But it is men themselves who make a Church, and
are the instruments of its ministrations. Its vigour varies with
the vigour of its servants. Writers like de Maistre, de Bonald,
Chateaubriand, might effectively support it in its mission; but
without organization much of their power would be lost. The
Roman Catholic Church is itself a grand organization; and
within it another organization, the Jesuit Order, was its great
drawing force in the early and middle nineteenth century.

The fall of the Jesuit Order, its dissolution by Clement XIV
in 1773 at the command of the *rois éclairés*, was the most striking
proof of the decline of the power of the Church, its yielding to
the disintegrating forces of the age. The restoration of the
Jesuits in 1814 by Pius VII was equally the proof of returning
confidence and revived purpose in the Church; and for the next
fifty years they were undoubtedly the right arm of the Papacy.
Writing in 1843, Michelet declared: " If you stop the first

passer-by in the street and ask him, '*What are the Jesuits?*' he will reply without hesitation, '*The Counter Revolution.*' [1]

The Church is founded upon a rock: "Thou art Peter, and upon this rock I will build my church." If the Pope is the successor of St Peter he is the rock, and his position leads logically to Infallibility. Renan says that all the young priests at the time he was in St Sulpice (about 1840) were going over to Papal Infallibility. But Infallibility was not a dogma of the Church in 1840, nor, indeed, for thirty years afterwards. There was not sufficient support for it in the Sacred College at Rome; only the Jesuit Order in its headquarters there seems consistently to have supported the claim of Papal Infallibility, and in the end to have brought about its proclamation.

The Jesuit Order, or Society of Jesus, is divided into national 'provinces.' A General of the whole order is elected for life. He resides at Rome, where are the headquarters of the order, in constant touch with the Vatican. The achievement of the order, which is vowed to fight for the Church, is due to its possession of an ideal of service and mission and its success in attracting ardent and intelligent young men into its ranks and in subjecting their will to the use of the order. Its work in the provinces of Europe, in the United States, and in the mission field is of high importance in the history of the modern Roman Catholic Church; but its work at Rome, the constant, powerful pressure of the Order in upholding and advancing the centralizing power of the Papacy, is more important still. It is one of the outstanding facts of Church history. It might be said of the work of the Society of Jesus in the nineteenth century, as Chateaubriand said of the work of Bossuet in the seventeenth, "The hydra of heresy was again struck to the ground [*L'hydre de l'hérésie fut de nouveau terrassée*]." [2]

The Jesuit outlook and system have much that is attractive and valuable in a changing and uncertain world. The Jesuits' faith is secure, their confidence in divine governance is complete, their subjection of their will is entire. The Order lives up to the

[1] Michelet, *Les Jésuites*, Introduction.
[2] *Génie du Christianisme*, Introduction.

ideal of the founder and of the Bull *Ecclesia militans* on which
the Order is legally based. The system satisfies all religious
people and yearners after religion who can make what Jesuits
themselves have called *il sacrifizio del intelletto*. It is not the
way of Geneva, which in the eighteenth and early nineteenth
centuries was regarded as the Protestants' Rome and (for Cal-
vinism had long given up ' predestination ') as the emblem of
religious freedom. There is a remarkable similarity, perhaps
even identity, of spirit between the Jesuit philosophy and the
' totalitarian ' philosophy of certain twentieth-century politics.
For these the individual is an instrument serving the whole
society or whole State; he is a means to an end. In the system
of Geneva the individual is an end in himself, not an organ or
function of a great society; Government exists for the good of
the individual, and unity in society is achieved by a harmony
of wills. This was the faith of two Swiss writers, Madame de
Staël, the Genevese, and Benjamin Constant, the Lausannois.
The Reformation, wrote Madame de Staël in *De l'Allemagne*,
made an epoch at which the spirit of man *could not believe
without testing*.

> The testing may enfeeble that customary faith which men do
> well to keep as long as they can; but when a man issues from
> the testing more religious than he entered into it, it is then that
> religion is immutably established; it is then that there is peace
> between it and enlightenment [*les lumières*], and they mutually
> serve each other. . . . Christianity was first founded, then altered,
> then examined, then understood; and these diverse periods were
> necessary to its development; they have lasted sometimes a hun-
> dred, sometimes a thousand, years. The Supreme Being, who
> works in eternity, is not economical of time after our manner.[1]

Benjamin Constant held, as Renan[2] did later, that man was
naturally *religious* in the same way as he was naturally social and
articulate. Sociability, religion, language, were essential qualities of man, not developed in him at a certain epoch, but innate
in him. This natural religion is individualist; it is a *place of*

[1] *De l'Allemagne*, Part IV, Chapter 2.   [2] Renan, *Vie de Jésus*, p. 2.

safety, a ' camp ' where he entrenches himself against external forces, against the omnipotence of the State.[1] This religion is a liberating agent. Constant will not have a Vatican in it. This religion is not a society organized for obedience, an empire, a law, a hierarchy. It is a personal right. Religion, for Benjamin Constant, is a form of individual liberty.[2] Gioberti, who was a secular priest, attacked in *Il Gesuita moderno* (1846), the " error " of the Jesuits in maintaining that the progress of science and other branches of culture is injurious to religion. *Il Gesuitismo . . . uno dei padri dell' incredulità*.[3]

All this, it must be admitted, is, from the point of view of the Roman Catholic Church, rank heresy. And it cannot be said of Madame de Staël and Benjamin Constant, as the Inquisitor says in *St Joan*, " Heresy begins with people who are to all appearance better than their neighbours." [4] Roman Catholicism was producing saintly lives in this period of the Ultramontane revival. The Protestants, Pestalozzi, the educator, who died in 1827, and Oberlin, the pastor, who died in 1826, are saintly figures who came over from the eighteenth century.

Ozanam, though not canonized, is a genuine saint of the nineteenth century. Antoine-Frédéric Ozanam was an admirable literary scholar and critic, who wrote important works on Italian literature, particularly on that of the thirteenth century. After holding a teaching position at Lyons he was promoted to Paris, and eventually became professor in the faculty of letters of the university. Deeply religious, a friend of Montalembert, he was one of the remarkable Catholic liberals of the eighteenforties. He will always be remembered as the chief founder of the great Catholic charitable society of St Vincent de Paul. It was in 1833 that Ozanam, at that time a student at the Sorbonne, with seven other like-minded students joined together to found this society.

The Lutheran communion had a deeply religious spirit in Madame de Krüdener. She was born in 1764 at Riga, the

---

[1] Faguet, *op. cit.*, p. 240. [2] *Ibid.*, p. 241.
[3] Gioberti, *Gesuita moderno*, Chapter 3.
[4] G. B. Shaw, *St Joan*, Scene 6.

daughter of Baron von Wietinghoff, a Baltic nobleman. At the age of eighteen she was married to the Baron von Krüdener, a Russian diplomatist. Madame de Krüdener was beautiful, romantic, passionate. Her novel, *Valérie*, published (in French) at Paris in 1804, is a kind of autobiography, sentimental and romantic, with lifelike pictures of the elegant and worldly life of High Society at Venice, where her husband was Russian ambassador. The book had a great success. Sainte-Beuve, who writes with great approval of it in his essays, thought it worth while editing it in 1855. In order to superintend the education of her son, Madame de Krüdener lived much in Germany, and became the friend of the beloved and unfortunate Queen Louise of Prussia. She was greatly attracted by the personality of Bernardin de Saint-Pierre, the author of *Paul et Virginie*; also by Jung Stilling, the Pietist physician and professor of economics, the friend of Goethe's Strasbourg days.

The events of 1813 made Madame de Krüdener. The elegant, fashionable Livonian noblewoman became a prophet of the War of Liberation. Like Madame de Staël, she had conceived a deep aversion to Napoleon, and was determined to pit her frail woman's force against the might of the tyrant. Her place in the high world of fashion and diplomacy brought her into contact with the Emperor Alexander. They met in Switzerland in the time of peace between the end of the War of Liberation and the beginning of the Hundred Days. Madame de Krüdener had foretold the crisis of 1815, the return of Napoleon from Elba, the collapse of the edifice of peace, and at last the restoration of order, the saving of Europe. After Waterloo she was at Paris in a house, near the Élysée palace where Alexander was lodged. The Emperor used to visit Madame de Krüdener and pray with her side by side. If she did not originate the idea of the Holy Alliance (leagues of peace were in many men's minds) she encouraged and inspired Alexander in his belief in his mission. If Alexander I wrote the text of the Holy Alliance Madame de Krüdener's mysticism supplied its spiritual character. At the Camp de Vertus in Champagne, the great review of the Allies, she was treated almost as a crowned prophetess.

Madame de Krüdener, inheriting her father's Latvian estates, was rich enough to live where she pleased. The Germans, wrote Madame de Staël in *De l'Allemagne*, are prone to enthusiasm.[1] Madame de Krüdener was a Baltic German. A genuine cosmopolitan, she resided in city after city, holding forth in public and private, urging people to deeds of charity, to faith in God, to mystical communion with the Unseen. For four or five years after the Restoration of 1815 she provoked a religious revival wherever she went. She died on December 25, 1824, in the Crimea, where she had gone to establish a penitentiary.

After the rationalism of the eighteenth century and after the destruction of all things medieval by the French Revolution, people turned, with a kind of homesickness, to the Middle Ages. There they found a refuge, an escape into a quaint and romantic world, where beliefs were firm, faith secure, and authority unchallenged.

> A great sigh of joy and satisfaction, a warm emotion of tenderness, welled up in and reanimated all breasts as, after so long a rationalistic ascesis, they again took to themselves the old religion, the old national customs, regional and local, again entered the old houses and castles and cathedrals, sang again the old songs, dreamed again the old legends.[2]

This nostalgia of the Middle Ages influenced culture in every direction. It can be felt in the ballad poetry of Bürger, the historical romance of Scott, the resumption of the building of Cologne Cathedral, the publication of chronicles and other texts of the *Monumenta Germaniæ Historica*, the theocratic feudalism of Haller, the glamorous *Christianisme* of Chateaubriand, the Papalism of Joseph de Maistre. It explains Dean Church's saying that Sir Walter Scott was responsible for the Oxford Movement.

In view of all this it is not surprising that there should be a flow towards the old faith of the Church. The Romantic

[1] Part IV, Chapter 10.

[2] B. Croce, *Theory and History of Historiography* (trans. D. Ainslie, 1921), p. 264.

movement, the Ultramontane movement, the conversion of many literary men to Roman Catholicism, the writing of histories of the Middle Ages, like Giesebrecht's *Kaiserzeit*, and of romances about the Middle Ages, like Scheffel's *Ekkehard*, are all manifestations of the same thing—reaction against eighteenth century rationalism and self-sufficiency. They are all escapes from the puzzles of modern life, from its lack of form, lack of security, lack of single purpose. There were three ways in which people met the spiritual and mental chaos of the nineteenth century. One was the world's way—to enjoy the pleasures of life with more or less refinement. The second was the Protestant way—to wrestle individually with the problems and reach a settlement, if one could, through individual judgment. The third was Rome's way—to accept the doctrine of the past and to found an unquestioning faith upon it.

Chapter XII

THE PENINSULA

RICHARD FORD, the writer of what is probably the best book on Spain since *Don Quixote*, has remarked that people are far too much under the tyranny of political frontiers. The Iberian Peninsula is politically divided between Spain and Portugal, but it is still the Iberian Peninsula. Napoleon, once he extended his power into the Peninsula, found it impossible to observe the political frontier between Spain and Portugal; and the war with England which followed was always called the Peninsular War. Continental travellers, visiting the Peninsula, practically always approached it from the landward side, from the direction of France; and they seldom went beyond Spain into Portugal, many not even beyond Madrid. English travellers, on the other hand, nearly always went by sea, either, as Ford did, to Gibraltar, which was something of a winter resort in the early nineteenth century, or, as Borrow did, to Lisbon, which has probably never been without some English residents since the fourteenth century. For historical, commercial, and geographical reasons the English who went to Spain or Portugal tended to acquire a juster notion of the Peninsula as a whole and of its peoples than did other Continental travellers; and throughout the first half of the nineteenth century the English name was very familiar in the Peninsula, and English travellers were accorded a spontaneous welcome. They seem, in a sense, to have felt almost at home, or at any rate in a socially friendly environment. The French, however, were not without interpreters of Spain—Gautier, Hugo. In one of his familiar letters to Victor Hugo Sainte-Beuve declared, " If I were to make a journey in Estremadura it would make less impression on me than your verses about Estremadura and Catalonia." [1]

[1] Sainte-Beuve, *Correspondance*, i, 155 (November 2, 1829).

Political and geographical frontiers cannot, however, be disregarded. The Peninsula, sea-girt and mountain-spanned though it be, contains two distinct states and two peoples whose historical traditions make them feel distinct from each other, and whose men of letters have established two distinct literary languages. Yet Borrow, when he passed from Portugal over into Spain, keen observer though he was, did not notice any abrupt transition, any particular break in social or geographical environment, although he found the passport examination very exacting. The passport is the great sign of the barriers of suspicion between men and men.

It is curious to notice how the political fortunes of Portugal and Spain have been linked together. That both were equally involved in the great European war is not in itself particularly remarkable. Once Napoleon had intervened anywhere in the Peninsula this was inevitable. Throughout the rest of the half-century political development or changes proceeded on almost completely parallel lines in each country. The Spanish and Portuguese peoples, or rather the educated laity among them, acquired, as the result of the French Revolution and the intervention of the British Government in the Peninsular War, the taste, indeed, the passion, for a constitution. For a constitution—Parliament, a responsible Ministry, an equal law for all citizens—both peoples have struggled persistently. According to Théophile Gautier, the name ' Plaza de la Constitución ' could be seen in every town written up on a crumbling wall of some public square. This struggle for a constitution was reflected in a dynastic contest. Queen Maria of Portugal, who came to the throne in 1826, relied on Parliament; her uncle, Dom Miguel, on ' Divine right.' Queen Isabella of Spain, who came to the throne in 1833, had a Parliamentary title, and was opposed by her uncle, Don Carlos, the upholder of ' divine right.' A long civil war in each country ended with the victory of the Parliamentary monarchy. In the last half of the nineteenth century a republican movement gradually grew in strength, and in the early twentieth century first Portugal, later Spain, became republics. This remarkable parallel development in the two countries cannot be explained by geographical contiguity : it has depended far more on similarity of social conditions, temperament, and political consciousness.

Borrow made his first journey into Portugal in 1835, the year after the end of the Miguelite war. Sailing up the Tagus to Lisbon, he saw the *Rainha Nao*, recently the flagship of the Miguelite fleet, captured by Admiral Napier at the battle of Cape St Vincent in 1833. " The *Rainha Nao*," Borrow wrote,

> is said to have caused him more trouble than all the other vessels of the enemy ; and some assert that, had the others defended themselves with half the fury which the old vixen queen displayed, the result of the battle which decided the fate of Portugal would have been widely different.

Lisbon had not even yet been completely restored after the damage done by the earthquake of 1755. Borrow judged it to be " unquestionably the most remarkable city in the Peninsula, and, perhaps in the South of Europe . . . quite as much deserving the attention of the artist as even Rome itself." George Ticknor called it " a rival for Naples." [1] The majestic river, the great harbour, the seven hills, the superb Roman aqueduct, the vast, silent palaces of the nobles, broad streets, open spaces, ruins—these were features which gave to Lisbon an air at once sad, grand, and romantic. It was perhaps more impressive in the age when all cultured travellers had the taste for melancholy.

The same impression of half-emptiness was made on Borrow by nearly every place he visited : the inn kitchen at Estremoz into which a drunken horseman came clattering and curveting ; the " enchanted region " of Cintra ; the rare schools ; the monasteries. George Ticknor, who was on the point of becoming a professor at Harvard, noted that the universities in 1818 were places to which men went as a matter of form, in order to have the privilege of a professional career. Bandits and smugglers were common. George Ticknor hired two to conduct him from Seville to Lisbon. " They were high-spirited, high-minded fellows," he wrote; " I easily accommodated myself to their

[1] *The Life of George Ticknor*, i, 244. The subsequent quotation is from i, 205.

manners, and, spreading my blanket on the ground, ate heartily and slept as soundly as the hardiest of them." Borrow visited some of their lairs and dropped religious tracts there for their edification. At Evora he found some Spanish *contrabandistas*, who came over the frontier into Portugal. Finding, in the course of conversation, that one of them could read, Borrow gave him a tract. The smuggler, a man of about fifty, read aloud the tract, which was in the Spanish tongue. The other smugglers gathered around him, listening to the reading and expressing approval. The strange scene lasted for an hour. When the reading was over the smugglers eagerly asked for more tracts, and Borrow left them with a good supply.

Richard Ford, writing in 1843, declared that the kingdom of Spain was a union, not a unity. As a single state it has kept together for over four hundred years. The people is, in fact, tough and cohesive. Yet there are several types of Spaniard; and the provinces are distinct units, geographically and socially. Ford observed that patriotism was provincial; that there was a powerful *freemasonry* of province and of town. The character of the inhabitants of each province was so distinct, wrote Ticknor, " that it seems as if you had changed country every time you pass from one to another." Yet there was community feeling among Spaniards as a whole, and they were immensely proud, not of their province, but of Spain; as the Duke of Wellington put it, " To boast of Spain's strength is the national weakness." As a matter of fact, the conjunction of provincial patriotism and central patriotism in the same persons was an attractive and wholesome feature; it contented the Spaniards, and they showed no tendency to develop *chauvinism*, an aggressive spirit in foreign policy.

In a century of progress Spain has been reputed backward. The provincialism probably retarded material development. The royal Government, though despotic, was weak. The kings, from Philip III to Philip V, did little for the country, though after this Charles III, king from 1759 to 1788, showed great energy; but one enlightened monarch could not compensate for the ineffectiveness of a whole line. Yet Spain was not so backward in the first half of the nineteenth century as it was reputed to be. George Ticknor wrote in 1818 that illiteracy was extremely rare. Borrow had no particular difficulty in having the New Testament printed in Madrid, and he found a bookseller, or several booksellers, in every town who were willing to sell it. At Lugo, which had only 6000 inhabitants, the bookseller was described as " wealthy." Literature and politics often went together. Compostela, the great centre of pilgrimage, with about 20,000 inhabitants, had the " most considerable " bookseller in Northern Spain, and he was eager to help in selling the New Testament. Toreño and Martinez de la Rosa, representative liberal statesmen, were known in their time, though not now, as distinguished men of letters. In fact literary Ministers were rather common in the early Cabinets of the regent Christina and Queen Isabella.

Spain in the early nineteenth century (1812) gave to the European peoples the word for which they were seeking, to express the new, vital force of the age. This word was liberalism; for it was liberty, the ' liberal ' mind and thought, that was making modern Europe. There is " no little irony," as Benedetto Croce has remarked, in the fact that it was this still almost medieval, scholastic Spain which coined the word *liberal*, " with its exact antonym *servil*." [1] For as a whole the Spaniards were ignorant and unpolitical. More difficulties are created in a country by a people being unpolitical than by their being politically minded. In a European country, like Spain, where the mass of the people were quite unpolitical, government was bound to be in the hands of a small group of individuals among whom high office rotated. There being no discernible public opinion, administration was weak and corrupt. " There is nothing that cannot be done by bribery," wrote George Ticknor. Changes in the *personnel* of the central Government were more often due to intrigue and conspiracy than to any expression of the voice of the people. Spain was almost without newspapers in the first half of the nineteenth century, except for the *Eco del Comercio*, the *Nacional*, and the *Diario*, which were read in

[1] B. Croce, *History of Europe in the Nineteenth Century*, p. 9.

the *cafés* of Madrid. News spread slowly and was inaccurate. Abuses went unchallenged. Ford wrote that it was the absence of a public Press which accounted for the persistence of the belief in witchcraft among the Spanish people. The Inquisition, though suspended from 1820 to 1825, was not finally abolished until 1835. The Peninsular War from 1808 to 1813 and the Carlist Civil War from 1833 to 1839 distracted the country, and habituated the people to the notion of war as one of the normal troubles of existence. For these wars were fought largely with foreign resources, and their direct effects were felt only locally, as the moving armies and guerrilla bands traversed particular districts. The Carlist War in particular was a local affair, or series of local affairs. But as long as the wars went on it was impossible for any common educational policy to be undertaken by the Government or any noticeable rise to take place in the standard of life, or in social and intellectual development. The people had little desire to improve their lot, or else they failed for want of the directing-power of an intelligent and energetic class of country gentry. The despotism and centralization of the royal Government since Philip II had prevented the development of a local ' squirearchy.' The lower orders, though not politically minded, were declared by Borrow to be more inclined to Liberal sentiment than were the landed gentry. Locally roads and bridges were left to fall out of repair. Travellers noticed something like Oriental ' incuriousness,' *incurie*, such as Lamartine remarked in the provinces of the Turkish Empire. The population of Spain was eleven to twelve millions, considerably less than it was in the sixteenth century. This fall in population had not been accompanied by any rise in the standard of living, for it was almost certainly due simply to bad government.

Spain was drying up. The navigable area of the rivers was diminishing. There are few lakes in Spain; " the fall is too considerable to allow water to accumulate." A policy of conservation could have remedied this condition of affairs; and Ford found projects in existence for digging artesian wells. Water companies had been promoted and shares were to be issued *at a premium*, "which," wrote this somewhat caustic observer, " will be effected, if nothing else is." In summer the flow of the rivers shrank, and their scanty streams ambled among pebbles and dry earth, uncertain, *capricieux comme des femmes*, as Gautier called them. Yet there were many splendid bridges, and one of the jokes of this age was for the visitor to a village or town to advise the inhabitants to sell their bridge in order to buy water. There were rivers without bridges; and owing to shifting of channels there were bridges without rivers. These bridges, wrote Gautier (1840)—their duties a perfect sinecure — remained " with imperturbable phlegm and patience, worthy of a better fate, waiting for a river, a thread of water, or simply for a little humidity." [1] At Coria there was a great bridge with five noble arches over dry meadows, while the Alagon river, a furlong or so away, had to be crossed by a dangerous ferry.

It is believed that owing to the energetic administration of Charles III Spain at the end of the eighteenth century had better roads than any other Continental state. These roads, however, were only between the great towns on the one hand and the seaports on the other, or else they went from the capital to royal palaces in the country. Yet Ticknor in 1818 found the road between Barcelona and Madrid to be " abominable." [2] Means of communication between the great roads were bad; and most of the internal trade of Spain went on the backs of mules. By 1830 or 1840, however, even the main roads had been allowed to fall out of repair. The road from Madrid to Toledo was ankle-deep in mud or dust.

Down to the end of the reign of Charles IV transportation for hire was a royal monopoly, although, of course, people could use their private carriages. Ferdinand VII (1808–33) gave up the royal monopoly, except for the carriage of mails. There were, accordingly, now three kinds of carriage. First, the post-chaise. This vehicle took passengers as well as the mails; it was comparatively light, and, having always fresh horses or

[1] T. Gautier, *Voyage en Espagne* (ed. 1911), p. 21.
[2] *The Life of George Ticknor*, i, 185.

N

mules, was driven at a tremendous pace: " the inside passenger feels like a kettle tied to the tail of a mad dog or a comet." The second mode of travelling was the public diligence, or stage-coach. Starting from Madrid, the diligences plied their way along the highways according to a regular time-table. The companies which operated the diligences made arrangements with inns along the routes for the reception of the passengers, so that a substantial meal and a clean bed could be reckoned upon. This lessened the fatigue of travelling, which remained, however, heavy; for not many hours were allowed for sleeping; the usual starting hour was dawn, and the day's journey ended only with nightfall. In this manner the traveller might have to proceed for ten days over a distance of five hundred miles. The third method was to hire a *calesa*, a carriage and six. This was the ' taxi ' of Spain, as it was also of Italy. Carriages and six could be hired where they stood in the public squares of towns and cities, and would go wherever their driver was paid to go. They were a sort of heavy closed *barouche*, could take a good deal of luggage behind or in the front boot, and had a picturesquely clad driver, called the *mayoral*, and assistant, called his *mozo*. The *calesa* offered the most comfortable mode of travelling long distances for those who could afford to spend time on the way; and, indeed, it was, apart from horse-riding, the only possible method off the main roads. For a vigorous single man horse-riding was the best means of travelling. George Borrow, in his journeys in Spain on behalf of the Bible Society in 1835–38, bought a couple of horses, one for himself and one for a manservant (easily engaged in any city), and so rode throughout the length and breadth of the country.

French *cuisine* and what Ford called " *café* civilization " were coming into the Peninsula from France, but the inns were little influenced by all this. Most of the larger towns had hotels, some of them kept by a Genoese or other North Italian. Less pre-tentious than the hotel, the *venta* was a tolerably good inn, with clean beds and abundant, if not very tasteful, food and wine. Stage-coaching had brought about a great improvement in the *ventas*. Humbler than the *venta* was the *posada*, which was very like the Oriental *kan*, and must have been introduced into Spain by the Moors. According to Théophile Gautier, the traveller who asked the host at an inn, " What can I have to eat? " was answered by the polite but impassive innkeeper with, " What have you brought with you? "[1] Spaniards had the reputation of supping off a cigarette. No experienced traveller expected to find anything at a *posada* except room for man and beast. The typical *posada*, which seemed to be just as it had been in the reign of Philip III or Philip IV, was a big stone building, with many and large rooms, paved with brick or stone, and with an alcove at the end of each room in which was a wretched flock bed. Behind the house was a court, and behind this a large stable for horses, mules, and donkeys. Travellers cooked their own food at the kitchen fire. In some cases the landlord would sell food or candles, to the travellers. The *posada* kitchen generally had much company, examples of all the types of people who were continuously moving on the roads of Spain—the broken soldier, the *contrabandista*, the gipsy horse-coper, the muleteer and pedlar, a motley, picturesque, talkative collection who delighted the soul of George Borrow.

The *ventas* and *posadas* were scarcely places of good living. Ford has many pages on " the imperfect gastronomy of the Peninsula." Bread was of various kinds, from *pan de candeal* for the affluent to *pan de munición* for the soldiery. *Pan de munición*, " sable as a hat, coarse and hard as a brickbat, would just do to sop the black broth of the Spartan military." Ford's experience was that few Spaniards were good cooks. The more aspiring tried to institute foreign *cuisine*; the rest, the ordinary people, cooked in old Oriental fashion. Fuel was scarce, so that roasting was unknown. The national dish was the *olla*, a pot of oily stew, which would be cooked in hot ashes. Another dish, often a very good one, was the *pollo* of chicken and rice, obviously a direct descendant of the celebrated Oriental *pillau*, which is a feature of every Mohammedan banquet. The wine at roadside *ventas* was often no better than " purple blacking ";

[1] Gautier, *op. cit.*, p. 15.

but Spanish hams at their best were incomparable, with " fat like melted topaz." Crabb Robinson, who was the *Times* correspondent in 1808 at Corunna, dined usually at the chief hotel, the Fontana d'Oro, and found the food execrable : " the only excellent meat was the Spanish ham, cured with sugar." [1] The salad too was usually excellent, for the Spaniards knew how to compound it. Four persons were required—" a spendthrift for oil, a miser for vinegar, a counsellor for salt, and a madman to stir it all up." Tea and coffee were little used, but chocolate could be had everywhere and was really the national drink. It was always good ; the best was made by nuns. Thick and satisfying it was, nevertheless, classed as a liquid, and therefore did not constitute a breach of a fast. The nuns of some convents also made and sold excellent confectionery. At Montemor, in Portugal, Borrow noted down a very good supper at an inn (kept by a Portuguese who had served in Wellington's army) of tea and cheese-cakes made by the nuns of the local convent ; and Gautier described at full length a magnificent *puchero*, a dish of many sorts of meat, served at the inn at Astigarraga, but actually obtainable anywhere between Irun and Cadiz. Yet after fairly wide experience he admitted ruefully, *La cuisine n'est pas le côté brillant de l'Espagne*.[2] There was a flourishing wine trade at Xerez, mainly in the hands of foreigners, because of the skill and forethought, and also because of the heavy capital which the sherry trade required. Each owner or firm had their own *bodega*, or warehouse and equipment. A *bodega* might contain anything from one thousand to four thousand butts of fine sherry. At £25 a butt the capital invested in the wine of only a single *bodega* might be £100,000. As few really fine sherries were exported before they were ten or twelve years old it is clear that only wealthy individuals or syndicates could finance the trade. The finest sherries were worth 80 guineas a butt in the *bodega*, and as much as 130 guineas in the cellars of the importer. The port-wine business at Lisbon and Oporto was conducted in much the same way as the Spanish sherry business.

[1] *The Diary of Henry Crabb Robinson*, i, 144.
[2] Gautier, *op. cit.*, pp. 23–24, 138.

As a strong Protestant, making his way on behalf of the
Bible Society through Spain, Borrow was naturally not much
prepossessed in favour of the Roman Catholic clergy. Nor was
he the kind of Protestant who was in the habit of concealing his
views and prejudices. Moreover, the high clergy were adverse
to the indiscriminate spreading of the Bible in Spain; and,
though generally not actively opposed, Borrow had one period
of very real trouble, and spent three weeks in a Madrid prison.
Nevertheless, Borrow's own narrative shows that he was, in
general, courteously and hospitably received by the clergy
throughout the whole Peninsula. He visited the English College
at Lisbon, and found the inmates—" these gentlemen," as he
calls them—" full of amiability and courtesy to their heretic
countryman." The communities of the Irish College at Salamanca, and of the Scottish and English Colleges at Valladolid
were all courteous and ready to speak with the heretic stranger.
The English College at Valladolid was conspicuous for its
" order, neatness, and system." Borrow concluded, " This is
by far the most remarkable establishment of the kind in the
Peninsula, and, I believe, the most prosperous." The priest of
a village near Cordova, who had a small library of the Fathers
and who fattened pigeons for the market, was particularly
friendly with him. This priest had been an Inquisitor, and
remembered the case of a Seville nun who was punished on
account of her habit of flying through the windows and over
the orange-trees. He seems to have formed the impression that
Borrow was a Roman Catholic himself. The *cura* of Pitiego,
near Salamanca, was under no such illusion. Nevertheless,
when Borrow found himself supperless at the end of a long
day's journey in that poor village the priest overwhelmed him
with attention and kindness. The pigeon-house was rummaged
for the best fare, and the good priest was distressed to find none
suitable. He brightened up, however, when Borrow, noticing
some flitches of bacon, said that this would do. " To tell you
the truth," said the kind old gentleman, " I have nothing better,
and if you can content yourself with such fare I shall be very
happy; as for eggs, you can have as many as you wish, and

perfectly fresh, for my hens lay every day." He pressed Borrow
to stay for the night, but the Englishman, refreshed by good
food and lively conversation (the old priest had picturesque
reminiscences of Wellington and the generals of the Peninsular
army), decided to push onward with his journey. On saying
good-bye Borrow presented a copy of the New Testament to
the good old man, who received it without a word and placed
it on one of the shelves of his study. At Madrid Borrow had an
interview with the Archbishop Primate of all Spain, and engaged in a long and interesting conversation. Though he does
not say so, the impression which Borrow leaves on the reader
of *The Bible in Spain* is that he could have agreed with Renan's
later remark: he had known none but *bons prêtres*. George
Ticknor, who moved in high circles, found in 1818 the bishops
and archbishops whom he met to be kindly, dignified, hospitable, and charitable.

The number of monasteries in the Peninsula had been greatly
diminished in the course of the secularizing Ministry of Godoy,
of the Peninsular War, and of the troubles which followed the
death of Ferdinand VII in 1833. An obvious result of the
decline of monasteries was the increased prominence of beggars
everywhere. Gautier found even soldiers commonly begging,
their pay being for years in arrear. The hospitals and asylums,
still managed largely by clergy, were sad affairs, suffering
both from poverty and mismanagement. Large sums in the
aggregate were still paid away in Masses for the dead—sufficient, wrote Ford, to have endowed Spain with a first-rate
railway system; for in 1843 there were still no lines, except
on paper.

Richard Ford declared Spain to be " the romantic, racy, and
peculiar country of Europe." Théophile Gautier, who was
there about that time, even welcomed the brigandage, as maintaining an element of romance in a world that was growing
drab: " It is something in a civilization so advanced as the
present, in this prosaic and untoward year 1840." [1] He added,
On ne peut faire un pas en Espagne sans trouver le souvenir

[1] Gautier, *op. cit.*, p. 137.

de Don Quichotte: the work of Cervantes is so profoundly
' national,' in the best sense of that word. Ticknor wrote (1818)
from Spain: " There is more national character here, more
originality and poetry in the popular manners and feelings,
more force without barbarism, and civilization without corruption, than I have found anywhere else." [1] It is remarkable that
Ford and Borrow, two Englishmen of different type, should
have been there about the same time and, without any contact
with each other, should form similar impressions. Anyone who
reads *Don Quixote*, *Gil Blas*, Ford's *Gatherings*, and Borrow's
Bible in Spain will realize the continuity of Spanish social life,
notwithstanding wars, revolutions, and modern inventions and
industry. He will realize too why revolutions in Spain have
never affected the rest of Europe—because Spain is the most
secluded country of the Continent. In 1823 the French Government had drawn a *cordon sanitaire* along the Franco-Spanish
frontier, to keep out the infection of plague and revolution.
This was unnecessary. The Pyrenees were an effectual barrier.
On the French side were roads, diligences, *tables d'hôte*, cooks,
cicerones, donkeys—all the apparatus of thriving tourist
society. On the Spanish side was the real, " hard land of
Iberia," given up to the smuggler and the lizard. Even the
Pyrenees, however, could not quite separate two not unfriendly
peoples from each other. When Théophile Gautier made his
journey from Paris to Spain in 1840 he wrote, when still far
from the frontier:

At Bordeaux Spanish influence begins to make itself felt.
Almost all the signs are in two languages; the bookshops have
at least as many Spanish books as French. Many of the people
brag [*hâblent*] in the idiom of Don Quixote and Guzman d'Al-
farache. This influence increases in proportion as one approaches
the frontier; and, to speak truly, the Spanish *shade*, in that half-
tint of demarcation, gains on the French shade. The dialect
which the people of the country speak has much more relation
to Spanish than to the tongue of their motherland. [2]

[1] *The Life of George Ticknor*, i, 188.
[2] Gautier, *op. cit.*, p. 13.

Travellers in Spain during the thirties and forties left it with real respect for the Spaniards. "The lower class," wrote George Ticknor in 1818, " is, I think, the finest *material* I have met in Europe, to make a great and generous people." " Spain is the true home of equality," wrote Gautier. Ticknor, a little paradoxically, said that the people had " a kind of instinctive uprightness which prevents them from equality. . . . A more quiet, orderly people, a people more obedient and loyal, I have not seen in Europe." Even beggars addressed each other politely and with dignity. Domestic servants were treated by their masters with natural gentleness and familiarity, a contrast to the affected politeness of the French and to the curtness which German servants received (and preferred to receive) from their masters. Living was cheap and easy. " With three or four *sous* a day an Andalusian can live splendidly," observed Gautier. There was thus little incentive to hard work, and the Spaniard felt no urging to undertake it. To a traveller, used to the devouring, whirlwind activity of London or Paris, Granada provided a singular spectacle, a life of leisure, conversation, siesta, promenade, music, dance. " One is surprised to see the happy calmness of the faces, the tranquil dignity of their expression." As no one could make money no one was ambitious. " Convinced of the uselessness of their efforts, they do not seek for impossible fortune, and pass their time in a charming idleness favoured by the beauty of the country and the ardour of the climate." And withal they were of extreme kindness and good nature.[1] Such was the much-travelled and observant Frenchman's experience; and that of Borrow and Ford, after due allowance is made for their rather more realist outlook, was not markedly different.

The tranquillity of Spanish social life was giving way in the capital, Madrid, before political interests. The *cafés*—Bolsa, Nuero, Levante, Malta—were frequented by eager politicians and ' intellectuals.' The Madrilenian climate was brisker than that of the south, and the population of Madrid more energetic. They were poor, however; a solid *bourgeoisie*, such as made revolutions conservative in seventeenth-century England and

[1] Gautier, *op. cit.*, pp. 246–247.

nineteenth-century France, scarcely existed as a class in Spain. Poor Madrilenian students in the eighteen-forties put up advertisements outside the Post Office offering services like polishing a gentleman's boots, in order to earn money wherewith to finish their courses in rhetoric or philosophy.[1]

Gautier returned from Spain to France with something like homesickness for the country that he had left behind him. He had a complete answer to the question which Heine, during a concert of Liszt, had spitefully put to him shortly before he set forth: " I wonder how you will speak of Spain *after you have been there?* "

[1] Gautier, *op. cit.*, p. 102.

CHAPTER XIII

THE NEAR EAST

THE peace of 1814–15 gave opportunity for the relief of a long-thwarted desire for travel. The cultured European gentry spread themselves over Asia, Africa, and America. Most of all, the Near East cast its spell upon them. They had all heard or read of the heroes of ancient Greece; and the more enterprising and imaginative would fain see Athens and Sparta. They would like to go farther and to visit Troas and other scenes of the *Iliad* or *Odyssey*. Religious sympathy inclined them towards Palestine; and Napoleon's expedition to Egypt had familiarized them with the notion of Cairo. The last volume of Gibbon's *Decline and Fall of the Roman Empire* had given them some conception of the grandeur and pathos of Constantinople, the majesty of St Sophia, and the bizarre magnificence of the Grand Turk. As in the time of the Roman Empire and of St Paul, the Mediterranean was still the centre of the world, and drew the Europeans to its farther shores with the enchantment of the East.

Classical antiquarianism was beginning to unveil the hidden and extinct civilization of the ancient Mediterranean world. Bonaparte's select band of scholars, led by the mathematician Monge, had prosecuted fruitful researches while the French army was cut off in Egypt from 1798 to 1801. The result was a magnificent and now rare work in two large volumes, profusely illustrated with plates, on the monuments of ancient Egypt.

In spite of widespread feeling for the ancient world, the governing classes of Europe as a whole, except in Russia, were in favour of the maintenance of the Grand Turk. Kinglake wrote in *Eothen* (1844) that Pitt would not speak to anybody who did not hold as an article of faith the integrity of Turkey. Lamartine, narrating his tour of 1832 in the Levant, wrote that the " jealousy of the Powers " would always come to the succour of the Turks, and would sow discord in any conquest made from them.[1] The successful Serbian revolt (1807–15), the first stage in the break-up of European Turkey, attracted no attention in Europe, although French and Russian agents tried to use the Serbs to further French or Russian interests. In the Greek War of Independence of 1821–32 the Powers, until almost the very end, had no thought-out policy at all. Chateaubriand, who went to the Levant in 1806 (the Great War did not quite put an end to travelling), remarked that the Turks were *campés en Europe*, but was not moved by the sight of Athens or Sparta to lament the fate of the Greeks. Chateaubriand was an exception. He wrote:

> To pretend to civilize Turkey by giving it steamships and railways, disciplining its armies, and teaching it to manœuvre its fleets, is not extending civilization in the East: it is introducing barbarism into the West; future Ibrahims will be able to bring back the time of Charles Martel or the time of the siege of Vienna, when Europe was saved by that heroic Poland, on which weighs the ingratitude of kings.

Even the Romantic poets gave little thought to the Near East. Byron was the great exception. Lady Hester Stanhope went out to the Ægean in 1810, and as her ship put in at Athens a man dived off the end of the mole. " It is hardly necessary to say that it was Lord Byron." [2]

Although the Great War did not interrupt all travelling—for instance, Lady Hester Stanhope, Michael Crawford Bruce, the Marquis of Sligo, and the rest of her party had no difficulty in visiting Athens and Constantinople in 1810—the peace naturally enormously increased it. But Chateaubriand had already made his " itinerary " in 1806. He saw nothing good to say of the Turks. They had a notion of order and justice, but it was

---

[1] Lamartine, *Voyage en Orient* (ed. 1913), i, 123.
[2] M. Armstrong, *Lady Hester Stanhope* (1927), p. 41.

very capricious. Osman Pasha of the Morea had fifty brigands killed, which was all to the good, but he killed three hundred peasants with them. There was not a single carriage road in the Morea; indeed, there were practically no made roads at all in Greece, although there were causeways over swamps. There were routes designated as post-roads. If a traveller had proper firmans (documents) from the pasha of the province the inhabitants were bound to provide him with horses and food along the road, free of charge; but Chateaubriand *s'obstinait à payer*, even for the miserable chickens which his astonished janizaries had collected. The *kans*, or inns along the roads, were public shelters put up by pious benefactors; all that the Government did was to license some Turk or other subject to show the hospitalities of the *kan* to travellers and to sell necessities to them. All the *kans* at which Chateaubriand lodged in Greece were in ruins. He refers to some of them briefly:

> In the evening one sometimes stops at a *kan*, an abandoned hovel, where one has to sleep among all sorts of insects and reptiles on a worm-eaten floor. They are not bound to supply you with anything in this *kan* when you have not a ' firman '; you have to procure yourself what victuals you can. . . . We entered the *kan* through a stable; a ladder in the form of an overturned pyramid led us up to a dusty granary. The Turkish merchant threw himself on a mat, exclaiming that it was the finest *kan* in the Morea.[1]

Food was cheap and fairly abundant, and very simple, but Chateaubriand was content with supper of melon, raisins, and black bread.

It was not merely the *kans* that were in ruins. There was desolation everywhere, a condition of affairs rather congenial to the Romantic temperament of the Western Europeans, who had the *goût de solitude*. Anyone who was wearied by revolutions in Europe, wrote Chateaubriand, could find peace among the ruins of Athens. The Morea (or Peloponnese) was almost wholly desolate. Chateaubriand's guide at the miserable village

---

[1] Chateaubriand, *Itinéraire de Paris à Jérusalem* (1893), p. 84.

at Sparta (then called Misitra) did not even know the name of Lacedæmon. Yet by one of those curious chances which every traveller meets Chateaubriand found, in the Greek archbishop's house at Misitra, a translation in modern Greek of his novel *Atala*. And there was an excellent *auberge anglais*, where roast beef and port wine were served. There were generally some Englishmen travelling along the road in Greece, and these travellers had brought about a great improvement in the accommodation " everywhere in Europe."

Lamartine was the most eminent Frenchman after Chateaubriand who visited the Near East and wrote a book on it. Quite a large literature was growing up on the subject. When that pleasant antiquarian the Honourable Robert Curzon, Junior, sat down to write the narrative of his journeys he apologized in the Preface for " presenting to the public another book of travels in the East, when it is already overwhelmed with little volumes about palm-trees and camels and reflections on the Pyramids." Yet the little volumes—some, in fact, rather large—preserved the memory of a way of life and a society which have passed away. Lamartine's is one of the bigger books. This royalist and sweet poet of solitude felt out of place in France after the July Revolution, and so set forth with his English wife, his daughter of fourteen (who died on the journey), three friends, and six servants in a 250 tons' ' brick,' the *Alceste*, from Marseilles in July 1832. It was a literary age. The voyage of the *Alceste* was to last two years; the captain had prepared for this not only by laying in large stocks of provisions, but also by accumulating a library of five hundred books—history, poetry, and volumes of travels.

The Mediterranean was still beset with pirates, not those of Algiers, who had been curbed by Lord Exmouth's expedition in 1816, and finally by the French conquest in 1830, but Greek pirates, the scum of the War of Independence, which had just been legally concluded. One shipload of pirates came close up to the *Alceste*, but sheered off when they saw the guns primed and the passengers and crew standing by to defend themselves. " Never have I seen faces on which crime, murder, and pillage were written in more hideous characters," wrote Lamartine. The captain of a British naval frigate, Edmund Lyons (later a distinguished admiral), offered to escort the *Alceste* to Nauplia; and as he sailed faster than the French ship lowered a boat and effected the difficult operation of attaching a cable and towing the *Alceste* along. Captain Lyons, to whom Lamartine was quite unknown, visited him and his family on the *Alceste* several times. *Voilà l'officier anglais dans toute sa générosité personnelle*, writes Lamartine; *voilà l'homme dans toute la dignité de son caractère et de sa mission.*

The War of Greek Independence had been concluded by the treaty of May 7, 1832, but the Turkish evacuation had not yet been effected. The Greek Parliament sat at Nauplia in a wooden shed. The deputies arrived on horseback, and took their seats on plain wooden benches raised up on sand. They spoke well, without confusion, without interruption, in terms firm, measured, harmonious. Outside Nauplia the country was filled with anarchy and civil war. The French army which had driven out the Egyptian troops of Ibrahim Pasha was still in the Morea. There was a Turkish commander in Athens, which was a little town of about 15,000 inhabitants, with one hotel. Lamartine found still greater ruin there than there was when Chateaubriand visited Athens in 1806; for in the war it had been " pulverized " successively by Greek and Turkish cannon. Although the long Greek War of Independence was over, and Greece declared free and independent by the Treaty of London, May 7, 1832, the Turkish garrison did not leave Athens until April 1833. Meanwhile Nauplia was the capital. The first King of Greece, Otto of Bavaria, resided there. On December 13, 1834, Athens was legally established as the capital of Greece, and Otto transferred his residence to it. The first Athenian gymnasium, or secondary school, was opened in 1836, and the University of Athens in 1837.[1] The Greeks were interested in their ancient history and in general culture, and were assisted by a fairly numerous foreign ' colony,' among which was the eminent

[1] See W. Miller, " The Centenary of Athens as Capital," in *History*, December 1834.

George Finlay, who had fought for Greece, and now adopted the country as his own, living in Athens until his death in 1875. Lamartine saw nothing of the development of Athens. He was only nine days there, and went from it in the ' brick ' to Beyrout. General Sir Richard Church, who began his experience of the Near East as an English officer commissioned to raise a regiment of Greek irregulars in the Napoleonic war on the Adriatic coast, " clung to the Mediterranean throughout his life." Commander-in-Chief of the Greek forces in the War of Independence, he spent all the rest of his life in Greece as his adopted country, and died, universally respected, in 1873. In his young days he had been prominent in " a band of distinguished men who represented a new enthusiasm in Europe " —the enthusiasm for the freedom of nations.[1]

Syria had just (1832) been conquered by Ibrahim Pasha, whose father, Mehemet Ali, Pasha of Egypt, had quarrelled with Sultan Mahmoud over the price of the Egyptian intervention in Greece in 1827. When Ibrahim was riding at the head of his army into Beyrout an enormous serpent slid out of some brushwood and raised its head almost under the horse's feet. Attendants hurried forward to kill the animal, but Ibrahim, waving them back, drew his sword and with one sweep cut off the serpent's head. This was looked upon as an augury of victory, for nothing in the Moslem world is regarded as mere chance. The campaign was going on all the remainder of the year in the extreme north of Syria.

Lamartine hired five little houses to make one decent dwelling for his family, for he was going to leave them for a while. He next bought fourteen Arab horses and formed a caravan and went off into the Lebanon. His chief object was to visit Lady Hester Stanhope, who had now been settled in her gloomy castle, Djoun, in the Lebanon for about fifteen years. Goethe said that " a man who has been among the palms is never the same again." [2] The career of this remarkable lady seems to confirm the remark.

[1] R. W. Church, " Sir Richard Church," in *Occasional Papers*, ii, 326 ff.
[2] Quoted by H. Temperley, *England and the Near East* (1936), p. x.

Hester Lucy Stanhope, a hard, neurotic woman, was niece of Mr Pitt, and had kept house for him during his last Prime Ministry. After the great statesman's death in 1806 Parliament voted her, in accordance with Pitt's wishes (for he left only debts), a pension of £1200 a year. Lady Hester was then thirty years old. She was not beautiful, though her plain countenance was not unattractive: " homogeneous ugliness " was what she called it. She disliked her own sex, and infinitely preferred the company of men. She was believed to have had one or two love affairs, and seems to have had a serious disappointment at the hands of Lord Granville Leveson-Gower, who was expected to marry her. Later Sir John Moore seems to have been in love with her, and his death at Corunna was a great blow. His last words, spoken to Lady Hester's brother, who was on his staff, were, " Stanhope, remember me to your sister."

In 1810 Lady Hester embarked at Portsmouth, and never returned to England. She took her physician, Dr Charles Meryon, with her. Two other young men, the Marquis of Sligo and Mr Michael Crawford Bruce, who were setting forth on their travels, joined her party. They sailed to Gibraltar, Malta, Athens, Constantinople. The Marquis of Sligo turned back there. Lady Hester took a house at Therapia. She became Bruce's mistress. From Constantinople she and Bruce and Meryon and her women servants went on by ship to Egypt; on the way, at Rhodes, she put on man's dress, Turkish, and wore it for the rest of her life. From Egypt, her *cortège* growing ever larger (for she was recklessly generous), she went into Palestine and visited Jerusalem and other cities; then into Syria, to Damascus, Palmyra, and the dangerous Bedouin-infested deserts. She had adventures with the Arab tribes, and made a great reputation among them as a fearless, generous, and rather mad woman. At Latakia Bruce left her and went home, and Lady Hester became more eccentric than ever. This was in 1813. Four more years passed, partly in wandering among the Arabs, partly settled in a disused monastery called Mar Elias, before she came finally to rest at Djoun, another deserted and ruined monastery in the Lebanon. She spent a lot of money on it, made quite a good garden, built cottages and stables, and filled the place with servants, slaves, and hangers-on of various kinds. She secluded herself like an Oriental, smoked a *chibuq*, and dabbled in magic and astrology. Djoun became a kind of sanctuary for fugitives from the Egyptian pashas, who probably respected the fearless, mad Englishwoman as one stricken by God. The most sensible thing she did was to spend some of her money (a good deal of which was borrowed) on keeping a stable of fine Arab horses, which could be regarded as an investment. One visitor, whose name has not been preserved, about the year 1827, was taken by Lady Hester to the stables, and was shown a horse which, she said, no one must mount. " God has saddled it for His own Son," she continued; " under my protection it awaits its true master." [1] Many travellers tried to visit her, but she only rarely answered their letters with an invitation. As the years went on she became poorer and poorer. No doubt her Oriental servants plundered her, and all the refugees and hangers-on traded upon her good-nature. Meryon, who had left her, but revisited her in 1830, found her living in absolute poverty. Yet she was as proud as Lucifer, and treated the rare visitors whom she admitted with dignified and liberal hospitality. When Meryon, who was a faithful friend, came back again in 1837 he found her seriously ill. She smoked interminably, covering the floor of her bedroom with tobacco and tobacco-ashes.

In 1838 a Turkish money-lender, who had for years been trying to get his money back from Lady Hester, applied to the Foreign Office for help. Lord Palmerston, who liked saving the Government from unnecessary expense, stopped payment of Lady Hester's pension. This only made her furious. She wrote to the Queen, to the Duke of Wellington, and to Palmerston, and vowed that if her pension was not paid she would wall up the gateway of Djoun and stay inside till she died. She believed that her name was familiar in England, and that everybody was still speaking about her; whereas, in truth, she was quite forgotten. In the summer of 1838 she had the gateway of Djoun

[1] Pückler-Muskau, *Tour in Germany, Holland, and England*, iii, 374.

O

walled and settled down to die. She kept up a correspondence with Meryon, and seems to have been moderately contented and cheerful. She had an Italian physician and some native servants. She died on June 23, 1839. The British Consul at Beyrout and William M. Thomson, the Scottish missionary, author of *The Land and the Book* (an excellent work on the Holy Land), rode through the mountains to Djoun and buried her. The Consul's duties as executor were easy: there was nothing of any value in the vast place.

Lady Hester Stanhope was not the only Englishwoman who found her last home in Syria. Lady Ellenborough, after being divorced in 1830 from Lord Ellenborough (later Governor-General of India) for adultery with Prince Schwarzenberg (later Austrian Chancellor), married a Bavarian nobleman, became successively the mistress of Count Theotokes and General Hadjipetros (heroes of the Greek War of Independence) and finally married a Bedouin sheikh and died at Damascus in 1881.

Lamartine wrote to Lady Hester, and obtained from her permission for a visit. He found, on arrival at Djoun, that her ladyship never appeared before three or four in the afternoon. He was given one of the little cells, or single-roomed cottages, of which Djoun consisted, and lunch was brought to him. At three o'clock he was shown by a small negro boy into Lady Hester's room, which was completely dark. A majestic figure, in Oriental clothes, rose from a couch, and Lamartine could just discern the grave, noble countenance of Lady Hester. " You have come far to see a hermit," she said; " be welcome." They had a long talk, chiefly about religion, partly about politics. " Europe is finished; only France has still a great mission to fulfil," said this Amazon who boasted that she had the blood of the Pitts in her veins. After some time a black slave took Lamartine back to his cell, where dinner was served for him alone. When he returned to Lady Hester's chamber she was smoking a pipe. The conversation was resumed, Lady Hester doing most of the talking and smoking pipe after pipe. Every quarter of an hour slaves brought in small cups of coffee. With-

out interrupting her monologue, she next took Lamartine down
into her particular little enclosed garden, a gem of beauty; and
then showed him her horses, including one, particularly graceful, which Lamartine believed that Lady Stanhope reserved for
her riding into Jerusalem when the Second Messiah should
come. The name of Bonaparte also, of course, came up. Lady
Hester seemed to have a fanatical interest in him. The conversation continued nearly all night, for her ladyship's habit of
late rising enabled her to turn night into day. At last she shook
hands with her guest. " We shall see each other frequently
during your travels," she said. " Go and rest, and remember
that you leave a friend in the solitudes of the Lebanon." But
the intrepid Frenchman was to have little rest that night, for
it had already gone; and after his ten hours of conversation with
the mystical Englishwoman he set off on a visit to Beschir, the
emir of the Druses, a Christian and Catholic, who governed the
Lebanon under the protection of Mehemet Ali of Egypt, as he
had formerly done under the protection of the Sultan.[1]

Three years after Lamartine, Kinglake, whose mother had
known Lady Hester's mother at old Lady Chatham's house,
Burton Pynsent, in Somerset, obtained an invitation to visit
Djoun. His experience, narrated in great detail in *Eothen*, followed precisely the same order as Lamartine's, lasted as long,
and was occupied by the same continuous, intense monologue
about religion, magic, politics, Bonaparte, Fox, Pitt, and the
rest of that vanished world in which Lady Hester's mind still
roamed. Prince Pückler-Muskau had audience with her in
1838.

Lamartine's *Voyage en Orient* was continued until July 1833,
when he was at Constantinople in time to see the departure of
the Russian fleet and army. Ibrahim Pasha had completely
defeated the last Turkish army at Konieh, in the Taurus (December 21, 1832), and had been stopped from advancing to
Constantinople only by the diplomatic intervention of the

---

[1] For Beschir, " one of those singular Oriental tyrants whose policy is
cruel and barbarous while their tastes are artistic and refined," see Temperley, *op. cit.*, i, 177–181.

Powers. At the same time, however, Nicholas II of Russia had sent a fleet and army, on invitation from the Sultan Mahmoud II, to the Bosporus. The Russian force remained about six months, departing in July 1833, after concluding a treaty, called the Treaty of Unkiar Skelessi (July 8), for mutual support of the Sublime Porte and the Tsar. It was feared in Europe that Turkey had thus become a protectorate of the Tsar, but the treaty, which was made to endure eight years, was never invoked, and peacefully expired at the end of its period.

Lamartine made his way back through what he called " the eternal forests of Serbia," to Belgrade and Semlin in September 1833. He was impressed with the simplicity and heroism of the Serbian people, who had lately won freedom from the Turks. " The history of this people," he said, " should be sung, not written. It is a poem which is still in progress." [1]

The Honourable Robert Curzon, Junior, belonged to an ancient Norman house which has produced no men considered by the world to be particularly eminent, except his distant kinsman the first and only Marquis Curzon, Viceroy of India under King Edward VII and Secretary of State for Foreign Affairs after the World War. Nevertheless, Robert, who was regarded by his friends as rather an average example of the sort of globe-trotter, took risks and endured hardships that few modern travellers would care to reckon upon as normal incidents of their travels. His work *Visits to the Monasteries in the Levant* gives an account of an aspect of Near Eastern life that is generally ignored. His chief object in visiting these almost inaccessible monasteries was to find ancient manuscripts. " I was the pioneer who first in modern times undertook this sort of literary campaign," he wrote. His investigations were made in 1833, eleven years before the enterprising German scholar Lobegott Friedrich von Tischendorff discovered the *Codex Sinaiticus* in the Convent of St Catherine at Mount Sinai. Robert Curzon found stores of liturgical manuscripts, but no classical works; " so thoroughly were these ancient libraries explored in the fifteenth century that no unknown classic author has been

[1] *Voyage en Orient*, ii, 267.

discovered." [1] The monastic libraries were in a very much neglected condition. Curzon heard of, though he did not visit, a monastery near Cavalla, in Bulgaria, where the monks stood on the bound folios while chanting in chapel, in order to keep their feet off the damp stone floor. Naturally, the damp had penetrated through a large portion of each volume.

The *morale* of the monks was a little difficult for a Westerner to understand. They maintained their religious services regularly and decently. They were hospitable and received the English traveller frankly and kindly. They were not anxious to sell their manuscripts, although themselves taking no interest in them; when they did sell they cheated the buyer " according to their gifts—that is, as far as a total want of principle and understanding enabled them to cheat." [2] Yet the same observer states, " Quietness, simplicity, and a complete ignorance of the world are the usual characteristics of all monks." [3] There was something, too, heroic about them, notwithstanding their unassuming ways. Perched on their crags, or in the wildest, most desolate regions, the monasteries and monastic communities had been repositories of the Christian faith through the centuries. Curzon writes :

From Mount Ararat to Bagdad the different sects of Christians still retain the faith of the Redeemer, whom they have worshipped, according to their various forms, some of them for more than fifteen hundred years; the plague, the famine, and the sword have passed over them, and left them still unscathed, and there is little doubt but that they will maintain the position which they have held so long, till the not far distant period arrives when the conquered empire of the Greeks will again be brought under the dominion of a Christian emperor.

The prophecy has come not very far short of fulfilment. The monasteries of Albania, Meteora, Mount Athos, and Bulgaria are no longer under Turkish dominion, nor are those of Syria, Palestine, Iraq, and Egypt, although there has been no restoration of an Eastern Christian empire.

[1] R. Curzon, *Visits to the Monasteries in the Levant* (ed. 1865), p. x.
[2] *Ibid.*, p. ix.   [3] *Ibid.*, p. 19.

Since Bonaparte's expedition of 1798 Egypt was one of the aims of every Near Eastern traveller. Robert Curzon went there in 1833, just after the end of Mehemet Ali's war with his master the Sultan. He took ship from Malta to Alexandria, touching on the way at Navarino, in Western Greece, where the harbour was still littered with the wreck of the Egyptian fleet, sunk by Admiral Codrington's fleet in 1827, when Mehemet Ali was still faithful to the Sultan and fighting for him in the Greek War.

A. W. Kinglake, a very adventurous student of Lincoln's Inn, not yet called to the Bar, made his great journey to the Near East from Semlin, the Austrian port on the south side of the Danube. Here, in 1835, wheeled traffic stopped, and after cross-ing the Danube the traveller entered into " the Splendour and Havoc of the East." Though the Serbs had become free, Bel-grade was still a Turkish fortress (the Porte's troops were there until 1867). Everybody going to or coming from the East by Semlin had to pass through the Austrian quarantine station.

> If you dare to break the laws of the quarantine, you will be tried with military haste; the court will scream out your sentence to you from a tribunal some fifty yards off; the priest, instead of gently whispering to you the sweet hopes of religion, will con-sole you at duelling distance, and after that you will find your-self carefully shot, and carelessly buried in the ground of the Lazaretto.[1]

Metternich used to say, " Behind the Landstrasse [a cele-brated Viennese street] Asia begins "; but the frontier was really at Semlin and along the Danube, for the whole Otto-man Empire was in quarantine, and the plague effectually divided it from ' Europe.' Armed pickets guarded the line, with the object of shooting ' compromised ' individuals (who in the medical jargon of to-day would be called ' contacts ') who tried to cross the line, as well as with the object of maintaining military defence.

---

[1] A. W. Kinglake, *Eothen* (ed. Routledge), pp. 1–2.

The Moslem quarter of a Serbian, Macedonian, or Bulgarian city was not very inviting.

> You go up, and down, and on, over shelving and hillocky paths, through the narrow lanes walled in by blank, windowless dwellings; you come out upon an open space strewed with the black ruins that some late fire has left; you pass by a mountain of castaway things, the rubbish of centuries, and on it you see numbers of big wolf-like dogs lying torpid under the sun with limbs outstretched to the full, as if they were dead: storks or cranes, sitting fearless upon the low roofs, look gravely down upon you; the still air that you breathe is loaded with scent of citron and pomegranate roots scorched by the sun, or (as you approach the Bazaar) with the dry, dead perfume of strange spices. You long for some signs of life, and tread the ground more heavily, as though you would wake the sleepers with the heel of your boot; but the foot falls noiseless upon the crumbling soil of an Eastern city, and Silence follows you still. Again and again you meet turbans, and faces of men, but they have nothing for you—no welcome—no wonder—no wrath—no scorn—they look upon you as we do upon a December's fall of snow.[1]

Kinglake had his first interview with a pasha at Belgrade. The Ottoman Empire enjoyed a curious quasi-democracy. There was no hereditary privilege, except for the Sultan's family, nor under the uncertain, arbitrary *régime* was there much hereditary wealth. Anybody, however poor or lowly born, might hope to rise to the highest posts if he gained entrance to a public office or to the family of some official. Promotion went by personal favour, and the art of rising was the art of pleasing a superior. High officials retained the manners which had served them well. " You will seldom, I think," wrote Kinglake, " find them wanting in that polished smoothness of manner and those well-undulating tones which belong to the best Osmanlees. . . . They preserve in their high estate those gentle powers of fascination to which they owe their success." [2] The pasha whom Kinglake met was highly interested in railways

---

[1] A. W. Kinglake, *Eothen* (ed. Routledge), pp. 5–6.
[2] *Ibid.*, p. 7.

(which he had never seen), and thought that everything could be done by wheels. He also knew a good deal about the doings of the East India Company, upon which the prestige of England in the East seemed largely to depend. But most of his conversation consisted of elaborate compliments.

Kinglake had a companion whom he calls Methley (the real name is said to be Lord Pollington), for part of his journey, and he had also, of course, a small retinue of servants and a guard as far as Constantinople. The journey from Belgrade to Constantinople, on horseback, took fifteen days. He considered the Balkans to be greatly overrated as a barrier. There was said to be a pyramid of 30,000 skulls, heaped up by the Serbs in their war of independence against the Turks in 1806–15. Kinglake—if it existed—passed it in the dark. The country was quite undeveloped, although the reigning prince, Milosh Obrenovich, was at this time (1835) keeping Baron von Herder, the head of the Saxon Government mines, prospecting in the Serbian mountains for three months.[1] There were no proper roads, and the travellers had to direct themselves largely by compass. After passing through Adrianople Kinglake made more " southing " than he intended, and turned up on the Sea of Marmora.

The party rode along the coastland to Constantinople. After staying there some time they rode by way of the Troas to Smyrna (called by Théophile Gautier *ville à la grace asiatique et voluptueuse*), whence Methley returned to England. Kinglake took ship to Beyrout, and found all the bazaars talking about Lady Hester Stanhope, though people in England had long since forgotten her.

Kinglake's great interest was military history and battles, but in Palestine and Syria he carefully observed the monks, and is very fair in his account of them. They were men of the peasant class, French or Spanish, who had been sent from their home convents to Palestine, as soldiers are quartered in one garrison town or another. They were well-conducted men, punctual

---

[1] *The Life of George Ticknor*, i, 478. Baron von Herder was son of the great Herder, critic and philosopher.

in their ceremonial duties, humble-minded Christians. They knew little about any place outside the Holy Land, except that they took a good deal of interest in Spain. For down to the year 1833 much of the funds for the maintenance of the Roman Catholic monasteries came from Spain, but since the death of Ferdinand VII this source had practically stopped. The Franciscans of Damascus had a very fine wine-cellar, and partook liberally from it. The Jerusalem Roman Catholic monks had shown devoted heroism during the recent great plague, daily ministering to the dying. Twenty-one out of a community of forty lost their lives in this service.

The Church of the Holy Sepulchre at Jerusalem was in possession of Greek monks. On Easter Saturday after prayer from monks fire issued from the Sepulchre. In the year before Kinglake's coming there was a serious riot in the church, caused by the excitement of the crowded mass of pilgrims over delay in the appearance of the fire. From 1833 to 1840 Palestine was subject to Mehemet Ali, and was in the government of Ibrahim Pasha. Although a Mohammedan, Ibrahim had chosen to be present at the ceremony in the church. He fainted in the crush of the riot, and had to be rescued by his soldiery. About two hundred people lost their lives. The Egyptian rule was not liked in Palestine. The Mohammedans of Bethlehem revolted. Ibrahim exterminated them. The Christian population of Bethlehem felt an immense relief, for the severe, Puritan decorum of Mohammedan manners had repressed all cheerfulness in the village.

From Jerusalem Kinglake rode to Cairo. The Palestinian *kans*, or caravanserais, as he described them, were more elaborate than those which Chateaubriand found in Greece. The Palestinian caravanserai formed four sides of a court. The ground floor was used as a warehouse; the first floor was for the guests; the camels were kept in the court, and loading and unloading and any mercantile business was done there. The guest-rooms on the first floor were a series of small cells, opening on to a corridor round the inner side of the court.

The journey across the desert from Gaza to Cairo took ten

days by camel. A travel agent in Gaza made all necessary arrangements beforehand with the Arab tribes along the route. About half-way across the desert Kinglake's party met that of an English officer who was returning home from India. The two Englishmen touched their caps and were passing each other without a word, as if they were in Pall Mall, but the servants all stopped with one accord and fell into conversation; so the masters had, rather shamefacedly, to stop and to exchange some rather formal conversation. Kinglake judged the officer to be a manly, intelligent fellow—" a worthy one of the few thousand strong Englishmen to whom the Empire of India is committed."[1]

Cairo, at this time, was a city estimated by Kinglake to have 200,000 inhabitants, and by Prince Pückler-Muskau to have 600,000, the capital of the *pashalik*, or rather of the empire of that hope of all those who believed in the progress of the Orient, Mehemet Ali. Kinglake hired apartments from Osman Effendi, a Scotsman who had invested in house property. Osman had come out to Egypt as a drummer-boy in " Fraser's force " in 1807. Captured by the Turks, he had been offered the alternatives of death or the Koran. He became a Mohammedan, and served in the Egyptian army which conquered the Wahabis of Arabia. He prospered and saved money. He was now settled down in Cairo, wearing Eastern dress, keeping a *harem* with two slatternly wives, but cherishing three shelves of books, among which was his especial proud possession, *The Edinburgh Cabinet Library*.

Kinglake did not have an audience with Mehemet Ali. The Honourable Robert Curzon was more fortunate when he visited Cairo in 1833. At the interview Mehemet Ali, who was sitting upon a cushion, felt in a pocket for his handkerchief, but could not find it. From the lower end of the room the voice of a servant came, " Feel in the other pocket." " I have not got a handkerchief," said the Pasha. " Yes, you have," insisted the servant. " No, I have not," maintained the Pasha. " Yes, you have," said the servant. At last the servant advanced up to the Pasha, felt in the pocket of the jacket, poked all round the

[1] *Eothen*, p. 184.

Pasha's waist, to see if it were under the shawl; then he took
hold of his master, turned him half over on the divan, and
looked under him to see that he was not sitting on the handkerchief; next pushed him over on to the other side; at last the
servant thrust his hand into one of the voluminous pockets of
the Pasha's trousers and brought out a snuff-box, a rosary,
and several other things. This would not do, so he went round
the divan and dived into the other trouser pocket, and brought
out the handkerchief. During all this handling and turning of
him the Pasha remained perfectly quiet and passive.[1] Disraeli,
who visited Mehemet Ali at Cairo in 1831, received the same
impression of a simple and gentle man.[2]

Prince Pückler-Muskau saw Mehemet Ali frequently, and
made a " land voyage " with him through part of Egypt.
Mehemet Ali, he says, was a " low-sized, kind-looking old
man "; his manners were simple and naturally dignified. Nor,
when Pückler knew him, was he swathed in masses of Oriental
drapery, but he wore " a simple brown-fur garb," and on his
head a fez. A more detailed description by the same author is:

> He is now a man past sixty years of age, with small and spark-
> ling eyes, the fiery and cunning, though somewhat unsteady, ex-
> pression of which he tries very characteristically to soften and
> conceal, as much as possible, underneath the shawl which forms
> his headdress and which is drawn down low over his forehead.
> He is without the least affectation of business importance, easy
> of access, though of indefatigable industry, affable to every one,
> an enemy to ostentation and pomp, discreet to an extreme, and
> certainly one of the most cunning of the cunning.[3]

Mehemet Ali's progressiveness did not extend to the abolition of slavery. There was a great slave market in Cairo, and
although white slaves could not be sold to Christians, they
could be sold to Orientals. Kinglake visited the market, and
saw one white slave, a woman, exposed for sale. No price was
advertised in this case, but apparently prices for slaves were

[1] R. Curzon, op. cit., p. 66.
[2] W. F. Moneypenny and G. E. Buckle, The Life of Disraeli (1929), i, 180.
[3] Pückler-Muskau, Egypt under Mehemet Ali (1845), ii, 39.

not high. Théophile Gautier saw at Smyrna a young negress exposed for sale for 250 francs.[1] The slave market, as described by Pückler-Muskau, was a loathsome and disgusting place. The female slaves, who were the greater number, were exposed for sale not with a view to domestic service, but concubinage, and were discussed and handled and bargained over with this in view. Pückler bought a beautiful Abyssinian slave, who, he says, as soon as she joined his party became free.

Mehemet Ali was efficient in his way, but he was a terrible monopolist. *Fermier et douanier impitoyable*, is Chateaubriand's description of him; but to Pückler-Muskau Mehemet vigorously defended himself, saying that unless his Government had gone into industry there would have been no industry in Egypt at all.[2]

It was natural for the Egyptian Viceroy to maintain an army, but the Egyptian navy must be considered something of a marvel. The rotting hulks and wreckage which Kinglake saw in Navarino Bay in 1835 had long since been written off. Pückler-Muskau, who visited the dockyards and knew the French officials there in 1837, declared that the Arsenal at Alexandria was a " colossal establishment," and that the fleet comprised 33 ships, with 200,000 *personnel*, and 1,482 guns.[3] Said Bey, Mehemet Ali's second son, his successor as ruler of Egypt, was trained as a sailor.

Pückler visited the State cotton manufactories operated by Mehemet Ali, and found them to be large and clean, well managed by capable Frenchmen; the cotton and sugar plantations of Mehemet and Ibrahim up the Nile were given similar commendation. The *fellahin* were forced to work, but Pückler says that they looked strong, cheerful, and well fed, and that they had wages, punctually paid.

In every province there were several " primary " schools maintained by the Government; Mehemet Ali had established

[1] Gautier, *Constantinople*, p. 61.

[2] Chateaubriand, *Mémoires d'outre-tombe*, v, 67; Pückler-Muskau, *Egypt under Mehemet Ali*, ii, 39.

[3] Pückler-Muskau, *Egypt under Mehemet Ali*, i, 92.

higher schools and also technical colleges—schools of artillery, marine, medicine, languages, and music. There was a system of State scholarships, to enable promising pupils to attend these higher educational institutions, of 100 to 200 piastres (25s. to 50s.) monthly. Pückler visited a high school which had 2000 pupils, well housed and well fed. A considerable number of Egyptian scholars were sent to study in Europe.[1]

Mehemet Ali's power was, probably, well established in Egypt, and his family still has the throne there. In Syria, however, in spite of his hosts of disciplined troops, Mehemet Ali's power was considered, even by the depressed Syrians, to be transitory. " Every peasant practically felt, and knew, that in Vienna or Petersburg or London, there were four or five pale-looking men who could pull down the star of the Pasha with shreds of paper and ink."[2] They saw too, " that the person, the property, and even the dignity of the humblest European was guarded with the most careful solicitude." In those days the West was dominant, and the fate of the East was in its hands.

Most observers seemed to hold that the Turkish Empire was doomed to disappear from Europe. In a remarkable memorandum on Turkey, submitted to Palmerston on December 19, 1832, when Turkey was being attacked by the army of Mehemet Ali, the British ambassador, Stratford Canning, wrote: " The Turkish Empire has reached, in its decline, that critical point, at which it must either revive and commence a fresh era of prosperity, or fall into a state of complete dissolution." It was the second alternative that he thought the more likely, at any rate if the British Government did not make up its mind to give Turkey immediate and direct support. " That Empire may fall to pieces at all events; and he must be a bold man who would undertake to answer for its being saved by any effort of human policy. But His Majesty's Government may rest assured that to leave it to itself is to leave it to its enemies."[3]

[1] Pückler-Muskau, op. cit., i, 203, 270.   [2] Eothen, p. 254.

[3] Stratford Canning's memorandum, December 19, 1832, which is a lengthy document and has never been published, is in the Public Record Office, listed as F.O. Turkey, 211.

The British Government decided to give no material support; and in the following year, June 8, 1833, the Russian Government concluded with the Porte the Treaty of Alliance of Unkiar Skelessi. This treaty, which became celebrated, seemed designed to make Turkey into the vassal state of Russia. Chateaubriand, writing about 1835, declared: *La Turquie d'Europe, devenue vassale de la Russie en vertu du Traité d'Unkiar Skélessi, n'existe plus.*[1] Nevertheless by 1839 the Russian Government had decided not to use its rights under the Treaty of Unkiar Skelessi, and two years later the alliance expired. Turkey in Europe continued to exist.

[1] *Mémoires d'outre-tombe*, v, 67.

CHAPTER XIV

RUSSIAN AUTOCRACY

THE Russians were the only European people whose condition was not materially improved in the late eighteenth and early nineteenth centuries. In some respects the condition of the people deteriorated. Catherine II (1762–96), by gifts of Imperial property and free peasants to favourites, added about 800,000 to the serf population, which already was about 90 per cent. of the whole people. Paul I (1796–1801) did something to ameliorate their condition; he forbade, by royal *ukase*, the nobles to employ their serfs on field-labour on Sundays and holidays. It appears to be impossible to discover how far this regulation was observed. The intention of Alexander I to forbid the selling of serfs away from the land to which they were attached was defeated by the opposition of the nobility. Serfdom could not be maintained without discipline, and the small class of noble-proprietors must have had considerable cause for anxiety in regard to the maintenance of their ownership over practically a whole population; but the inhuman beatings, of which there is ample evidence, were more than were necessary for disciplinary purposes, and were due partly to the proprietors' fears, partly to the callousness which the system engendered, and largely to the low state of civilization of the whole country, itself the result of the horrible servile system. For this did not merely keep the peasants in a brutal condition; it brutalized the proprietors. These might, and in many cases did, according to their riches and inclination, acquire some culture; but as a whole their moral condition seems to have been debased through their practically uncontrolled power over the bodies of their tenants, a power which killed the sense of responsibility and, indeed, of humanity. Further than this, it was the servile system which produced not merely a general low condition of morality among the proprietors, but also made possible the existence of the occasional " monsters " whom Alexander Herzen describes in his memoirs, hedonistic, sadistic monsters of the worst medieval and Bluebeard type.

> My uncle was one of those monsters of eccentricity which only Russia and the conditions of Russian society can produce. A man of good natural parts, he spent his whole life in committing follies which often rose to the dignity of crimes. . . . He was nearly murdered by his serfs for interference with their daughters and for acts of cruelty; he owed his life to his coachman and the speed of his horses. After this experience he settled in Moscow. Disowned by his relations and by people in general, he lived quite alone in a large house on the Tver Boulevard, bullying his servants in town and ruining his serfs in the country. He collected a large library and a whole *harem* of country girls, and kept both these departments under lock and key. . . . Our servants would not walk past his house, for fear of meeting him, and turned pale at the sight of him; the women dreaded his insolent persecution, and the domestic servants had prayer offered in the church that they might never serve him.[1]

Serfdom was widely recognized in Russia to be the plague of the whole country. Adam Smith's *Wealth of Nations* was circulating in Russian translation, and convinced readers that forced labour was uneconomic. In the years 1816–19 Alexander freed the serfs in the Baltic provinces of Estonia, Curland, Livonia, without, however, securing them any land at all. This was all that the ' liberal ' Tsar accomplished for freedom; and the Crown still kept its twenty million State serfs, as compared with forty-five million privately owned serfs. Servile mutinies were common, and because they were feared were repressed with all the more cruelty. Philoret, Archbishop of Moscow, preached in 1831 that no man should be merely the instrument of another; he was influenced by " the vague Christian social-

[1] *The Memoirs of Alexander Herzen* (trans. J. D. Duff, 1923), p. 21. The period referred to in the passage quoted above is the reign of Alexander I, 1801–25.

ism of Lacordaire." [1] His courage was rewarded. In 1833 Nicholas I forbade the selling of serfs without the land; and in 1840 manufacturing companies were authorized to set free serfs who so desired, and were paid by Government thirty-six roubles *per head* for loss of property. Textile factories were developing in Russia, and the manufacturers readily availed themselves of the authority to free their serfs and to employ paid labour, which was more productive. Landed proprietors always had power to free their serfs (receiving no State indemnity), but had made very little use of this power; the vast majority of the mass of serfs had to wait until 1861 for their freedom. Not all serfs were badly treated. Herzen's father paid his house serfs wages, and seldom had them beaten; instead he had refractory serfs enlisted in the army for the full period of twenty years, a fate which they dreaded infinitely more than beating. Some serfs prospered. Herzen's uncle had one who cooked very cleverly and was allowed to seek his fortune; he became *chef* of the English Club in Moscow and saved money— " but with the noose of serfdom still round his neck." Another of this enlightened proprietor's serfs passed through the College of Medicine and became a physician. But serfdom dogged him as it dogged the *chef* at the English Club, and both came to a bad end.

Education in Russia was only for the nobility and *bourgeoisie*, who numbered altogether about five million out of the total population of fifty million. There were some secondary schools, gymnasiums; but the children of the nobility were mainly educated by tutors and were largely brought up by serfs. They were never left alone; a servant even accompanied them down stairs. German tutors, men of very inferior education and culture, were kept in the noble families, to take the boys out for walks and to converse with them, rather than to teach them anything. Governesses were also employed, and visiting tutors (men) of better attainments than the resident Germans; priests also were employed to give instruction in religion and Latin. If a young noble became a student at the university he had a

---

[1] *Op. cit.*, p. 153.

P

valet with him who accompanied him to the lecture-room and waited for him in the entrance-hall.

Russia was fairly well supplied with universities. There were in Russia proper Moscow, Petersburg, Kharkov, Kazan; Vilna, in Poland (suppressed in 1831), and Dorpat, in Livonia. Moscow University had six hundred students; the total number of university students would be between 4000 and 5000. Herzen says that down to 1848 the universities were " purely democratic." They were open to every one who could pass the entrance examination—" provided he was not a serf, or a peasant detained by the village community." The universities were, in fact, fairly free, and were the soundest institutions in Russian life, although official " curators " kept an eye on students and teachers, as was the case also in German universities under the Carlsbad Decrees of 1819.

Moscow was the most eminent Russian university. The ancient capital had recovered its prestige as a consequence of the events of 1812. By the year 1820 the university had become famous, and was exercising a profound influence upon Russian youth. The repression of opinion which took place after the Decembrist rising of 1825 checked the progress of Moscow, but it resumed its advance after a few years, and in 1840 was at the height of its fame. " Moscow University," writes Herzen, who was there for four years in 1829-33, " was a successful institution." Nearly all the professors were zealous, highly instructed, and efficient. They were open to ideas from the West, and when Alexander Humboldt, the naturalist and traveller, visited Moscow they gave him an enthusiastic welcome. Arriving at the university hall in a simple blue coat, he was rather taken aback to be met by all the professors " wearing full uniform and their orders, looking most martial, with swords, and three-cornered hats tucked under their arms "; still more at being greeted with " Humboldt, Prometheus of our time! " Trying to see some of the records of scientific observation made by the university *savants*, he was put off by the rector with a relic plaited out of the hair of Peter the Great; but he did ultimately have some scientific conversation.

The great era of Moscow University came to an end in 1848. The Revolution in France and Central Europe alarmed Nicholas I. He reduced the numbers attending the universities to three hundred students each, reinforced the control and inspection, and forbade the study of constitutional law. The great days of the university were over.

The most characteristic features of Russian life in the nineteenth century were the autocracy and the bureaucracy. No other country of Europe had anything really like them. The Tsar was in theory quite absolute; and Alexander I and Nicholas I, both very strong-minded men, made the theory into fact. The only effective check on their absolutism was the unwillingness, laziness, or corruption of the bureaucracy; but the Tsar, provided that he could have his orders properly transmitted through the bureaux and their agents, was omnipotent. Constitutional check on the Tsar there was none. In 1809–12 Speranski, " the most remarkable Russian statesman of the nineteenth century," son of a village priest, professor of philosophy at the ecclesiastical academy of Petersburg, was Alexander's chief adviser, head of the Imperial office, or ' Chancellery.' In a series of studies and memoranda Speranski elaborated a constitution for Russia, with central executive council, legislature, judiciary, and with a system of local government. Only the first step was taken in the execution of this design. The administrative boards, or ' colleges,' established by Peter the Great were suppressed and departmental Ministers were instituted, meeting together under the Tsar as a Council of Ministers. Before any further steps could be taken the Napoleonic invasion of 1812 caused a reaction against Western enlightenment, and Speranski was dismissed. As the Council of Ministers was composed exclusively of high bureaucrats (there being no legislative assembly to provide politicians) the bureaucracy was practically unchecked. The nobility met occasionally in provincial assemblies under the local ' marshal of the nobility,' but these were merely deliberative bodies, without authority to make acts or to issue orders.

After the death of Alexander I the bureaucratic *régime*

became more elaborate, more complicated, more interfering. Nicholas I, alarmed by the Decembrist rising of 1825, and devoutly convinced both of the necessity of autocracy and of the corruptibility of the bureaucracy, added still more bureaux to transmit his commands and to control his officials. The result was more writing, reporting, " memorializing "—more *paperasserie*. And in the long chain of routine, with human agents of inferior moral calibre reporting on every request of the citizen at every stage, the opportunities for miscarriage of justice were infinite. Herzen has described the typical bureau and inferior bureaucracy. He wrote:

> One of the saddest consequences of the revolution effected by Peter the Great is the development of the official class in Russia. These *chinoviks* are an artificial, ill-educated, and hungry class, incapable of anything except office work, and ignorant of every-thing except official papers. They form a kind of lay clergy, officiating in the law-courts and police-offices, and sucking the blood of the nation with thousands of dirty, greedy mouths. . . .
>
> There, in those grimy offices which we walk through as fast as we can, men in shabby coats sit and write; first they write a rough draft, and copy it out on stamped paper—and individuals, families, and whole villages are injured, terrified, and ruined. The father is sent to a distance, the mother is sent to prison, the son to the army; it all comes upon them as a clap of thunder, and in most cases it is undeserved. The object of it all is money. Pay up! If you don't. . . .[1]

And they were tyrants too. When a Jack-in-office " hears himself shouting," wrote Herzen, " he turns into a wild beast." The only way to prevent this is to begin shouting at him first, and then he is cowed.

Yet the prime cause of all this horror of misery and terror was not the bureaucracy, but the autocracy—the lack of self-government, of freedom—the fact that official leave had to be obtained for almost every sort of activity, so that opportunities for procrastination, vexation, blackmail, and petty tyranny were innumerable. Even in later years, with the help of the telephone

[1] *The Memoirs of Alexander Herzen*, pp. 307–308.

and telegraph, it was almost impracticable for the central offices, which were fairly honest, to keep control; before the days of rapid communication it was quite impossible. The vast petty official class, spread over all Russia and Siberia, was really sovereign. " All measures of the central Government are emasculated before they get there, and all its purposes are distorted; it is deceived and cheated, betrayed and sold, and all the time an appearance of servile fidelity is kept up, and official procedure is punctually observed." Herzen adds, " Two things are needed to cope with it—publicity and an entirely different organization of the whole machine."

Alexander I's *velléités* towards liberalism, never very strong, disappeared altogether about the year 1820. His former tutor, César-Frédéric Laharpe, had influence with him in the liberal direction down to 1814 or 1815, but not afterwards. Laharpe, who had the rank of a general, outlived his master, and was visited by Ticknor at Bern, his home, in 1835. He retained his interest in Russia, and talked much about Russian affairs, but was never consulted. Alexander in his last years, and after him Nicholas I, tried to shut out the West. The ideas of the West, however, had already entered—in 1789 and the following years, and particularly in 1814, when the Russian officers returned from the War of Liberation. Some Guards officers formed in 1816 a society for the enlightenment and education of the people, beginning with their own troops, whom they treated in a humane manner. This society and another of the same kind attracted considerable support. They made little headway, however, in face of the uncompromising resistance of Arakcheev, an ill-educated but capable reactionary to whom Alexander gave his confidence after the fall of Speranski. Driven underground, the societies became secret and revolutionary. The death of Alexander I on December 1, 1825, anticipated a revolution in favour of a constitution. There was an ambiguous period of three weeks when people did not know whether the Archduke Constantine (elder brother), who stayed at Warsaw and sent a renunciation of the throne, or the Archduke Nicholas was Tsar. The plotters pushed on their preparations, and Nicholas, warned about them, hastily had himself proclaimed Tsar (December 26, 1825). On the same day the plotters raised a rebellion in the garrison of St Petersburg; only one Guards regiment and a few isolated companies rose, and the rebellion was easily suppressed. Its main importance is that it confirmed the absolutist tendencies of Nicholas, and made him the unswerving opponent of every liberal idea. After this Russia became the complete police state. Herzen wrote, " If you spoke above your breath you would spend the whole day wondering whether the police would be down upon you." The division or opposition between Government and intelligentsia made the Government ignorant of the public opinion of the country; it had to rely solely on the bureaucracy for information. The fear of revolution haunted Nicholas. The revolt of Poland, 1830–31, which was suppressed only after hard fighting and with the greatest difficulty, naturally strengthened his bias. The Polish constitution, of course, was suppressed. The legend of Russian invincibility, the belief abroad in the inexhaustible resources of Russia, and the personal autocracy of this handsome, strong-minded man made Nicholas I the most powerful statesman of Europe for thirty years, the head of the conservative and, as they called themselves, the anti-revolutionary forces. In Germany and, indeed, all over Central Europe there was a veritable Russian domination. Lonely and conscious of being hated, Nicholas was filled with self-pity, and regarded himself as a martyr to duty. " *Je suis né pour souffrir*," he said. Although his intervention in Hungary in 1849 was fatal to the revolution there, and though his word, down to the Crimean War, was unchallenged in Central Europe, he knew at last that he was a failure. His sudden death in the middle of the Crimean War was imputed, no doubt wrongly, to suicide. *Tædium vitæ*, disgust at life, was the chief cause of his, as of Alexander I's, death.

For some fifteen years before Nicholas died the Russian intelligentsia, the product chiefly of Moscow University, without caste, made up from nobles and *bourgeoisie*, was divided between the Slavophils and Occidentals. Curiously, both groups, Slavophil and Occidental, were the product of foreign influence.

The Slavophils were led by German philosophy, by Schelling, to believe in their peculiar spirit, their mystic personality—in a word, to be race-conscious. They held that Russia's religion marked her off from the West. Orthodoxy supported autocracy; and the Slavophils recognized a mystical communion between autocracy and the people. Orthodoxy, autocracy, nationality—these ideas expressed the Slavophil creed, and they entirely concurred with the view of the Tsar and the high bureaucracy. Thus, Slavophilism was in the ascendant in 1850.

The Occidentals denied the primacy of religion in defining national life; they averred (and experience seems to have justified them) that there is no need artificially to cultivate the national spirit, " for the national character manifests itself ineluctably in the popular genius." Civilization, they contended, was a universal thing; the Russians did not differ fundamentally from other peoples, but were only less advanced. The reform movement of Peter the Great was in the right direction; it only needed to be continued.[1]

Some young men were feeling the influence of French Socialism. " The simple liberalism of 1826, which, by degrees, took in France the form sung by Béranger and preached by men like Lafayette and Benjamin Constant, lost its power over us after the destruction of Poland."[2] Saint-Simon, Fourier, and Enfantin, French Radical Socialists, began to be regarded as prophets. But the views of the 'advanced' present and former students of Moscow and Petersburg were really political rather than social: they thought that a federal system for Russia was the cure for the evils of bureaucracy and the police state; and they advocated, of course, the freedom of the serfs.

The police, naturally, were alive to the ferment. In 1835 Alexander Herzen was condemned at Moscow to penal servitude in Siberia, because he was suspected of socialism and kept company with suspected people. In 1840 Slavophils and Occidentals were alike powerful at Moscow University, then in its most brilliant period. It was now no longer Guards officers, as

[1] Milioukov, *Histoire de Russie*, ii, 791.
[2] *The Memoirs of Alexander Herzen*, p. 188.

in the years 1815–25, who supported the cause of progress, but students, professors, and journalists, although there was no political Press, but only a few literary journals. St Petersburg too was having a brilliant period. In 1849 a number of young men had a ' study-group ' for reading and discussion of the works of Fourier. The police broke it up, and the members were condemned to Siberia. Among them was a man of twenty-eight, Feodor Dostoievsky, who after a brief experience of service in the army had settled down to the career of writer in St Petersburg. He spent seven years there; and on his return became Russia's most ' Russian ' novelist.

Herzen is a type of the young socialists; Dostoievsky, though condemned as a socialist, was really, or at any rate soon became, a passionate Slavophil. Turgeniev was a ' Westerner,' or Occidental. Tolstoi was all three things.

The nineteenth century among its many achievements has the long social novel, *Pickwick*, *Vanity Fair*, *Soll und Haben*, *War and Peace*, *Les Misérables*. The last two are the biggest —in theme, conception, size. Both *War and Peace* (first volume, 1864) and *Les Misérables* (1862), published in the latter half of the nineteenth century, belong really to the earlier half—in scene, in material, in treatment. Tolstoi and Victor Hugo were grown men by the year 1848. Hugo describes the post-Napoleonic age which he lived through in his fervid, observant youth; Tolstoi describes the war of 1806 and 1812, but the war he knew by experience was the siege of Sebastopol in 1855. Hugo's book belongs to the literature of revolt; his theme is the outcast, the just man condemned by law, hunted by Society. Tolstoi's theme is something finer—courage, self-forgetfulness, family life, the ideal of the gentleman, and the spirit of the common man.

War and Peace has almost no beginning, and certainly has no ending: it just breaks off, unfinished. It is a story of two families, the Bolbonskis and the Rostovs, their friendships and loves, good and bad fortune, and the whole vivid life which makes a family a social world in itself. The other big aspect of the book is war decided in the long run, not by the generals who make plans and mismanage them, but by the dumb, wise spirit of the people; and the successful commander is not the brilliant, decisive genius Napoleon, but the aged Kutusov, who sits quietly in his chair, ruminating, receptive, in touch with his soldiers, in touch with the people, gradually forming his decision upon their unspoken behest.

There is no artistry in the book; it is no *chef-d'œuvre* of elegance and finish, like Turgeniev's *Fathers and Children* or *Virgin Soil*; nor is it the red-hot outpouring of a volcanic nature, like Dostoievsky's *Idiot* or *Crime and Punishment*. It is Slavophil in its rather mystical view of the spirit of the people; it is Occidental in its liberalism; it is cosmopolitan in its large humanity. In its neglect of the classical, its carelessness of form, its abundance of feeling, it is Romantic. Like *Les Misérables* it contains essays and aphorisms, portraits, descriptions, the great stage of history. And like *Les Misérables* it is a human work, in which its age lives and the men and women speak, think, feel, and act. Goethe, Hugo, Tolstoi, though most of their active life and work fell outside the Romantic Age, are its biggest interpreters: *Wilhelm Meister* has the spirit of youth; *Les Misérables* the spirit of revolt; *War and Peace* the spirit of humanity, the common joys and sorrows and creative activity of the family and of the nation—the nation which is the particular or personal manifestation of universal humanity.

CHAPTER XV

TOURING

THE first half of the nineteenth century had, at any rate
from the point of view of social history, much in common
with the eighteenth century, which in many respects seemed to
stop not in 1789 nor 1800 nor 1815, but only in 1848. Society,
in the large sense of the word, was mobile. It is true that careers
were not so international between 1815 and 1848 as they were
between 1715 and 1789. There was nobody in the nineteenth
century like Casanova, who flitted from city to city literally
throughout the length and breadth of Europe, made a good
income, lived softly, and was received into the best Society.
Europe in the eighteenth century was essentially cosmopolitan;
and, however high the praises of nationalism may be sung, it
is a pale thing compared with the brilliance of cosmopolitanism, the highest social expression of civilized man. The Romantic Age could not escape the consequences of the Great War,
which left its poison behind it. Yet the people of the early nineteenth century still retained something of the reasonableness,
the humanity, and the urbanity of the Age of Reason. And they
still roamed over Europe out of sheer curiosity and intellectual
and social interest. The Peace of 1814 came as a great release
of the peaceful energies of people. Eager, observant Americans
came over to Europe. " They are treated," wrote George Ticknor, " with the most distinguished kindness and courtesy wherever they are known to be such." [1]

It was not only the rich who travelled. Students wandered
up and down the Rhine, knapsack on back, like Longfellow's
Hyperion. Henry Crabb Robinson was an articled clerk preparing for the Bar when an uncle died, leaving him £100 a

[1] *The Life of George Ticknor*, i, 54 (Letter of May 26, 1815).

year. The young man (he was then twenty-five years old) left the law for the time being and went to Germany in 1801. This visit, one of several, lasted for five years. Crabb Robinson resided first at Frankfurt, where he was admitted into the stimulating if rather Bohemian literary circle of the Brentanos. A little later he went to Weimar. There he met Wieland, aged, but still witty, vigorous, and a somewhat terrifying freethinker: " He is not less universally admired in Germany than Voltaire was in France." After Wieland Goethe, " the most oppressively handsome man I ever saw." The next visit was made to Herder, who in any place but Weimar would have held the first rank, and who in his person and bearing impressed every one with the feeling that he belonged to the highest class of men. Next Friedrich Gentz, a distinguished ' publicist,' to use the German term, the eminent political writer and statesman. After Gentz Schiller: " There was in him a mixture of the wildness of genius and the awkwardness of the student." Finally Kotzebue: " I drank tea with him, and found him a lively little man with small black eyes." Besides these great men, Crabb Robinson was also received in very friendly spirit by a student of the University of Jena called Kölle, who took him to a concert of students and talked with him enthusiastically about the poets and philosophers.

Leaving Weimar, he walked with two German friends through the Fichtelgebirge, and then went to Berlin. From there in 1802 he journeyed to Ansbach, Würzburg, and Erlangen, a university town, where he was " pleased with the gentlemanly appearance of the students, though they had not the dashing impudence of the Cantabs or Oxonians "; Nuremberg, " one of the most curious and national of cities "; and so back to Frankfurt, where he had a long talk about Wordsworth and the English poets with Friedrich Schlegel. The next journey of Crabb Robinson was to Giessen, an " uninteresting " university town; next, to the university town of Marburg, where he lodged in the same house as Savigny, at that time a young *Privat Dozent* of the university, soon to be the most famous professor of law in Europe; " he became head of the historical school of law, as opposed to the codifying school, of which in modern times Bentham was the most eminent advocate." After about six weeks at Marburg Robinson went with Christian Brentano to Jena and entered himself as a student at the university. " I took up my residence in agreeable apartments (at an annual cost of rather less than seven pounds), and was at once introduced to a social circle which rendered my stay there, till the autumn of 1809, one of the happiest periods of my life." [1] All this on £100 a year!

Victor Cousin was a young professor of the Sorbonne. He was travelling in Germany in 1825, and was arrested as a political suspect. Students and scholars have always managed to travel since the time of Abelard, or, indeed, much earlier. Parents could generally provide something towards expenses, or the home university might offer a *bourse*, or there was always the possibility of a private tutorship in a foreign family or in charge of a rich young traveller.

Besides student travellers, who are never rich, there were other mobile, observant, and invariably cosmopolitan travellers, the painters. J. M. W. Turner throughout the first half of the nineteenth century went about in France, Germany, Switzerland, and Italy, mostly on foot, painting *The Rivers of France* or making illustrations for *Childe Harold's Pilgrimage*, painting Rhineland or Venetian scenes. And besides students and painters there were always adventurous and inquisitive young men, like Bayard Taylor, who left a Pennsylvanian printing-house at the age of nineteen and began (in 1844) his travels afoot over Europe. Even artisans had opportunities for travel and for foreign residence. The career of William Cockerill, the great ironmaster of Liége, is well known. He was a Lancashire artisan who travelled through Sweden and Russia, earning his living as he went, before he settled down at Seraing, on the Meuse, and began to make cannon for Napoleon I. Henry Crabb Robinson in 1801 met a Welshman at Chemnitz, by trade a watchmaker, who was in charge of a factory belonging to the Elector of Saxony, and was making " £200 a year and

---

[1] *The Diary of Henry Crabb Robinson*, i, 39-65.

perquisites." [1] The German traveller Kohl at St Petersburg about 1840 noted that " a multitude of German, English, and French mechanics and tradesmen had hung out their signs." English engineers were numerous on the Continent; but commercial travellers were seldom or never met with before 1850.

Although people of fairly moderate means, and even some poor people, could travel, it was in the main the comfortable class, the *bourgeoisie aisée* or nobility, who engaged in this wholesome activity; and on the whole the *bourgeoisie* rather more than the nobility. Thackeray in *The Newcomes* has described a family of this comfortable, middle-class kind travelling to Baden-Baden about 1835:

> They all travelled to Coblentz, Mayence, and Frankfurt together, making the journey which everybody knows, and sketching the mountains and castles we all of us have sketched. . . . The family travelled with a pair of those carriages which used to thunder along the Continental roads a dozen years since, and from the interior, box and rumble, discharge a dozen English people at the hotel gates. [2]

John Ruskin describes his actual experiences of travelling to Switzerland about the year 1833 in *Prœterita*. The first thing which the Ruskin family had to do was to choose a carriage from " the hireable reserves at Mr Hopkinson's, of Long Acre."

> The poor modern slaves and simpletons who let themselves be dragged like cattle, or felled timber, through the countries they imagine themselves visiting, can have no conception whatever of the complex joys, and ingenious hopes, connected with the choice and arrangement of the travelling carriage in old times. The mechanical questions first, of strength—easy rolling—steady and safe poise of persons and luggage; the general stateliness of effect to be obtained for the abashing of plebeian beholders; the cunning design and distribution of store-cellars under the seats, secret drawers under front windows, invisible pockets under padded lining, safe from dust and accessible only by insidious slits, or necromantic valves like Aladdin's trap-door; the fitting

---

[1] *The Diary of Henry Crabb Robinson*, i, 51.
[2] Thackeray, *The Newcomes*, Chapter XXVII.

of cushions where they would not slip, the rounding of corners for more delicate repose; the prudent attachments and springs of blinds; the perfect fitting of windows, on which one-half the comfort of a travelling carriage really depends; and the adaptation of all these concentrated luxuries to the probabilities of who would sit there, in the little apartment which was to be virtually one's home for five or six months;—all this was an imaginary journey in itself, with every pleasure, and none of the discomfort, of practical travelling.[1]

Ruskin does not say how much all this cost. Crabb Robinson and Wordsworth, for their Continental tour in 1837, purchased a second-hand *barouche*, " which had been considerably used," for £70. When they crossed over to Calais with it they had to pay 400 francs customs duty (£16), but three-fourths of the duty was returnable when the travellers left the country.[2]

A carriage of this kind required four horses, which were driven, if they were steady, by a postilion who rode one of the shaft-horses. If the horses were young and troublesome there might be a postilion riding one of the leaders too. The travellers had all the carriage to themselves. When the Ruskin family journeyed to Switzerland in 1833 the front seat was occupied by Ruskin *père* and a niece, the dicky at the back by the courier and the children's nurse, and the four inside seats were at the disposal of Mrs Ruskin and John (aged fourteen), or for any of the outside passengers if the weather were bad. Every post-house kept half a dozen teams of horses, ready to be inspanned on the arrival of any carriage, notice of the coming being sometimes brought in advance by a courier. The postilion driver, a clever, young, not too heavy rider, got into his place by walking along the pole barefooted. His heavy riding-boots were slung from the saddle like two buckets, and the postilion inserted his feet in them and settled down into the saddle.

The courier (his proper title was *avant-courier*), though a seat on the dicky might be reserved for him, might have the duty

---

[1] *Præterita*, i, 150–151.
[2] *The Diary of Henry Crabb Robinson*, ii, 187.

of riding in advance to the next post and ordering a fresh team
to be ready. The party largely depended for the comfort and
harmony of their journey, as well as for intellectual enjoyment,
upon the courier, for he acted as factotum, guide-book, and personal conductor. He reserved rooms at the inns for his patrons,
and saw that the rooms were good; he made bargains and paid
bills. " He (my father) perfectly well knew," writes John Ruskin, " that his courier would have his commission, and allowed
it without question." The courier knew what were the chief
sights in every town and (a very important matter in those days)
how to obtain leave to see them. He went shopping with the
family, and saw that it was not overcharged. If he were a good
representative of his class he knew all the other good couriers
on the road, and by gossiping with them was able to tell his
patrons who were the guests of consideration staying at each
inn every night. Ruskin's father, though reasonably affluent,
had habits of economy, and would not spend his money on pro-
viding the courier with a horse to ride in advance; besides, a
riding *avant-courier* had too much the appearance and style of
a nobleman's party. So he kept the courier on the dicky, and
ordered fresh teams in advance through the postilion of a pre-
ceding carriage; or else, being in no great hurry, he gave no
warning to the next inn on the stage, but waited on arrival for
a fresh team to be produced and harnessed to the carriage.

The mode of journeying of the Ruskins probably did not
differ much from that of any other comfortable middle-class
family. They reckoned to cover forty to fifty miles every day,
starting while the dew was still on the grass, about six o'clock,
and doing a stage or two before breakfast. The day's journey
ended about four o'clock, when the party dined. With the help
of the courier it was always possible to find an inn where large,
clean rooms could be had, on the first floor, with a good view,
and good cookery. All this, of course, meant that there must
be no limitation of expenses. " To all these conditions of luxury
and felicity," writes Ruskin, " can the modern steam-puffed
tourist conceive the added ruling and culminating one—that
we were never in a hurry? " Although six in the morning was

the usual hour, the party started when it pleased: the horses could always wait. Breakfast was taken about eight o'clock, and the journey was resumed about nine. After the day's forty or fifty miles had been done, and a leisurely dinner taken after four o'clock, there were two hours for delicious exploring before tea at seven; afterwards the travellers trifled with a book, wrote up their journal, finished off a sketch, and so to bed about nine-thirty.[1] Down to about the year 1846 practically all travelling was done either by private carriage, Government postchaise, or large public diligence, operated by a diligence company, a sort of omnibus which carried fifteen passengers and was drawn by five or six horses.

Prince Pückler-Muskau describes the diligence in which he travelled from Calais to Paris in 1829.

I approached the wonderful structure which in France people have agreed to call a diligence. The monster was as long as a house, and consisted, in fact, of four distinct carriages, grown, as it were, together; the *berline* in the middle; a coach with a basket for luggage behind; a *coupé* in front; and a cabriolet above, where the conductor sits, and where I also had perched myself. This conductor, an old soldier of Napoleon's Garde, was dressed like a wagoner, in a blue *blouze*, with a stitched cap of the same material on his head. The postilion was a still more extraordinary figure, and really looked almost like a savage; he too wore a *blouze*, under which appeared monstrous boots coated with mud; but besides this he wore an apron of untanned black sheep's-skin, which hung down nearly to his knees. He drove six horses, harnessed three and three, which drew a weight of six thousand pounds over a very bad road.

The journey by diligence from Calais to Paris, 160 miles, occupied two days and one night, travelling continuously, stopping only once every twelve hours for a meal, and then only for half an hour; dinner was at 1 P.M., supper at 1 A.M. This was Pückler-Muskau's way of travelling; but when Crabb Robinson and Wordsworth went on tour in 1837 Wordsworth refused to travel by night; nevertheless, though they rested two nights on

[1] Ruskin, *Præterita*, i, 32–34, 150–160.

the way, they arrived in Paris from Calais on the third day. To a traveller coming from England the journey was rather dull: " The whole country, and even its metropolis appears somewhat dead, miserable, and dirty, after the rolling-torrent of business, the splendour, and the neatness of England."

When you look at the grotesque machine in which you are seated, the wretchedly harnessed cart-horses by which you are dragged along, and remember the noble horses, the elegant, lightbuilt coaches, the beautiful harness ornamented with bright brass and polished leather of England, you think you are transported a thousand miles in a dream.

On the other hand, four things are manifestly better here— climate, eating and drinking, cheapness, and sociability.[1]

Passports were necessary for travellers in foreign countries then as now. It was not unusual for the traveller to procure a passport both from his own Foreign Office and from the Consul in his own country of the country which he was going to visit. For instance, an Englishman going to France would receive a passport from the Foreign Office (for 7s. 6d.), and one also from the French Consul in London. Earlier in the century, however, it was apparently possible to live abroad without a passport, for Crabb Robinson was at Jena in 1802, and, desiring to make a trip to South Germany, applied to Elliot, British Minister at Berlin, for a certificate of identity. Elliot " refused it civilly on the ground that I had not a single letter or paper to corroborate my declaration."[2]

The English were the greatest travellers in the early nineteenth century, as they are now. They were everywhere, on the Continent of Europe, in Asia Minor and Palestine, in tropical Africa, in North and South America, and they were beginning to find the way to the North Pole. Men of other peoples travelled too, and wrote like Prince Pückler-Muskau in England and Egypt in 1837, Théophile Gautier in Spain and Turkey, and lesser known men like J. G. Kohl of Bremen, whose voluminous

[1] A Tour in England, Ireland, and France in the Years 1828 and 1829, by a German Prince (Pückler-Muskau) (1832), i, 248-249.
[2] The Diary of Henry Crabb Robinson, i, 64.

Q

and conscientious travel narratives are a splendid source for the
social history of the period in Austria and Russia.[1]

In the first half of the nineteenth century people travelled
without any very definite purpose. They were not investigat-
ing politics or economics; they were seeing the world—men,
things, works of art and of Nature; they were *humane*, in the
Renaissance sense of the word. Travel books were popular and
were frequently translated. It was the age of Murray's *Hand-
books for Travellers*, which, without pretending to be anything
more than guide-books, have a good deal of terse description
and literary flavour.

A pleasant international society gathered at every capital and
at spas, and was beginning to be found along the Riviera. The
great Corniche Road, from Nice to San Remo, cut in the high
country, and, following the line of the coast, was the chief fac-
tor in opening up the Riviera to travellers. It was begun by
Napoleon as a military road, but he completed only about a
fifth of it; the rest was constructed by the Sardinian Government after the fall of the French Empire. Nice was in the kingdom of Sardinia until 1860. Lord Brougham, the celebrated
English reformer and humanitarian, settled in Cannes, on the
French Riviera, in 1835, and contributed to that pleasant town's
popularity. Besides well-to-do travellers and visitors at capitals
or spas or seaside resorts, there was at many Continental towns
an ' English colony' of half-pay officers and their wives and
families who lived there for years; in some German cities, such
as Hanover or Dresden, or in French cities, Paris, Nancy, Mont-
pellier, English families resided for years in order to take advantage of the cheap and efficient foreign education; and they might
have a social centre in the English Church. The international
society of Baden-Baden, as described by Thackeray, was less
innocent than that which would be found in educational centres
like Lausanne or Dresden. Thackeray wrote of the Newcome
family:

> So they travelled by the accustomed route to the prettiest town
> of all places where Pleasure has set up her tents; and where the

[1] J. G. Kohl, *Austria* (trans. 1843) and *Russia* (trans., abridged, 1844).

gay, the melancholy, the idle or occupied, grave or naughty, come
for amusement, or business or relaxation; where London beauties,
having danced and flirted all the season, may dance and flirt a
little more; where well-dressed rogues from all quarters of the
world assemble; where I have seen severe London lawyers, for-
getting their wigs and the Temple, trying their luck against fortune
and M. Bénazet; . . . where you meet wonderful countesses and
princesses whose husbands are almost always absent on their vast
estates—in Italy, Spain, Piedmont—who knows where their lord-
ships' possessions are?—while trains of suitors surround those
wandering Penelopes, their noble wives; Russian Boyars, Spanish
Grandees of the Order of the Fleece, Counts of France, and
Princes Polish and Italian innumerable, who perfume the gilded
halls with their tobacco smoke, and swear in all languages against
the Black and the Red.[1]

Compared with modern ways, travelling was a slow business,
which possibly helped people to be more observant socially than
they are now. Sir Robert Peel, summoned from holiday at Rome
to be Prime Minister of England in 1834, took two weeks, travelling as swiftly as he could, to reach London—not much quicker
than the postal couriers travelled over the same route in the
ancient Roman Empire. Boxed up in the lumbering diligence,
passengers were like a ship's company, sharing delays, discom-
forts, hopes, expectations, and not infrequent dangers. A family
travelling like the Ruskins, in its own carriage, could scarcely
proceed in otherwise than a leisurely way, ending the day's
journey after doing their forty or fifty miles with dinner about
four o'clock and a long ramble afterwards round the town. As
a means of appreciative approach to a beautiful, historic town
the carriage could only be equalled, if the town was on the sea,
by boat. Better still was the approach by both means, carriage
and boat, as described by Ruskin at the end of the first book
and the opening of the second of *The Stones of Venice*: the
carriage's exit through the dark gates of Padua; the smart trot
along the level road between elms and vine festoons; the short,
slow climb to the embankment above the Brenta; the drive

[1] *The Newcomes*, Chapter XXVII, *ad fin.*

along the dike on the river's northern side, the distant tall white tower of Dolo trembling in the heat mist; brief rest in the inn-parlour at Mestre, with the smell of garlic and crabs and the smoke of roasting chestnuts; and then the walk of two hundred yards to the low wharf on a canal, black with the boats of Venice. We enter one of them and glide away. " Stroke by stroke we count the plunges of the oar." The sea air blows keenly by, as we stand leaning on the roof of the floating cell. " To the west, the tower of Mestre is lowering fast, and behind it there have risen purple shades, of the colour of the dead rose-leaves, all round the horizon, feebly defined against the afternoon sky— the Alps of Bassano." The endless canal bends at last, reveal-ing the fort of Malghera; another, and another prospect of canal, but not interminable. Next the low, monotonous dock-yard wall, with flat arches to let the tide go through it (now the railway bridge); four or five domes rise behind it, and a sullen cloud of black smoke is issuing from the belfry of a church. It is Venice. But this is no unique experience: the view of Oxford or Florence, as the coach tops the last hill on the in-ward journey and the traveller looks down upon the dreaming city, or of St Peter's dome hanging in the sky, seen afar from the carriage rumbling over the Campagna, were better known then than they can be in the railway age.

Distance could not be vanquished, but there was compensa-tion through power of deliberate survey and the happiness of evening hours—" hours of peaceful and thoughtful pleasure, for which the rush of arrival in the railway station is perhaps not always, or to all men, an equivalent." [1] Kohl of Bremen, being a progressively minded man, judged the railway to be an im-provement—that is, the horse-railway. He was immensely pleased in 1841 by his journey over the Linz-Budweis line; he calls it " the grandmother of all the railroads in the European continent." He adds, " The trains on this railroad are drawn by horses, and owing to the inequalities of the ground over which it passes there is little likelihood that steam locomotives can ever be introduced there." Travelling by the horse-railway

[1] Ruskin, *Stones of Venice*, ii, 1.

was quiet and comfortable, affording excellent opportunities for conversation and for tranquil survey of people and country.

The increase of travelling brought about an improvement of hotels. Pückler-Muskau in 1826–28 found the English inns excellent, far better than those on the Continent; the fare was more abundant; cleanliness, order, and decency reigned throughout. The waiters expected to make at least £2 a week in 'tips.'[1] On the Continent conditions had also improved. J. G. Kohl remarked that during the years of peace an enormous number of hotels sprang up in Germany (including Austria). The casino, or coffee-house, which was becoming quite an institution in Central Europe, added greatly to the amenity of travelling, if the visitor was staying a few days in one place. Kohl, about 1840, found a magnificent casino at Pesth; it was comfortable, brilliantly lit, and had several reading-rooms with books and most of the foreign as well as all the Hungarian journals. The casinos, or coffee-houses, were places where people could meet socially and could discuss whatever matters interested them. As people tend to find their friends and associates among those of congenial views, the coffee-houses had helped to develop political parties and groups. In England the open coffee-house was gradually changed into the exclusive club. In 1824 the Athenæum was founded for the accommodation of literary men and scholars; in 1836 the Reform. These clubs were not expensive—Crabb Robinson paid £5 entrance-fee and £4 annually to the Athenæum—but they were of no use to ordinary travellers.

Travel by railway was only beginning in the eighteen-forties, but steamships had been popular for twenty years on the Rhine and Danube. Thackeray takes the Newcomes up the Rhine to Cologne by steamer in 1835. The Danube steamships were very popular, particularly for the journey between Vienna and Pesth. Kohl described the passengers on the *Archduke Stephen* in 1841:

There were Englishmen who spoke not one word of German, monks with shaven crowns, ladies with children, whiskered

[1] *A Tour in Germany, Holland, and England*, ii, 48.

Hungarians, Vienna dandies with eyeglasses instead of eyes in their heads, Berlin travellers with *Donnerwetter* in their mouths, and many others laden with cloaks and wraps, hats, bandboxes, parasols and umbrellas, sticks, pipes, chests and trunks.

The steamship undertaking began when two Englishmen, Andrews and Pritchard, who were engaged in shipbuilding at Venice, applied to the Austrian Government for a concession. They obtained a charter of monopoly, and in 1830, with the help of two Hungarian noblemen, Baron Puthon and Count Stephen Szechenyi, and of Vienna bankers, formed a company. The undertaking grew rapidly, and soon had a large fleet of passenger steamers and cargo-steamers. The fastest boats took thirteen or fourteen hours downstream between Vienna and Pesth, and about twice as long upstream. There were clean and comfortable berths on the boats and good cuisine, but the surface of the deck was spoiled by much spitting, the Hungarians being the worst offenders in this respect.

The conditions under which travelling was done varied very little from country to country. Victor Hugo described a post-chaise journey through Eastern France in *Le Rhin*. Borrow's *Bible in Spain* and Ford's *Gatherings from Spain* minutely describe travel conditions in that country. Prince Pückler-Muskau tells about the state of the roads in Germany, the good *chaussée* from Leipsig to the Dutch frontier, and the dust and mud of the road in Holland. Kohl went through Austria, Bohemia, Hungary, and Russia. Kinglake's vivid narrative *Eothen* describes a ride through Turkey in Europe. Only here was there no system of diligence or postchaise; even private carriages were practically unknown outside Constantinople; for Turkey was not European, though it was partly in Europe.

The social influence of travelling was undoubtedly considerable, though difficult to define or assess. The educated classes of the eighteenth century had been great travellers, inspired by curiosity, by interest in men, manners, and mind, by *humanity* or humanism, in the classical sense of these words. The philosophic, socially interested men and women of the eighteenth century had their *reasonableness* increased by travelling, had their cosmopolitanism strengthened by it. They belonged to the Age of Reason. The men of the Romantic Age lived in a time when means of communication were beginning to be speedier; the railway train and the steamship were beginning —though only just beginning—to revolutionize travel. Eighteenth-century means of communication, eighteenth-century reasonableness, lingered on; among the travellers of the Romantic Age there is, as yet, little or no indication of the nationalist outlook. For the most part travelling was still confined to Europe, although the more adventurous voyagers went to Palestine or to Egypt, which Mehemet Ali had brought very much into public notice. The study of classical archæology was being added to motives for travelling; in 1821 Colonel William Martin Leake published *The Topography of Athens*, in 1824 *Journal of a Tour in Asia Minor*, in 1830 *Travels in Morea*, and in 1835 *Travels in Northern Greece*. Missionary enterprise was making Africa known to Europeans. In 1795 the London Missionary Society had been founded, and in 1816 a young Scotsman, Robert Moffat, who was to be one of the Society's greatest missionaries, sailed for Cape Town. In 1825 he fixed his permanent mission-station in Kuruman, in Bechuanaland, north of the Orange River. In 1840 David Livingstone sailed for Africa, to take up his missionary work at Kuruman and thence to penetrate into the dark interior of the continent. It was in this year 1840, that Samuel Cunard sent his first steam-packet, the *Britannia*, from Liverpool to America in fourteen days. This began the great era, still in progress, of travel between Europe and the United States, though before this travellers had not been exactly scarce, and books of travels in the United States, such as Captain Basil Hall's *Travels in North America* (1829) and Mrs Trollope's *Domestic Manners of the Americans* (1832), attracted very considerable, though not always favourable, attention.

Social habit is always in process of development and change. The view that people take of the world changes. The educated people of the eighteenth century regarded ' Europe ' as the world, and a rather small Europe at that, which they called the republic of letters. The people of the early nineteenth century had lost this tradition; there was no European republic of letters for them. The *salons* of Paris had declined considerably from their eighteenth-century glory. Under Louis XVIII, Charles X, and Louis Philippe Paris was not the brilliant cosmopolitan place it had been. London, Holland House, the Pall Mall clubs (to which distinguished strangers might be admitted), outstripped Paris, and were a kind of social centre for Europe. There was another kind of cosmopolitan society, growing in size between 1830 and 1848—the society of political *émigrés*, exiles from Berlin and other German capitals; from Venice, Milan, Florence, Genoa, Rome; and particularly from Poland. And, lastly, there were the knight-errants of freedom, English, Irish, Italian, French, who were found serving in the Greek army, in South American navies, wherever there was risk and romance and the cause of free peoples to be served.

CHAPTER XVI

GERMAN SOCIETY IN THE REACTION

THE years from 1819 to 1848 were called by Duke Ernst of Saxe-Coburg the great *remora* of German history. The *remora* was, according to classical marine biology, a sucking-fish which adhered to moving ships and delayed their course through the water. The German people is a little unfortunate. Its immense fund of energy, its immense capacity for developing the powers of the mind and spirit, have suffered from time to time a setback such as other peoples—for instance, the French or English—have somehow escaped. German development is less continuous, the rhythm of progress of German civilization less steady, than that of their western neighbours.

This was the time when the *bourgeoisie* all over Central and Western Europe was beginning to assume the leadership of public life. The *bourgeoisie*, sometimes rather ambiguously called the middle class or classes, developed from the towns-people of the Middle Ages, who, deprived, owing to feudal law, of the chance of making their living through land, created a place in society for themselves between the landed peasantry on the one hand and the landed nobles on the other. It was the townsmen who steadily broke up the ' feudal ' system, found means to accumulate movable wealth, and were the main-springs of private enterprise and capitalism in Europe in the seventeenth and eighteenth centuries.

After the Napoleonic wars were over the influence of the *bourgeoisie* in society and politics was greatly increased. The enfranchisement of the peasantry, brought about in the Rhine-land during the French occupation and in Prussia by the reforms of Stein, had a stimulating effect upon society in general, and seems to have quickened the energies of the *bourgeoisie*. The prestige and power of the nobility, since the shocks of the French Revolution and the Declaration of the Rights of Man, were declining. The enduring peace after 1815 provided the necessary condition for the accumulation of savings for capitalist enterprise. The *bourgeoisie* entered into this world of peace and fruitful enterprise in 1815 as into a promised land. In the War of Liberation against Napoleon sure hopes of a liberal franchise and Parliamentary government had been held out to them; and where constitutions were granted, as in Saxe-Weimar, Baden, Bavaria, Württemberg, between 1815 and 1820, the *bourgeoisie* took full advantage of the opportunity and began a political ascendancy which looked like extending over all Germany, as it was certainly doing over France, Italy, Spain, and Great Britain.

The *bourgeoisie* of that period, 1815–48, was of a well-marked kind. It comprised what are sometimes called the ' professional classes '—the lawyers, doctors, university professors, school-masters, students, and journalists. Along with these should be included the mercantile *bourgeoisie*, men who owned their own business or were part owners of a family business. If not mer-chants, they might be owners of a small-scale industry, employ-ing from fifteen to thirty workmen. All these formed the genuine political *bourgeoisie*; they were, as a class, intelligent and well-educated people, not wealthy, but well-to-do, with moderate property and strong traditions. There was also a *petite bourgeoisie*, the shopkeepers and small-salaried men, whose social affinities or sympathies were with the higher *bourgeoisie*, although their economic interests might seem rather to be with the wage-earning workmen. The high capitalist, ' captain of industry,' the director and general manager, drawing a high salary and large sums in dividends and profits, was scarcely known then. He is a feature of grand-scale industry and of the enormous development of the joint-stock company which took place after 1848, and still more after 1870.

Social connexion of England with Germany (as also of Eng-land with France and with Italy) was very close in the years

1815–48. A large number of English people, individually or in families, settled in Germany for longer or shorter periods for the sake of their health (at spas and baths), of economy, or of education. And there were many Germans in England. London, it was estimated, had some forty to fifty thousand; Manchester ten thousand. They were described as " close, practical, fast-sticking fellows, who, like the Scotch, are enthusiasts regarding all that belongs to their own country, yet never care to return to it." [1]

The Rhine was the great thoroughfare of tourists, being easy of access and offering charming country to the visitor. A regular service of steamboats had been going up and down the river since 1827. Carriages were, of course, used by the wealthier travellers, and vigorous young men went on foot. The young Pennsylvanian Bayard Taylor walked up the Rhine in 1844–45, and wrote an admirable description of his journey. Longfellow travelled twice in the Rhineland, in 1835 and 1842. His novel *Hyperion*, published in 1839, is based on the later journey. It was still (and for a good many years to come) the old-fashioned Rhine, practically clear of industrialism, though, away from the river, in the Ruhr valley and round Aix-la-Chapelle, there were factory chimneys. " Of all the rivers of this beautiful earth there is none so beautiful as this," wrote Longfellow. Apprentices and craftsmen were still often met with, on holiday or on the business tour which by custom they had to undertake. Paul Flemming, in *Hyperion*, near Rolandseck passed a band of apprentices with knapsacks, singing, " The Rhine! The Rhine! A blessing on the Rhine!" Little progress had been made with Cologne Cathedral since the Middle Ages. As Murray's *Handbook for Travellers* of 1843 stated, " It has remained up to the present time in a condition between a fragment and a ruin." Frederick William IV, however, who came to the throne in 1840, soon succeeded in advancing the construction. Twenty miles above Cologne the traveller enters upon a region of rare loveliness and of romantic and historical association which was as celebrated in the early

---

[1] W. Howitt, *German Experiences* (1844), p. 8.

nineteenth century as it is now, or even more. Byron's verses
were echoed in many hearts:

> The negligently grand, the fruitful bloom
> Of coming ripeness, the white city's sheen,
> The rolling stream, the precipice's gloom,
> The forest's growth, and Gothic walls between—
> The wild rocks shaped, as they had turrets been,
> In mockery of man's art: and these withal
> A race of happy faces as the scene,
> Whose fertile bounties here extend to all,
> Still springing o'er thy banks, though Empires near
> them fall.[1]

Perhaps because it was so frequented by strangers, the Rhineland was not the most characteristic part of Germany, or, if it
was characteristic, this was in a way which they did not expect
or appreciate. Germany was a cheap country to live in, and
the Rhine was the dearest part of it. Yet the sums of money
demanded do not impress a reader of to-day as large. The
steamboat fare from Cologne to Strasbourg was 28s. 3d. A
good dinner on the steamer cost 16 groschen, or about 1s. 6d.
A bedroom for the night at a good inn cost only about 1s. 6d.
according to the tariff authorized by the police, although the
innkeepers often tried to charge more. The Rhineland cities
and towns, compared with the rest of Germany, were considered
to be socially corrupt.

> They do not offer the advantages of capitals, but they offer
> more than their expenses . . . with the addition of the greatest
> curse of social existence, the most rampant gossip, scandal, and
> personal interference of small towns—that social pestilence which
> the Germans call *Kleinstädterei*, or Little-townism.[2]

Frankfurt was the most respectable, but also the most expensive. Bavaria was the cheapest of German countries; Munich
had the advantage of cheap living and social graces—art, opera,
university, schools. An excellent furnished house could be
rented in Nuremberg for £40 a year; in the Rhineland it would

---

[1] *Childe Harold's Pilgrimage*, Canto III, Stanza 61.
[2] Howitt, *op. cit.*, p. 18.

be £90. Even this sum would not now be considered dear. In Heidelberg, in the " expensive " Rhineland (according to Murray's *Handbook*), there was an Englishman about 1834 who lived there on £380 a year, including horses, carriages, and servants. Beef, as late as 1843, was 4*d.* a pound, butter 8*d.* or 9*d.*; brown bread was 2*d.* the quartern loaf, compared with 6*d.* in contemporary London; but lump sugar was 7*d.* a pound. Maidservants, who could " do anything you want doing," had wages of £5 a year, an excellent cook £8. Fees for education in the splendid Heidelberg high school (*Gymnasium*) cost £5 a year; university fees were about £10 a year. A good seat in the opera cost 5*d.*, and the best seat about 1*s.* 8*d.* Strauss's open-air concerts at Vienna could be attended for 4*d.*

German life at its best was to be found in the small gay capitals of the minor principalities. " They have all the gaiety and charms of a capital, with the enduring freshness and suburban leafiness and retirement of a village." [1] Opera, the theatre, gardens, libraries, *cafés*, and clubs could all be enjoyed there at the most moderate cost. Weimar was the most famous, although not the most beautiful. It was the happiest, because everybody was free there. Talent was encouraged and supported; even the poets lived comfortably, indeed, affluently.[2] Dresden and Munich, rather bigger (Dresden had 70,000 inhabitants in 1843, Munich 166,000), had much the same kind of charm as the small capitals. The Germans were a great waltzing people, and this too was an attraction for many visitors, though not for all, as the dancing parties, over one's head in an apartment house, were destroyers of slumber.

The externals of German life had a distinctly pleasant aspect. The amenities of the towns and, in many respects, the convenience and enjoyment of the public were carefully fostered by the authorities, especially the civic authorities. Stein had established self-government in the cities of Prussia in 1808, and the other German states made similar advances about the same time. Already by the year 1840 German cities and towns were

[1] Howitt, *op. cit.*, p. 21.
[2] *The Diary of Henry Crabb Robinson*, ii, 62.

noted for their parks and promenades. The old walls and ramparts were made into walks where citizens could stroll and enjoy near and distant prospects of the countryside. Lime-trees grew along all the promenades and in the parks, and seats were placed in their shade. If there was an old castle in or near the town it was preserved and its garden opened to the public. The reigning princes' parks and gardens were, for the most part, public. The princely courts gave a certain quality of colour or romance to urban life, where the princes were seen every day. The Courts cannot have been rigidly exclusive, for Crabb Robinson dined three times in 1829 at the Court of Weimar. He found an atmosphere of dignified courtesy there.[1] The coffee-house (*casino*) and the orchestra made leisure cheerful. Life among the honest burghers, as described by Freytag in *Soll und Haben*, seemed to be divided between the counting-house, with its long hours of honest, scrupulous application, the home, with its eager, keen-minded children, busy at school or university, the open air, with walks and talks under the trees or boating on the town lake. The German *bourgeoisie* were docile, religious, hospitable people, essentially domestic, peace loving, cosmopolitan. They read the ' European ' Press, which to them meant the *Augsburger Allgemeine Zeitung* or some other local journal of more than local note which had correspondents from Paris or London and quotations from *The Times*, the *Journal des Débats* or the *Indépendance Belge*. They hated the idea of war, because it seemed to have no reason for itself in an otherwise reasonable world, and it was connected in their minds with the tyrannies and annexations of the first Napoleon. War, in their eyes, was simply Gallic aberration and instability. They had no conception of German race, because they were Bavarians, Saxons, Prussians, Hanoverians, Hessians, Mecklenburgers, or citizens of free cities—Hamburg, Bremen, Lübeck, Frankfurt. They were conscious of the community of all Germans who spoke the same tongue (with many local differences) and who had contributed to European religion and literature so many noble things. The State, the political organization in

---

[1] *The Diary of Henry Crabb Robinson*, ii, 80.

which they lived, was something which they just took for granted. Its power and dignity was no concern of theirs: their prince or king represented all that, and it was his affair. The word *Machtfreudigkeit*, joy in the consciousness of the State's power, was not invented yet, and the thing itself was not thought of; but they had a conception, vague yet pervasive, of *Weltbürgertum*, of the European or universal citizenry, the *bourgeoisie*, for they did not despise French expressions.

There was, however, a dark side to the life of the German *bourgeoisie*. They were censor-ridden and police-ridden. Trials were held in secret. There were no juries (before 1848). The darkness of prisons hid deliberate suffering imposed on prisoners to extort confession; cudgellings and worse abuses in prison were believed to occur.[1] As late as 1841 breaking on the wheel was inflicted upon a murderer in Prussia.[2] After the adopting in the *Bundestag* of the Carlsbad Decrees of 1819 this police tyranny had been intense for seven or eight years, and had then been relaxed. It revived again after 1830, when the July Revolution in Paris had awakened similar stirrings in Germany, and particularly after 1832 (May 27), the date of the Hambacher Fest, a celebration of friends of liberty held in Baden, something like the Wartburg Festival of 1817. *Streng verboten* was the current police phrase in the ' eighteen-forties,' just as much as it is now. The intensity of police surveillance varied, to some extent, from state to state, and was greatest in Austria and Prussia—most of all in Prussia, for the severity of the Austrian police system was tempered by the easygoing good-nature of the average man which was absent in the harsher Prussian official. There were, of course, a few advantages to be obtained from an all-pervasive and omnipotent police system. A stranger who was overcharged at a hotel or cheated by a cardriver might have his grievance summarily and sternly redressed on complaint to the local police-bureau perhaps more quickly than would happen in a free country.

The essential test of a police state is the use made of the

[1] Howitt, p. vi, quoting Welcker, *Allgemeine Zeitung* for April 26, 1844.
[2] *Ibid.*, p. 184.

passport and the censorship. Not only travellers from outside Germany, not only Germans travelling between state and state of the Confederation, but Germans travelling within their own state, moving, for instance, from one Prussian town to another, required passports. The apprentice wandering in search of experience had to have a 'wander-ticket,' and the student changing his university (a good old custom) had to have a certified identity-card. Travellers were under surveillance all the time, and reports were made from the local police to headquarters upon any who attracted attention.

The omnipresence of secret police and informers made people distrust each other and fear the authorities. It was turning the Germans, wrote Count Auersperg (the famous poet Anastasius Grün), into a race of hypocrites. In music alone could the artist express his love of freedom completely, and only because the authorities could not understand it or prove it against him. The poets had to be more careful. Uhland, the poet, who was a liberal member of the Württemberg legislature, wrote in 1838:

> *Wohl werd ich's nicht erleben;*
> *Doch an der Sehnsucht Hand,*
> *Als Schatten noch durchschweben*
> *Mein freies Vaterland.*[1]

Uhland inherited a considerable property, and could live without a professorial chair. Arndt, suspended from his chair at Bonn in 1820, was restored to it by Frederick William IV in 1840; he was too old to be dangerous now. The race of old poets who remembered Schiller and who as young men had sung their songs of liberty in the War of Liberation still lingered on in a few survivals—Tieck, Chamisso, Freiligrath. They were reconciled to despotism or took care to sing in very cautious tones. Heine lived in Paris. Younger singers published their books in neutral places—from Zürich, Bern, Schaffhausen, in German-speaking Switzerland, or from Hamburg, Frankfurt, free cities. Count Auersperg belonged to a powerful Austrian

---

[1] " I may not live to see it, yet, led by longing, I may wander as a ghost through my fatherland set free."

noble family, and the pen-name of Anastasius Grün provided a nominal covering which the authorities winked at. Nevertheless he published his *Walks of a Viennese Poet* (*Spaziergänge eines Wiener Poeten*) from Hamburg in 1831. When Ticknor met Count Auersperg at Von Hammer's house near Vienna in 1836 the poet was in trouble with his Government on account of his liberalism, but not so much in trouble as to be unable to visit his friends.[1]

The newspaper Press was fallen upon evil times. Under the heavy hand of the censor they could scarcely be lively, interesting, or even informing. The *Allgemeine Zeitung* or *Kölnische Zeitung* maintained something of a European reputation; but not until 1848, when the censorship was swept away, did the German journals really have a chance to justify themselves and to develop. It was not until 1856, however, that the celebrated liberal journal *Die Frankfurter Zeitung* was established.

Education was in chains. Frederick William IV gained great credit in intellectual circles by establishing universal elementary education in Prussia on his accession in 1840. But education, the grand means of freeing the spirit of man, may be employed as a means of enslaving it. The teachers were Prussian Government servants; their instruction and the books which they used were ultimately dictated by the Government.

The universities had long since been taken under official control, and though the student or the professor sometimes manages to keep his mind free, it is a hard thing to do if freedom of expression is not permitted. By 1840 university life had sunk markedly as compared with the great years before and after the War of Liberation. The noble sacrifice which seven professors of Göttingen, all famous men of learning,[2] made of themselves in 1837, when they protested against the suppression of the Hanoverian constitution by the King, had won sympathy in every university, but had not been copied. Their summary dismissal by the King of Hanover was all the more shocking

---

[1] *The Life of George Ticknor*, ii, 2.
[2] The brothers Grimm, philologists; Weber, physicist; Dahlmann and Gervinus, historians; Albrecht, jurist; Ewald, Orientalist.

R

because Göttingen, throughout the period of connexion between Hanover and England (which had lately terminated with the death of William IV), had been a place of the most liberal atmosphere. Foreign students were numerous, were encouraged to come, and were made to feel thoroughly at home.[1] The universities of Germany, indeed, were in better plight than the Austrian, which were kept by Metternich in the condition almost of high schools; but this was about the best that could be said of them. " Shun small towns as you would shun the plague, but pre-eminently and most especially a little university town," is the advice of a qualified observer[2]; he believed that they were saturated with gossip and spite. Heidelberg, in Baden, although its university was famous, was quite a small town in 1840, with about 12,500 inhabitants; and, wrote the same observer, it was " perhaps the most wretched, as to the general tone and quality of its society, of all the little university towns." The university had eight hundred students. Their opinions and discipline were so suspect to the Prussian Government, since students had engaged in political troubles at Frankfurt in 1833, that Prussians were not allowed to study at Heidelberg. It was, however, still one of the most famous, one of the most traditional, of German universities, and after Berlin probably still had the best professors.

German professors, in general, had the reputation of being ponderous and industrious. They were conscientious teachers. George Ticknor, who was a graduate of Dartmouth, a New England college of sound tradition, was impressed by the thoroughness of the professors under whom he studied when he proceeded to Göttingen: " Here for the first time he was made to understand and to feel what is meant by instruction."[3] They were mighty in research; in no country, it was said, were so many systems of philosophy composed and so many universal histories written. It would be unfair, however, not to point out that it was a very notable school of historians that was at work— Gervinus, Ranke, Giesebrecht, Gregorovius; only Gregorovius,

---

[1] *The Life of George Ticknor*, i, 75.   [2] Howitt, *op. cit.*, p. 23.
[3] *The Life of George Ticknor*, i, 71.

however (and he lived all the time at Rome), had much literary ability. Professors, like all other German officials, had small salaries: about 2000 gulden, or £180, a year was considered to be a good stipend. On this they lived well, had good apartments, dressed suitably, had large families, went frequently to the play, opera, or *café*, riding in a hired carriage, and took an annual holiday at some spa or in a pleasant hill or valley resort. Nobody but themselves could say how Continental professors and Government officials lived with so much dignity on their modest remuneration. Increase in the salary of a professor came if he was ' called ' to a chair in another university. He either accepted the call, at a higher salary than he was receiving, or the Government controlling the university which already employed him increased his present salary to the amount of the new offer. University boards were not left free to do their own ' calling.' If a professor's political opinions were disliked by his Government he might not only lose his employment there, but, by arrangement, other German Governments could be induced to refuse employment. Starvation or emigration to a foreign country were the only alternatives offered to an independent professor of advanced political views.

The student bodies were controlled in much the same way. The great avenue of employment for them after leaving the university was Government service. It was calculated that one person in every 630 in Germany was employed at the public charges; and many more, in the service of municipalities or charitable bodies, were in effect controlled by Government. As the student class supplied the bulk of the public servants, the proportion of students who looked forward to public service was extremely high. It might be said that practically every student, including Protestant and Catholic theological students, hoped to obtain work through Government nomination or approval. Princes and Government, accordingly, had very effective means for disciplining the students. They could threaten to prevent them from obtaining public employment after leaving the university if their record was not satisfactory. More effectively, they could dismiss a student before his studies were completed, and could mark his passport so as to prevent any other German university from admitting him. To be *relegiert*, as it was called, or ' sent down ' permanently, spelled simply ruin for a student. Nevertheless, the *Bursch*, the undergraduate, lived a happy and almost carefree life at the university. He was said to be the only free person in Germany. He was cheerful, companionable, open-minded, tolerant, and industrious. The students, said a close observer, in spite of all their extravagance, were " the most estimable class in Germany." [1] But the *Bursch*'s freedom did not last for long. His university years past, he went out into a harsh official world, hemmed in by regulations and closely observed by the police and the censors.

The servitude in which the German mind and body were held was all the more remarkable as the Germans had been great diffusers of freedom—*the* great diffusers, many people held. Since the time when Tacitus described, for the benefit of tyrant-ridden Roman society, the self-governing assemblies of freemen in the forests of ancient Germany, through the time of the Reformation, when Luther made his grand and successful stand for spiritual freedom, to the recent days of Kant, Schiller, and Goethe, Germany had been for Europe a lamp of liberty. In the ' eighteen-forties ' there were many German lovers of liberty, but they had to remain silent or eat their bread in exile. It was said that champions of freedom married women of fortune, so as to have an independent income on which they could live in a foreign country. The German ruling princes respected their own laws, and did not attack the private incomes of the wives of political opponents. But every exile cannot have been so fortunate as to have a rich wife.

For the most vigorous-minded Germans, the younger, more optimistic men, America was the promised land. Hoffman von Fallersleben (1798–1874), author of *Deutschland, Deutschland über alles*, has a rousing poem which the traveller William Howitt translated. It begins:

> Hurra! Hurra! Hurra! Hurra!
> We're off to America!

---

[1] Howitt, *op. cit.*, p. 317.

What shall we take to our new land?
All sorts of things from every hand!
Confederation protocols;
Heaps of tax and budget rolls;
A whole shipload of skins to fill
With proclamations just at will.
Or when we to the New World come,
The Germans will not feel at home.[1]

The Middle West of the United States—Ohio, Illinois, Wisconsin, and neighbouring territories or states—benefited enormously by the influx of Germans of the ' eighteen-forties,' healthy, vigorous, free-souled men who were a most valuable element in building up the sturdy and progressive democracies of those regions. Of the liberal and vigorous elements who stayed at home in Germany many became revolutionary in 1848. The intensity of their feeling can be gauged from Herwegh's *Hymn of Hate*, breathing fire and brimstone against the police state system, represented at that time particularly by Prussia.[2]

The German people has been dogged by bad luck. Vigorous in body and mind, with an appreciation of the mysteries of life, they have sought for forms of government consonant with their genius and temperament. And every time that they have been near the realization of this aim, after the War of Liberation, for instance, or in 1848, they have been thrown back into the old limits of government or forced into new forms of State regulation, into the adoption of new State ideals. The choice before the German people (or peoples) in the ' eighteen-forties ' has been clearly explained in Meinecke's book of history and philosophy *Weltbürgertum und Nationalstaat*.

[1] Howitt, *op. cit.*, p. 201.
[2] It was translated into English and published in Howitt, *op. cit.*, p. 269.

CHAPTER XVII

1815 AND 1919

GREAT wars, fortunately, do not occur very often. Consequently, when they have been fought and are finished there is great uncertainty about the best method of making peace. Precedents are lacking, or, if they exist, they are very old precedents. In 1919 for precedents of a general peace conference the diplomatists had to hark back beyond the Crimean War to the Napoleonic period and the peace conferences of Paris (1814–15), and the Congress of Vienna.

The aims and methods of diplomacy are limited by the social condition, by the structure and level of civilization, of the age. Society and civilization have not altered fundamentally in the last hundred and forty or fifty years, since the French Revolution. Accordingly, it is not surprising to find a considerable degree of similarity between the peace conferences at the end of the Napoleonic war and at the end of the World War and between the treaties of 1814–15 and 1919; and also considerable differences, which were due not only to the passage of time and to altered circumstances, but to a deliberate effort of the negotiators of 1919 to avoid what they regarded as the mistakes of 1814–15.

Both wars were conducted with loans, subsidies, and secret agreements. The financial transactions, however, of the Napoleonic war did not enter much into the post-war history. Direct subsidies, given by Great Britain, were more numerous than loans, which were also made by Great Britain; and the loans were quickly written down and paid off after the war. After the World War the British Government proposed a similar policy towards inter-State loans, or, rather, went further along the same line and proposed complete cancellation, but

this was found to be impracticable, because there was now
not one lender only (Great Britain), but other lenders (particularly the United States), and a common policy regarding
loans could not be adopted.

Combinations of Great Powers can only be made and maintained by agreement, sometimes by secret agreement. Napoleon's empire did not really begin to fall until the retreat from
Moscow took place and the Tsar Alexander I made the decision
to follow the French Grand Army over the Russian frontier
into Germany. All the Prussian young men, who had for years
been secretly plotting and drilling, were ready to rise against
the French oppressor, but King Frederick William III held
back; many of his fortresses were still occupied by French
troops. He met the Tsar at Kalisch in February (1813), and
received a guarantee for joining in the War of Liberation of an
amount of territory equal to what Prussia had lost after the
battle of Jena. The Treaty of Kalisch, naturally, was kept
secret at first. Its promises were carried out at the end of the
war in the treaties of 1814–15. Bavaria likewise, the chief
member of the Napoleonic Confederation of the Rhine, joined
the Allies on terms negotiated between the Bavarian Minister
Montgelas and Metternich and known as the Treaty of Ried.
The Treaties of Kalisch and Ried of 1813 are like the Treaty
of London (April 26, 1915), by which the Italian Government
agreed to join in the World War after receiving from the Allies
a guarantee of its territorial claims.

The Allies of 1914–19 were bound together throughout the
War by the Pact of London, made on September 5, 1914, in
which they each undertook not to enter into a separate peace
with the enemy. And in the last years of the War a Supreme
Council of the Allies, comprising heads of Governments, their
representatives and military advisers, directed and co-ordinated
policy. There was no such body among the Allies of 1813, and
as they continued their chequered advance towards Paris there
was a danger of the Alliance breaking up, until Castlereagh,
the most energetic of the Allied statesmen, persuaded them
to sign the Treaty of Chaumont, March 1, 1814. This bound

the Allies to continue the war against Napoleon in common; and, in effect, it established a Supreme Council among them which remained in being throughout the duration of hostilities and of the peace negotiations.

The circumstances in which hostilities were concluded in 1814 and 1918 have a common similarity. In each case the defeated country was represented by a new Government which hoped to escape responsibility for the acts of the previous *régime*. Talleyrand's Paris revolution of April 2, 1814, just after the Allies entered the capital, his proclaiming of Louis XVIII, and Louis's previous issue of the *Charte constitutionnelle* enabled the peace treaty to be negotiated by a legitimate royal Government with which the Allies had no quarrel. In 1918–19 the German Government which negotiated the Armistice and signed the peace treaty of Versailles was likewise a new and— from the points of view of the Allies—a ' legitimate ' *régime*. A revolution in Berlin had resulted in the fall of the militarist Empire and the establishing of a democratic republic—and the Allies had been fighting for democracy against Prussian militarism. The Allies in 1919, however, were not prepared to be as moderate in their demands on the new German Republic as they were in 1814 in their demands on the ' restored ' Louis XVIII. In 1814 the responsibility of the war was laid upon Napoleon; in 1919 upon the whole German people.

The peace settlement of 1814–15 was made in three stages— the First Treaty of Paris (May 30, 1814), which concluded the war with Napoleon; the Treaty of Vienna (June 9, 1815), which restored or redistributed the territories liberated from the fallen French Empire; and the Second Treaty of Paris (November 20, 1815), which made peace after Napoleon's escape from Elba, the Hundred Days, and the battle of Waterloo. In the three conferences (or congresses) which negotiated these three treaties the enemy or ex-enemy, France, was admitted as a full member—that is, the peace of 1814–15 was a negotiated, not a dictated, peace. After the Allied army entered Paris on March 30, 1814, Talleyrand proclaimed

Louis XVIII. The peace negotiations were undertaken between Talleyrand, as French Foreign Minister, on the one hand, and the Allied plenipotentiaries (Castlereagh, Metternich, Nesselrode, Hardenberg, and the rest) on the other. The ensuing treaty (May 30, 1814) made peace on the basis of the " ancient limits " of France, the frontier of 1792, with the important additions of the Saar and Chambéry–Annecy, which the French Revolution had taken from Prussia and Bavaria, and from Savoy.

The reduction of France to her " ancient limits " left thousands of square miles of territory and thirty millions of people (chiefly German and Italian) unallotted, formerly included in the Napoleonic Empire. It was to deal with this that the Congress of Vienna met, from September 25, 1814, to June 9, 1815. This was not, strictly speaking, a peace congress, for peace had already been made at Paris. Nevertheless, although there was now, technically, no ' enemy,' and although the French Government had been a full and equal negotiator at Paris, the Allies decided that France should not be admitted to the Congress of Vienna, and a secret article to this effect was incorporated in the First Treaty of Paris. Talleyrand, however, went to Vienna, lived in a hired house there, as he had a perfect right to do, and met the plenipotentiaries of the Congress Powers on social occasions. He was not long in finding a rift in the apparently solid front of the Allies, and he ended by seeing the Congress divided into two diplomatic camps, with himself, as representing France, partner of Great Britain and Austria against Prussia and Russia (January 1815). " *Sire, the Alliance is dissolved, and dissolved for ever,*" wrote Talleyrand in triumph to Louis XVIII. It was only the escape of Napoleon from Elba (February 26, 1815) and the re-emergence of the French Empire which healed the division of the Congress of Vienna and restored the united front of the Allies. The success of the enemy (or ex-enemy, technically) as a participating Power, almost breaking up the Congress of Vienna, was remembered in 1919, and was probably the reason for the unfortunate decision of the Allies to exclude Germany from the Peace Conference of Paris which drafted the Treaty of Versailles.

The two great conferences—the Congress of Vienna (1814–15) and the Conference of Paris (1919)—worked according to similar methods. At Vienna in 1814–15 all the princes and Governments of Europe or their representatives were assembled; at Paris in 1919 all the states (and several would-be states) of the world were represented or were ' unofficially ' present. But orderly and reasonably rapid business was impossible in such huge assemblages. Strictly speaking, the Congress of Vienna never met at all. The princes and high Ministers danced and played, but Metternich, Castlereagh, Hardenberg, and Nesselrode (or their substitutes), the plenipotentiaries of the " Big Four Powers," with later the addition of Talleyrand, undertook all the discussions and made all the decisions. Even the formal signature of the general Treaty of Vienna was undertaken by the representatives of only eight states; but the effective business sessions of the Congress had been simply the meetings of the four, or ultimately the five—the plenipotentiaries of Austria, Great Britain, Prussia, Russia, and France. At the Conference of Paris (1919) circumstances were strikingly similar. It is true that, nominally, the Conference comprised the representatives of some twenty-seven states, who were, in fact, convened on certain rare formal occasions, and who at the last appended their signatures to the Treaty of Versailles; but all the vital discussions and decisions were exclusively in the hands of a committee of the ' Big Four ' (Clemenceau, Wilson, Lloyd George, Orlando, or their alternatives), or the ' Big Five,' when the Japanese delegate took part. Only, it must always be remembered, there was no delegate of the enemy Powers, of Germany or Austria, at Paris. The Peace Treaty of Versailles was a dictated peace.

The exclusion of the enemy or ex-enemy Powers from Paris did not wholly prevent internal dissension and even division. At the Congress of Vienna difference of opinion on the subject of Poland became so wide that for a time the Congress fell apart into two camps (as mentioned earlier), for on January 3,

1815, Metternich, Castlereagh, and Talleyrand signed a secret treaty of alliance, binding themselves, in certain eventualities, to place 60,000 troops in the field against Russia and Prussia. Napoleon's escape from Elba consolidated the general alliance again into a ' united front.' At Paris in 1919 there was violent disagreement among the ' Big Four ' over the question of territories to be assigned to Italy; and in May the whole Italian delegation was withdrawn from the conference. A compromise, however, was achieved, and the Italians returned to Paris and signed the final treaty.

The congresses of 1814–15 and 1919 had each their project not merely for the making but for the maintenance of peace. In each case during the war thinkers and statesmen had been preparing the way. Kant published his *Project of Perpetual Peace* in 1795; Pitt had a plan, which he put into a State paper in 1804; and the Tsar Alexander worked upon Pitt's plan and made a scheme of his own. These efforts resulted at the final peace conference, which was held after Waterloo, in Paris, in the adoption of two acts—the Holy Alliance of September 26, 1815, and the Quadruple Alliance of November 20, 1815. Together these acts were the basis or constitution—a very loose and indefinite constitution—of the Concert or ' Federation ' of Europe, which had considerable, though not very lasting, success. A hundred years later, in the World War of 1914–18, President Wilson, General Smuts, Léon Bourgeois, and others were thinking out schemes for another ' concert ' or ' federation,' which resulted, at the Conference of Paris, in the drafting and adoption of the Covenant of the League of Nations. The makers of the League in 1919 profited by the mistakes of the makers of the Federation of 1815: they adopted a more precise and systematic statute (the Covenant), and they created a standing organization and *personnel* at Geneva. An outstanding difference between 1815 and 1919 was that in 1815 the United States was unnoticed; it was a weak republic in another hemisphere, another world. In 1919 the United States was present at Paris, vitally interested and influential in the person of President Wilson. Unfortunately, having intervened so potently to help solve Europe's and the world's troubles, the people of the United States cut loose again (or tried to do so), and did not join the League of Nations which their President had founded.

The Metternich–Castlereagh–Alexander I Federation or Concert of Europe was little known to the public, for there was no cosmopolitan Press in the first quarter of the nineteenth century, and it had no geographical centre, no secretariat, no ' Geneva,' to keep it before the public mind. The great adventure of 1919, the League of Nations, has had better prospects, because of the great European Press, and because of its permanent organization, its regular assemblies, its seat at Geneva. There is apt, however, to occur in the life of every big movement a dull period, when the first *élan* has been exhausted. The Federation of 1815 met this period about the years 1820–22, and never won through it. The withdrawal of Great Britain from the Federation in 1822 was practically fatal to it. The League of Nations met its dull period in the ' economic depression ' of 1932–34, and with difficulty passed through the crisis, only to meet another, the Italo-Abyssinian war. The notices of withdrawal served by Japan in 1932 and by Germany in 1933 were, to some extent, balanced by the entry of Russia in 1934.

It is a coincidence, perhaps only interesting as a curiosity of history, that the Congress of Vienna in 1814–15 and the Conference of Paris in 1919 lacked each one of the ablest of the contemporary statesmen—in the first case Canning, in the second Briand. Canning fought a duel with Castlereagh in 1809, and since then had been out of office. Briand was Premier in 1916–17, and then was out of office until 1922. Canning was small-minded enough to refuse to serve under Castlereagh, but there appears to be no adequate reason for the failure of the French Government in 1919 to utilize the services of Briand.

It is possible to emphasize too much the similarities of the two great peace settlements. There are striking differences. In 1814–15, as Talleyrand tells in his memoirs, the *mot d'ordre* was ' legitimacy '—that is, restoration. In 1919 the *mot d'ordre* was self-determination. In practice neither the principle of legitimacy nor the principle of self-determination was carried through to its limit. There was a good deal of compromise both at Vienna in 1815 and at Paris in 1919. Where the two peace settlements differed most was in the treatment of the conquered.

The first peace treaty, made on May 30, 1814, at the end of the War of Liberation, was, although the French did not like it, generous to France. It recognized not merely the frontier of 1792, but actually a substantial increase (noted above—the Saar, Chambéry-Annecy, and some less important areas on the Belgian frontier). Next, the territories liberated from the French Empire were considered and reallotted at the Congress of Vienna, 1814–15. Suddenly, however, while the Congress was still dancing and the Allies, with Talleyrand's skilful help, were covertly quarrelling, Napoleon escaped from Elba. This healed all breaches in the Allies' ' front '; they proceeded, with far more success than previously, to draft and discuss a General Treaty of Vienna; and they resumed hostilities against Napoleon, on the basis of ' no compromise.' The battle of Waterloo, June 18, 1815 (nine days after the signature of the General Treaty of Vienna), settled the question of Napoleon. He was shut up on the island of St. Helena. But the French people had accepted Napoleon on his return from Elba, and had thus inflicted another terrible war upon Europe, just after the close of the long series of wars which began in 1792 and ended with the War of Liberation in 1813–14. Naturally the French could not expect to receive peace after this on the generous terms of the First Peace of Paris. The Second Peace Treaty was (like the First Peace) negotiated between the Allies and the restored Government of Louis XVIII at Paris, and was signed on November 20, 1815. It detached from France the chief increments—the Saar, Chambéry-Annecy—of the peace terms of 1814, but still left France with more than her pre-Revolution area; it exacted the return to their owners, chiefly Italian and German princes and cities, of the pictures and sculptures removed by Napoleon; it imposed an indemnity of 700 million francs, to be paid quarterly over a period of five years; and it placed an army of occupation in North-eastern France, to be paid for at fixed rates by the French, until the indemnity should be discharged. This peace settlement, the Second Treaty of Paris, November 20, 1815, must be regarded as essentially moderate. The indemnity proved to be within France's capacity. The Saar, which reverted to Prussia and Bavaria, had really no French affinities; Chambéry–Annecy had been part of the Duchy of Savoy (kingdom of Sardinia) since the early Middle Ages. The return of the objects of art, which was quite a reasonable demand, was not advertised in the Main Treaty of the Second Peace of Paris, but, to spare French susceptibilities, was inscribed in a secret protocol. Real distress was caused in France by the heavy taxation rendered necessary in order that the indemnity might be paid, but by 1819 all the instalments were discharged; the transfers of territory were completed; the army of occupation withdrawn; and France, without humiliation and without sense of grievance, was an effective member of the Concert of Europe.

Opportunity was taken of the assembly of representatives of great and small states in 1815 and in 1919 to enact provisions of universal importance. In 1815 there was the provision for a Concert or Federation of Europe (Holy Alliance and Quadruple Alliance); in 1919 there was the Covenant of the League of Nations. In 1815 there was provision for freedom of " international rivers "—that is, navigable rivers which flow through or between the territories of two or more states. Naturally, it only bound states which were parties to the Treaty of Vienna. In 1919 this freedom was applied to the international rivers of all the signing parties; and, conformably with the advance of science, conditions were established for inter-state railway communication—for instance, across the Polish ' Corridor.' In 1815 a ' wish ' was adopted that the states, parties to the Treaty of Vienna, would abolish the trade in slaves. In 1919 humanitarianism was written into the Covenant of the League of Nations, and the principle of a world-wide effort at social amelioration was adopted in the statute of the International Labour Organization. In both years the advisability of some measure of disarmament was recognized. In 1814 France undertook in the *Charte* of Louis XVIII to discard conscription in her defence system; as did Germany in 1919, when a general disarmament ' wish ' was also adopted for all the Powers. The experience of both peace settlements, 1815 and 1919, has shown that there is nothing of which Governments are more afraid in practice than of reducing their defence forces even in agreement with all other states. The victor Powers could not agree to reduce their ' effectives,' and both the 1815 and 1919 " no-conscription " clauses of the peace settlements were a dead-letter within a few years.

Naturally, there are many points of difference between the two great peace settlements. The most outstanding has already been noticed: France, the vanquished, took part in negotiating the Treaties of 1814–15 as a full member of the conferences; in 1919 Germany was not admitted to the " dictated peace." In 1815 peoples and territories were transferred by the treaties without plebiscites being undertaken to approve the transfers; in 1919–20 the principle of ' self-determination ' and plebiscites was adopted for a large number of comparatively small areas (Eupen, Malmédy, Allenstein, Northern Schleswig, Upper Silesia, Teschen), where the disposition of the inhabitants was doubtful, but not in the big " restored " territories, such as Alsace-Lorraine, Posen, Galicia, and the rest.

In 1814–15 monarchy was the accepted basis of government; and the monarchs personally took part in the congresses at Paris and Vienna. No monarch, except Albert of Belgium, appeared at Paris in 1919. The end of the World War and the making of peace in 1919 involved the extinction of twenty-four monarchies (1 Russian, 1 Austrian, 22 German). In 1814–15 even an old republic which was restored to independence, Holland, was given a king. In 1919 it was taken for granted that all the new or even the restored and formerly monarchical states, like Poland, Czechoslovakia, were republican.

In 1815, though certain journals, like the *Rheinische Merkur*, and certain writers on public affairs, like Görres, had been fairly influential, there was no national or European Press to make insistent demands on Governments and peace-makers. In 1919 the Press of all the Great Powers had a definite, and sometimes sinister, influence upon the terms of peace. In 1814–15, down to the return of Napoleon from Elba, there was no attempt to fix ' war guilt ' upon anyone. In 1919 there was much more than the fining of the vanquished, which to a greater or less extent happens at the end of every war : there was a distinct and avowed dogma of war guilt against the vanquished and a formal indictment of ' war criminals ' from ' William of Hohenzollern ' downward. Perhaps most striking of all the points of difference was this : In 1814–15, except with regard to Italy, everything was done to make larger units out of small ones—Belgium was joined to Holland, Norway to Sweden, Genoa to Sardinia ; Germany was made into a federation of thirty-nine states, as against some three hundred and fifty of the Holy Roman Empire or forty-four of the Napoleonic reorganization. In 1919 the break-up of great states, which was the result of the exhaustion of Russia and Austria in the last year of the War, was accepted, and six states (Finland, Esthonia, Latvia, Lithuania, Poland, Czechoslovakia) were added to the number of states with which the Great War started.

It is no difficult task to discern many points of difference between the peace settlements of 1814–15 and a few points of similarity. The differences are not to be explained simply by the interval of rather over a hundred years. The task of the peace-makers of 1814–15 was simplified by the absence of nationalist sentiment. But it must also be admitted that they were wiser than their successors of 1919. The handling of the Saar territory shows this. In 1792 this territory belonged chiefly to Prussia and Bavaria. It became part of the French Grand Empire. At the peace conference of 1814 it was left within the frontiers of France ; but in 1815, in retribution for the French having accepted and fought for Napoleon after his return from Elba, it was given back to Prussia and Bavaria. The inhabitants do not appear to have greatly cared under whatever sovereignty they were placed.

less need
for Public
Pressure/opinion.

In 1919 the peace-makers, all of them avowed champions
of nationality, made a provisional settlement of the Saar question, involving an indisputably German population, which was
bound at its final stage to create enormous trouble. The territory was not left with Germany; nor was it given to France;
nor was it placed permanently under an international authority.
An extraordinary *régime* was established, under which the
French Government was given the Saar mines in private
property; it was included in the French customs frontier; it
was placed under an ' Allied ' governing commission subject
to the authority of the League of Nations for fifteen years;
and at the end of the fifteen years a plebiscite was to be taken
to ascertain whether the Saar population would prefer to return
to German sovereignty, or to be annexed into France, or to
remain under the League of Nations. Thus the way was opened
up to a tremendous agitation, bound to promote most dangerous
excitement inside and outside the Saar as the period of fifteen
years drew to an end. By reason of the self-restraint of the
French and German Governments, and of the presence of a
body of international troops, the plebiscite of 1935 took place
peacefully, and the Saar territory was restored to Germany.

It is, therefore, not a sufficient explanation of the more states-
manlike peace of 1814–15 to say that the men of 1814–15 had
no national problem to trouble them, or that they were aristocrats and had no democracies to make insistent demands on
them. Somehow or other the Great War of 1792–1814 ended
in a very much quieter atmosphere than that of 1914–18. There
had been propaganda in the earlier war, but it was high-class
propaganda, with the dignity almost of history and literature,
penned by Wordsworth, Gentz, Görres, and Chateaubriand.
Napoleon was not a gentleman, but the Allied statesmen certainly were; they fought the war and they made peace like
aristocrats (as they were) of the eighteenth century. I do not
mean, in saying this, to imply that the men who conducted
the World War and made the peace of 1919 were not gentlemen; but war and peace were certainly made in an ungentle-
manly way, of which the contemptuous locking of the peace

S

conference doors against Germany was the overt expression. The origin of this complete abandonment of good manners in the World War and the peace-making is to be looked for, must be looked for, in the invasion of Belgium, the deliberate breaking of a plighted word and the sacrificing of a small neutral state.

Compared with 1919, the peace settlement of 1814–15 had practically no ' reparations ' question. Napoleon had levied tribute, but the aristocrats who made peace disdained to do so. It was not that they understood the theory of political economy better than the men of 1919; it only means that they were less rapacious. In 1919 the United States Government declined to share in reparations, but all the other states participating in the peace settlement handed in enormous and minutely itemed bills for damages, which, if fully met, would have ruined the economic system of victor as well as vanquished.

The truth is that the statesmen of 1814–15 were not merely aristocrats; they were also pacifists—not Quakers, for they were ready enough to use force, but pacifists in that they hated war, and regarded armies as strictly police agencies. Metternich and Alexander and Castlereagh not only disliked war as they actually saw it, but disliked the thought of it. They never idealized fighting. Rightly or wrongly, they saw nothing fine about war; and they wanted to banish it entirely and to keep states fixed and stable by policing the frontiers with international armies. It was a system of stable frontiers and police armies which they endeavoured to set up in 1814–15; and though their system broke down after some thirty years, it was by no means unreasonable. It is time that the peoples of twentieth-century Europe learned the lesson.

INDEX